IMAGES
of America

BUCKHORN
MINERAL BATHS AND WILDLIFE MUSEUM

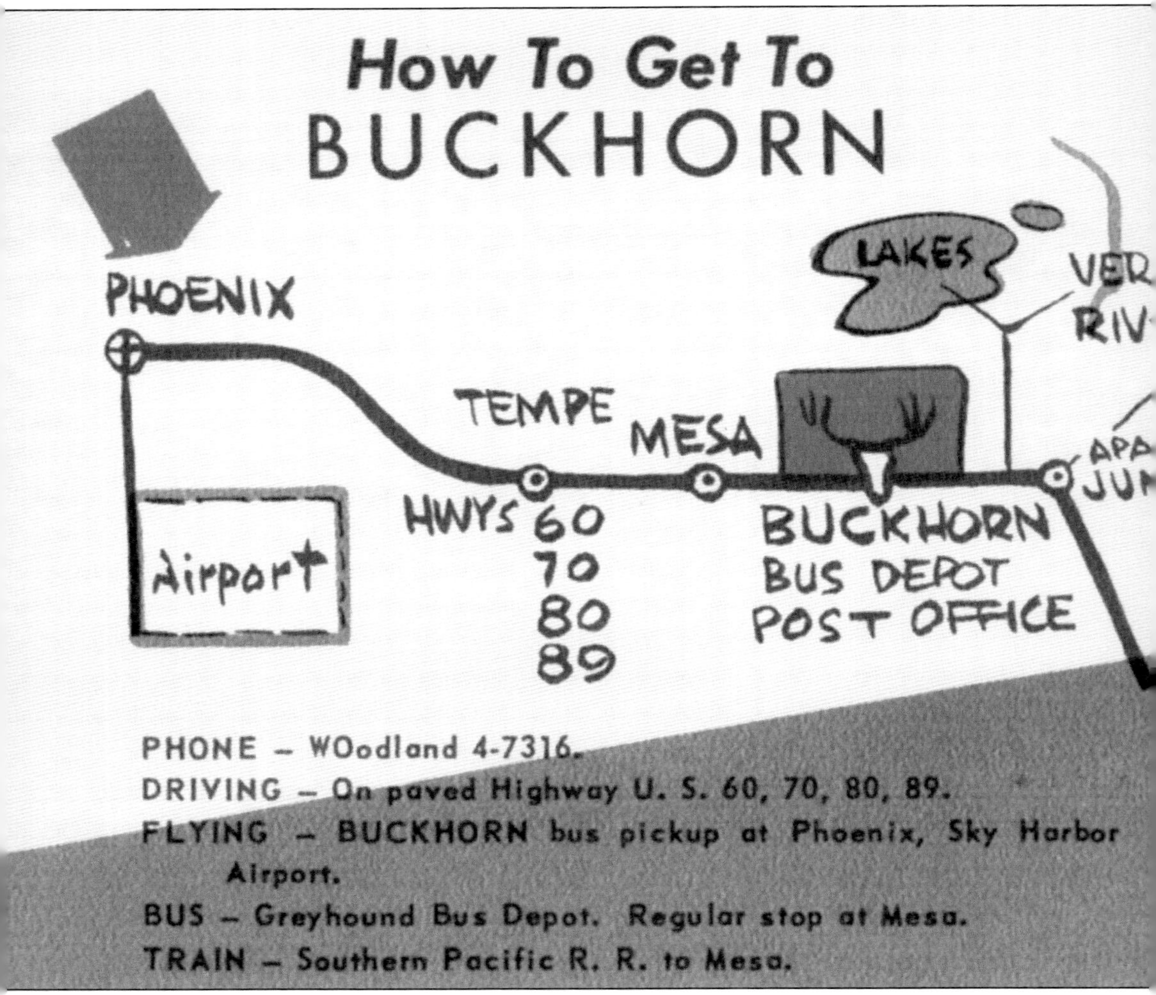

The Buckhorn began in 1936 as a two-pump gas station and small tourist stop drawing in motorists along US Highways 60, 70, 80, and 89—three of which ran from coast to coast. With the discovery of mineral-laden hot springs in October 1939, the business quickly expanded into a much broader enterprise that included a bathhouse, cottages, motel units, and an enlarged Wildlife Museum. This simple, hand-drawn map in an early brochure contained important reference points for travelers. (Courtesy Mesa Preservation Foundation.)

On the Cover: For six decades, the Buckhorn Hot Mineral Baths was a fixture on East Main Street in Mesa, Arizona, once the route of four federal highways. Erected in 1949, its monumental neon sign, topped by a 10-point antlered stag and visible at night from nearly a mile away, has remained the resort's most iconic feature. Closed in 2007, the Buckhorn remains an intriguing time capsule. (Courtesy Mesa Preservation Foundation.)

IMAGES
of America

BUCKHORN MINERAL BATHS AND WILDLIFE MUSEUM

Jay Mark and Ronald L. Peters
Foreword by Ted Newton Sliger

ARCADIA
PUBLISHING

ISBN 978-1-4671-2696-0

Published by Arcadia Publishing
Charleston, South Carolina

Printed in the United States of America

Library of Congress Control Number: 2017934239

For all general information, please contact Arcadia Publishing:
Telephone 843-853-2070
Fax 843-853-0044
E-mail sales@arcadiapublishing.com
For customer service and orders:
Toll-Free 1-888-313-2665

Visit us on the Internet at www.arcadiapublishing.com

For Ted and Alice Sliger's visionary inspirations, Alice's longtime friend Robert Brinton, Alice Jung at the Mesa Historical Museum, and all who treasure the Buckhorn.

Contents

FOREWORD

For a boy, growing up at the Buckhorn Baths was an experience like no other. Far from downtown Mesa at the time and surrounded by desert, it was a marvelous, ever-changing, vibrant oasis that my parents never really finished. They were forever adding new and unusual attractions. It gave tremendous opportunities for a young lad's imagination to soar—exploring and playing games. Of course, there were endless chores to help with at such an active place.

Maybe the best thing about living at the Buckhorn was the continual parade of celebrities. Hollywood stars were regulars, as were artists and other important and famous people. It was the best resort in the valley. But nothing was more exciting than all the baseball stars I got to meet every spring before Cactus League games began. Where else could you be up close to some of the greatest players baseball has ever produced? For a kid to play catch with the likes of Ty Cobb, Willie Mays, Gaylord Perry, Willie McCovey, and so many others was priceless.

I also remember exciting hunting and fishing trips with Dad, his friends, and hotel guests. It was always fascinating to watch Dad's taxidermy expertise turn those hunting acquisitions into an ever-expanding assemblage. The Wildlife Museum, containing his collection of more than 450 species, sent my imagination soaring.

The Buckhorn has always been a part of my life, my home. While its future remains uncertain at the time of this book's publication, it represents a wonderful, lasting tribute to the more than seven decades my parents invested in creating one of Arizona's most unique resorts and roadside attractions. Here is a permanent record that is sure to keep alive the special history of this unique place—something my mother had always wished for. Leafing through the pages that contain so many rare photographs has brought back many long-forgotten memories. I hope that you enjoy it as much as I have.

—Ted Newton Sliger, son of Ted and Alice Sliger

ACKNOWLEDGMENTS

Even though only two author names appear on the cover, the preparation of *Buckhorn Mineral Baths and Wildlife Museum* was very much a collaborative effort. Without the expertise and encouragement of others, the book could never have materialized. Numerous individuals assisted with images and shared valuable historic details. Special appreciation to Ted and Jerri Sliger for their exhaustive work digging through family records to uncover long-forgotten photographs, lending their unique family perspectives, and providing unwavering support and invaluable assistance. Thanks to the Mesa Historical Museum, which has archived much of the Buckhorn story—president and CEO Lisa Anderson and collections curator Angie Sullivan spent considerable time scanning images—and to Tom Wilson and Jerry Howard at the Arizona Museum of Natural History. Ann Empie Groves laboriously searched through her father's prolific catalogue of cartoon art to provide invaluable information about Hal Empie. We are indebted to Rebecca Ranan Aikins, a theatrical costume and puppet designer, who researched Buckhorn artists-in-residence George Frederick and Arnold Krug for a Mesa Historical Museum exhibit. Rodney Johnson, president emeritus of the Arizona chapter of the Society for American Baseball Research, lent his incredible skills in identifying elusive baseball celebrities. Tim Jelinek used his automobile knowledge to accurately date cars in the photographs. Our gratitude to former *Mesa Tribune* and *Arizona Republic* photographer Larry Ward for the use of his historic photographs, Jack Ellwood who unearthed scarce material, and to Greg Marek and Jared Smith.

Unless otherwise noted, all images are courtesy of the Mesa Preservation Foundation archive. MHM refers to the Ted and Alice Sliger Collection at the Mesa Historical Museum. AzMNH refers to the Arizona Museum of Natural History.

Introduction

Long before there was a Ted and Alice, as in the 1969 movie *Bob & Carol & Ted & Alice,* there was a real Ted and Alice. The Ted was Theodore William Sliger, and the Alice was Alice Annette O'Barr. Their story, which led to the creation of an empire, is the stuff of Hollywood—a fairy-tale chronicle of luck, pluck, and one big buck. It is a remarkable tale of changing circumstances, fortuitous discovery, and innovative enterprise—all converging as if by destiny at the same time and place.

Born in Thurber, Texas, in 1903, Ted Sliger moved to Arizona with his father in 1923. He spent his early years trapping and hunting; in the late 1920s, he opened a gas station and store on the corner of the old Bush Highway and Main Street.

After a three-year, on-again, off-again courtship, Ted married a 28-year-old schoolteacher, Alice O'Barr, in September 1935. Alice moved into a "homesteader's shack" the couple purchased for $125 and relocated to the property behind the gas station. Tragedy struck just three months later, on Christmas Eve, when a kerosene stove caught fire in the service station as Ted was melting wax for his taxidermy work. It left him with serious burns.

The misfortune would forever change the lives of Ted and Alice Sliger. With the gas station destroyed, the couple temporarily sold fruit from a makeshift roadside stand—while debating their future. Rather than continue on leased land, they decided to purchase their own place a couple of miles closer to Mesa. The decision was fortuitous, coming at just the time when four national highways converged along the Apache Trail (Main Street).

The Homestead Act of 1862 provided many Arizona settlers an opportunity to own land on which to begin a new life in the West. The original owners of the property that became the Buckhorn Baths were Charles and Florence Mitten, publishers of the *Mesa Journal-Tribune*. These early Mesa pioneers sold their property (originally 160 acres) over a period of years to Ted and Alice Sliger for the princely sum of $50 an acre.

As the 20th century dawned, the United States was experiencing major social and technological changes. The introduction of the automobile provided Americans with independent mobility that the horse and buggy could never achieve. It was not long before long-distance travel in personal conveyances became routine.

The Good Roads Bill of 1917 led to the construction of the first federal highway in 1923. The Lincoln Highway helped jump-start an auto-dominated society. Gas pumps were in use as early as 1885. By 1921, there were over 12,000 gas stations around the country providing Americans with fuel for the places they were looking to visit. California became the home to the first "motel" in 1926—the name derived from combining "motorist" and "hotel." From the 1930s to the 1940s, over 400,000 motorist cabins were constructed throughout the United States to accommodate the ever-increasing number of travelers.

Just months after the disastrous 1935 fire, the Sligers were pumping gas again and providing tourist services and novel attractions. Just seven miles east of Mesa, they began building an unparalleled business empire that, with success, expanded into the Buckhorn Mineral Wells and Wildlife Museum, popularly known as the Buckhorn Baths.

The first structure on the bare desert was the tiny homestead house they moved from the old site. It still remains a historic part of the property. The first permanent structure was erected in 1936 with bricks purchased from the demolished Mesa Irving School (old North School, c. 1894). With continued growth, construction continued apace until 1947.

By the end of March 1936, the Buckhorn consisted of just a two-pump gas station and small store from which Indian jewelry and rugs, fishing tackle, and hunting and fishing licenses were sold. Ted Sliger continued offering taxidermy services to local sportsmen. In 1938, he built a large addition onto the store to display his growing collection of Arizona wildlife. The "Buckhorn" was born. When they first moved to the well-less property, water had to be hauled from a well in Apache Junction by horseback or Model-T Ford. Tired of transporting the liquid to the business, Ted began drilling a well in 1939. The water he reached was 112 degrees and filled with minerals. Not good for drinking, but possibly good for business. Ted sent a sample to California for analysis. The report came back with just what the Sligers hoped for—mineral-laden contents ideal for a health spa. Soon after, the couple began taking advantage of the tourist value of hot baths. With the initial construction of a four-tub bathhouse and guest cottages soon after, the Buckhorn Baths and Mineral Spa was poised to take off.

The Sligers' world forever changed in 1947 when the New York Giants baseball team came to town. Discovery of the Buckhorn Baths led team owner Horace Stoneham to make the Phoenix area his spring training home, giving birth to the Cactus League. For the next 25 years, the Buckhorn was the Giants' home away from home. Ted and Alice welcomed the likes of Ty Cobb, Willie Mays, Gaylord Perry, Leo Durocher, Mel Ott, and Juan Marichal—all of whom became part of the Sligers' extended family. In 1952, when the Chicago Cubs arrived in Mesa for spring training, they too became fans of the Buckhorn, returning year after year.

The vernacular Pueblo style the Sligers used in the design of their buildings was part of the Southwestern lure tourists craved—along with the baths and, of course, the Wildlife Museum. Over the years, the somewhat remote Buckhorn provided essential conveniences—post office, Greyhound bus station, beauty salon, cottages, bathhouse, and restaurant that operated from several locations but finally closed in 1975. Other features included one of the most extensive collections of metates (Indian grinding stones), used in the construction of landscape walls throughout the campus. Hand-painted signs abounded, many of which are still in place today. Ted and Alice Sliger's business acumen over a 70-year period helped make the Buckhorn Baths one of Mesa's most significant and enduring local historic landmarks.

Alice continued operating the Buckhorn for 15 years after Ted's death in 1984. In 1999, at age 93, she closed the baths, saying they were just too much work at her age. Determined to carry on at a lesser degree, she kept the motel and museum going until 2007—the year she turned 101—and finally had to close the Buckhorn for good, although the public continues stopping by daily to take photographs. Alice died peacefully in 2010, just a month before her 104th birthday.

Today, while the future of the Buckhorn is uncertain, it is the authors' wish that this book serve as a valuable memory, providing a rare tour of a remarkable enterprise. With more than 200 photographs, many previously unseen, within its covers is a chance to explore the numerous intriguing facets that made the Buckhorn a unique, national, quintessential, and iconic example of the golden age of American roadside businesses.

Buckhorn Milestones

1903 Theodore "Ted" William Sliger is born in Thurber, Texas.
1906 Alice O'Barr is born on Christmas Eve in Mesa, Arizona.
1923 Ted Sliger arrives in Arizona with his father.
1926 Together, they open the Desert Wells gas station at the Apache Trail and Usery Pass Road (Bush Highway) in an existing 24-foot-by-24-foot building, from which they sell gas and souvenirs. Ted also provides taxidermy services.
1935 Ted and Alice marry. They move a small house onto the leased land. A Christmas Eve fire destroys the gas station and taxidermy business. Afterwards, they temporarily operate a fruit stand on the site.
1936 The Sligers buy five acres from Charles Mitten. They relocate their Desert Wells house from Usery Pass Road to the new site. Their first building is constructed with bricks purchased from the Irving School demolition. Buckhorn opens at Recker Road and Main Street.
1939 When drilling for drinking water, the Sligers hit a hot mineral-laden fissure instead. While digging the well, metates are discovered on the property.
1940 Mineral baths open with just four tubs.
1942 The Buckhorn gets electricity for the first time.
1942–1972 The Sligers operate a Greyhound bus depot.
c. 1942 A sign on the newly built wishing well is installed, reading, "Coins on which you make a wish will go to the War efforts." Following the war, proceeds go to the March of Dimes.
1945 Daughter Marilyn Alice is born.
1947 New York Giants baseball stars visit Buckhorn for the first time. The Sligers begin embedding metates in landscaping walls.
1948 Son Ted Newton Sliger is born.
1949 Paul Millet completes the monumental, iconic neon sign
1952 The Chicago Cubs discover the Buckhorn after arriving in Mesa for spring training.
1956–1984 The Sligers operate a contract post office.
1958 The Sligers sell back part of their 160 acres to Joe Farnsworth, developer of Dreamland Villa retirement homes to the northwest.
1961 The Sligers travel on a goodwill tour to Japan with good friend Horace Stoneham and his New York Giants.
1974 Buckhorn and surrounding areas are annexed into the City of Mesa.
1984 Ted dies at age 81.
1999 Due to her advancing age, Alice shutters the bathhouse portion of the business.
2007 Alice closes the motel and the remainder of the business to the public.
2010 Alice dies a month short of her 104th birthday.

One

The Original "Ted and Alice"

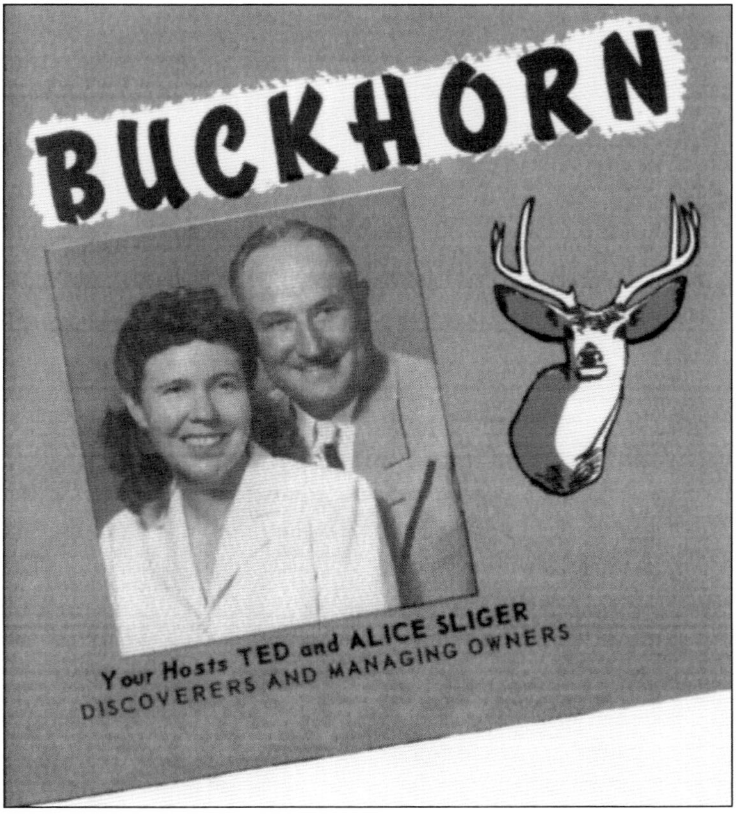

The story of the Buckhorn mineral wells is the tale of a truly remarkable couple. The path "the discoverers and managing owners" traveled to build an extraordinary enterprise represents an unparalleled six-decade journey of amazing tenacity, innovation, and entrepreneurship. Both Theodore William Sliger—everybody just called him "Ted"—and Alice O'Barr Sliger—"Alice" to her friends and guests—would probably have admitted what they accomplished far surpassed anything they could have ever dreamt.

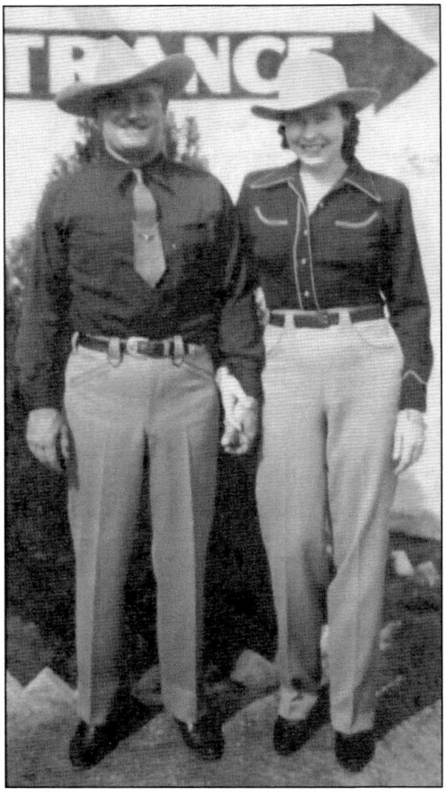

Ted and Alice Sliger enjoyed providing guests with an authentic cowboy experience, right down to their own attire. Ted routinely sported a pricey Stetson hat and cowboy boots that were often worn with a more traditional tie. Alice, who had emerged as a "liberated" woman of the 1940s, wore Western pants, shirt, and hat. The hospitable Sligers spent a lifetime making a home for people away from home. (Courtesy MHM.)

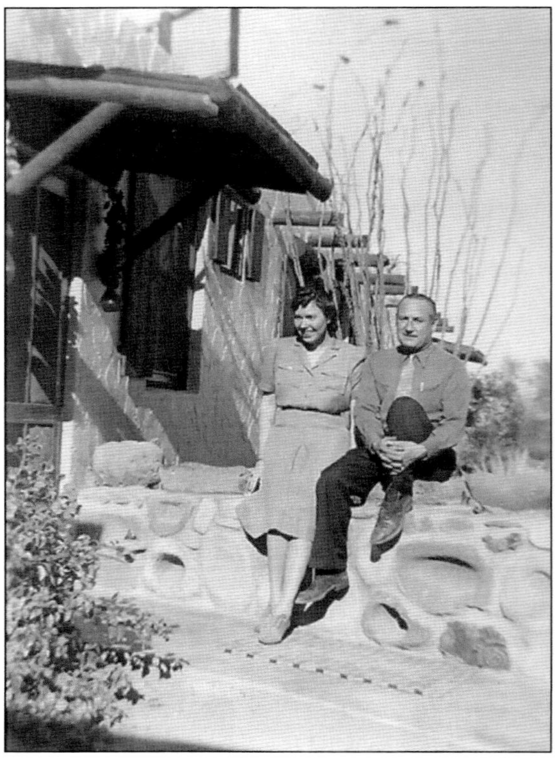

In 1942, Alice and Ted pose casually atop their newly completed landscape wall leading to the bathhouse entrance. Freshly embedded metates, part of an enormous collection, can be clearly seen. (Courtesy Ted and Jerri Sliger.)

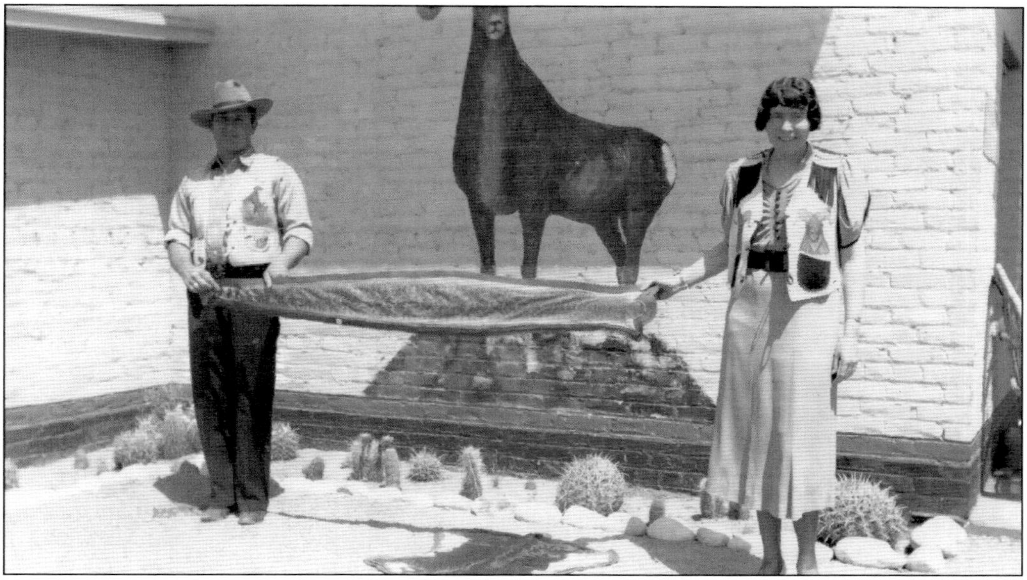

Although no photographs of Ted and Alice Sliger definitively showing their first business are known to exist, this undated image of the newlyweds posing with a rattlesnake skin in front of a wall painting of a Bighorn sheep likely provides an intriguing glimpse of that location. (Courtesy Ted and Jerri Sliger.)

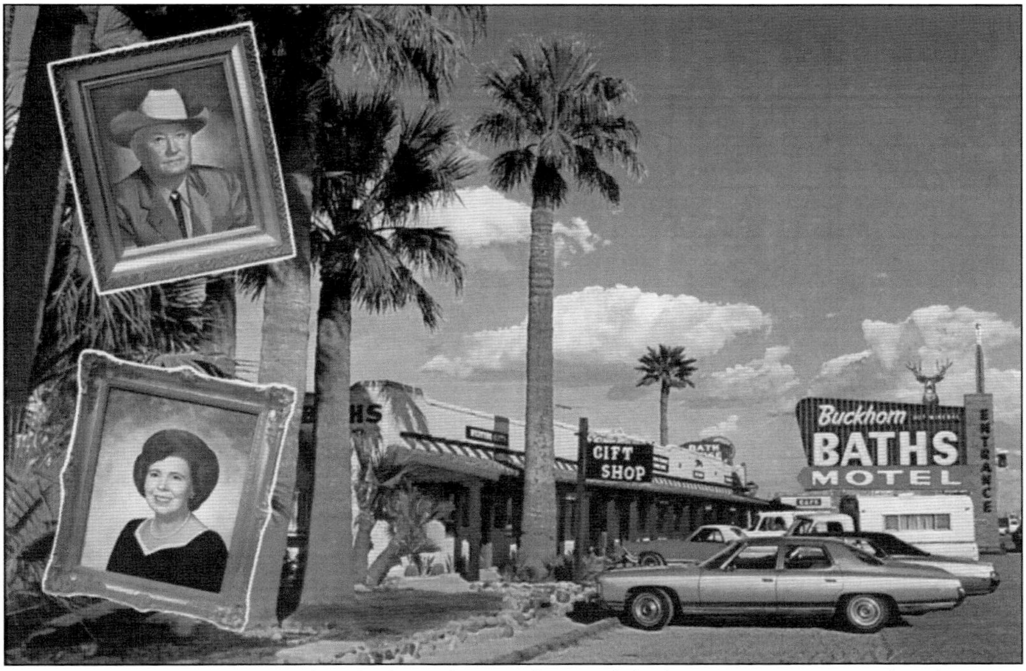

From the very beginning, Ted and Alice Sliger understood the best way to promote their business was to promote themselves—demonstrating they were part of the community. Both Ted and Alice were active participants in local organizations and events. After the installation of the large neon sign in 1949, most advertisements depicted Buckhorn founders Ted and Alice and their iconic sign.

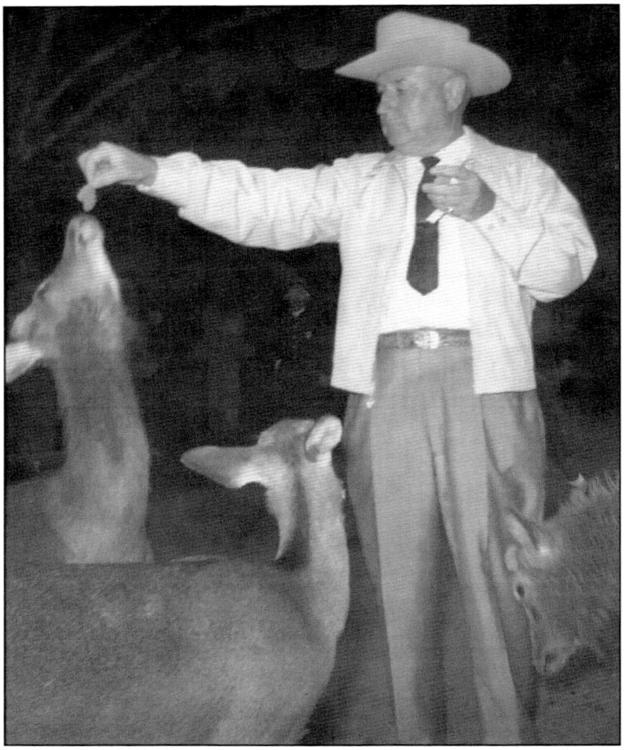

From the 1920s and 1930s, when he began running traplines in the desert and foothills east of Mesa, Ted Sliger became a lifelong avid hunter and trapper, which led him to start a taxidermy business. A growing accumulation of Arizona wildlife inspired Ted to create the Wildlife Museum at the Buckhorn. During the resort's early years, the remote desert, about seven miles from Mesa, was abundant with wildlife. Rattlesnakes, deer, javelinas, coyotes, and other animals freely roamed the area. (Courtesy MHM.)

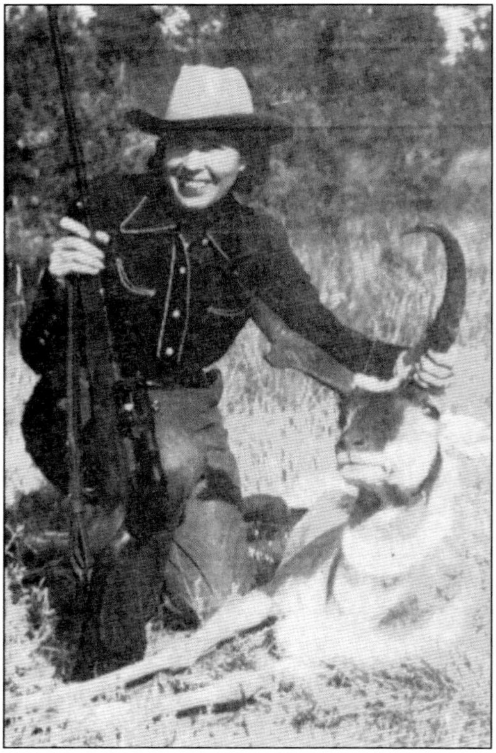

For Alice, hunting was not just a man's sport. She was an accomplished hunter in her own right, often accompanying Ted on his "safari" expeditions. In the early years, the couple traveled throughout Arizona collecting specimens for the museum. The handsome antelope shown in this late 1940s photograph was processed, stuffed, and mounted by Ted and placed on display in the museum. It remains there today. (Courtesy MHM.)

Although Ted and Alice Sliger appeared in countless photographs, most often with their celebrity guests, they seldom posed as just a couple. In 1942, they took time for a portrait at the Buckhorn entrance. Classic Western rattan chairs are placed out front for visitors and guests to sit and watch traffic along the highway. (Courtesy Ted and Jerri Sliger.)

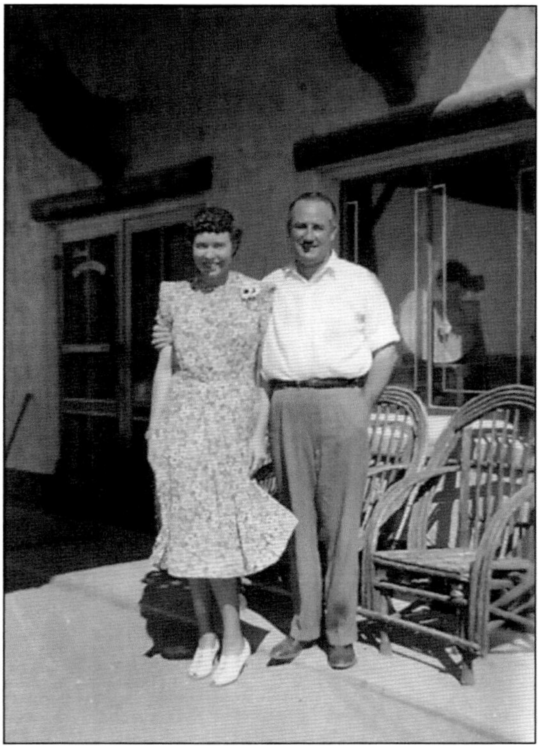

The Buckhorn's expansive grounds and celebrity guests offered an ideal playground in which to grow up. Being far from town meant isolation for the children, with few friends nearby. Lots of stimuli, however, let imaginations soar. In addition, the Sliger children were often included on frequent hunting and fishing trips to the mountains. Always busy, Ted and Alice seldom sat still long enough for a family portrait. That makes this image with infant Ted Newton and young daughter Marilyn very special. (Courtesy MHM.)

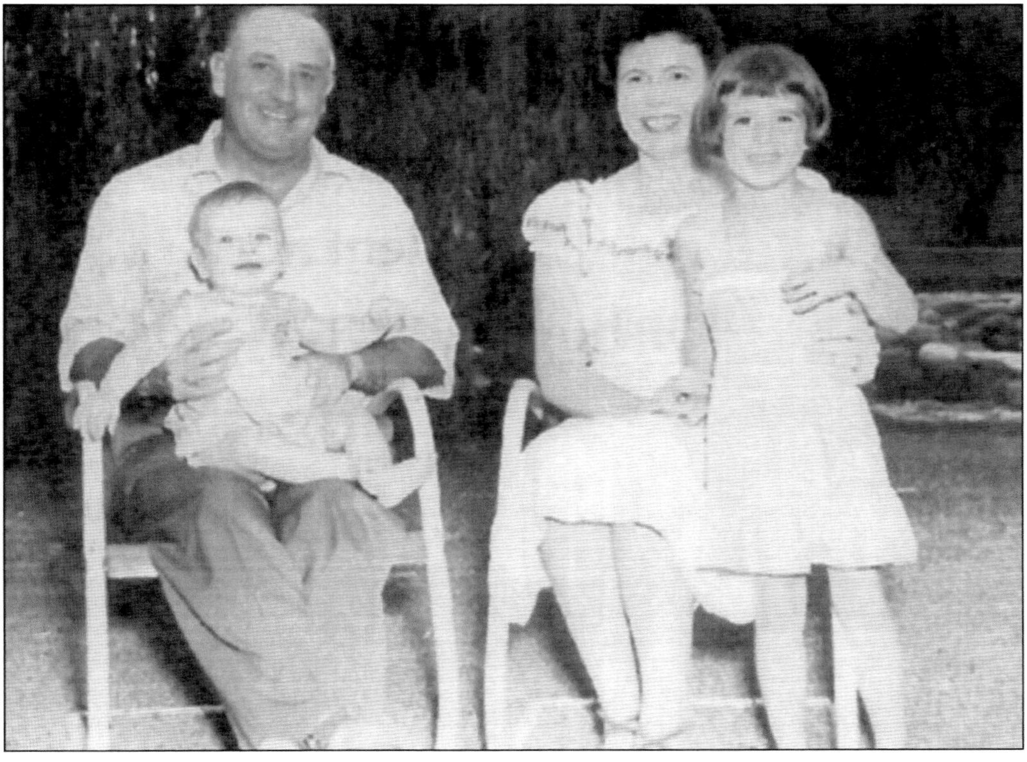

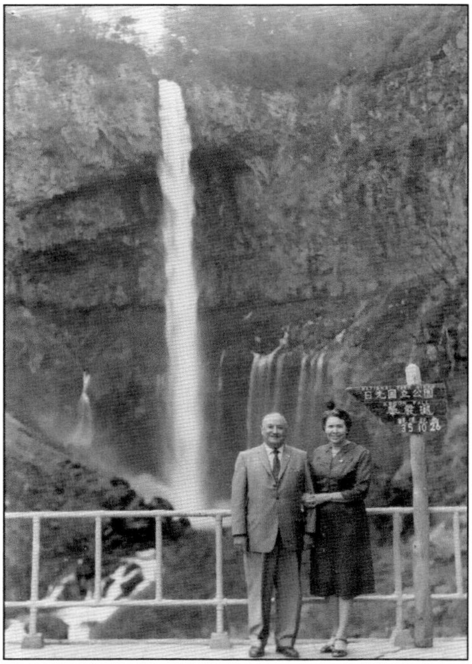

After New York Giants owner Horace Stoneham first discovered the Buckhorn, he sent his star players for spa treatment each spring for more than two decades. A lifelong friendship developed with the Sligers. It culminated in 1961, when Stoneham invited the couple to accompany the team on a goodwill tour of Japan. While there, they traveled the country extensively, visiting Hiroshima and many Japanese sites and landmarks. Posing in front of a Japanese waterfall and clad in conventional suit and tie and simple dress, Ted and Alice were a world away from the Western Buckhorn. No Stetson, no cowboy boots, no Western garb. For one of the few times in their long career, Ted and Alice could relax far from home and enjoy being taken care of rather than being the caretakers. (Courtesy MHM.)

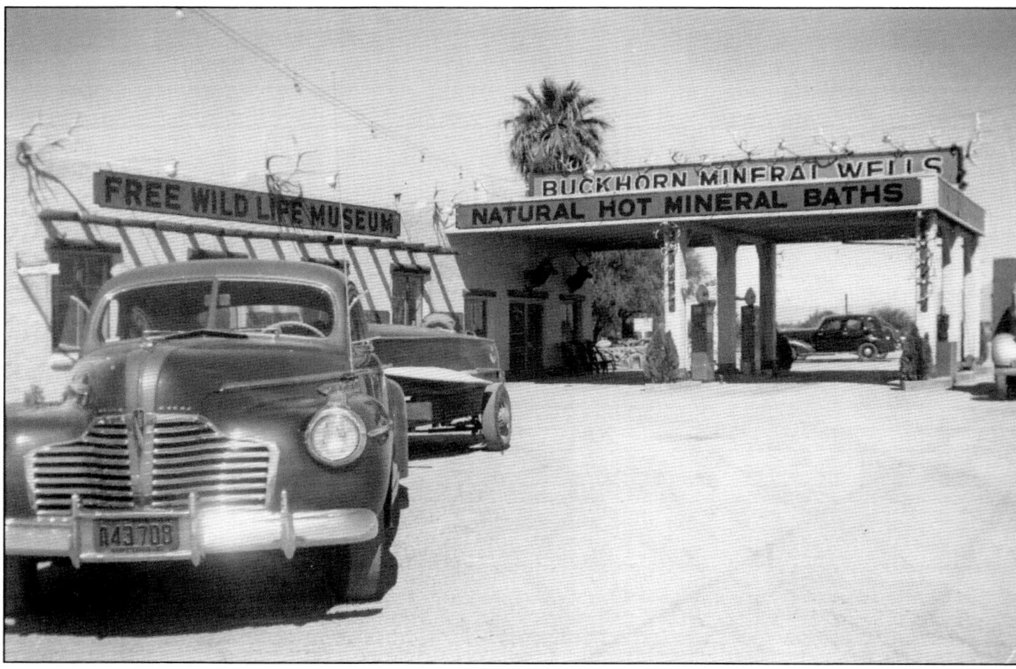

When the Giants moved their spring training headquarters to Casa Grande in 1961, Buckhorn barbecues, potlucks, and parties seemed to slow down, Alice recalled in a 1991 interview. Yet the parking lot was still often filled with cars. Along with onsite activities, the Sligers provided guests with frequent trips for big-game fishing in Mexico, with the catch brought back for big fish fries. Nearby javelina hunts provided meat for all—sometimes numbering in the thousands. The Buckhorn never stopped being east Mesa's biggest attraction. (Courtesy MHM.)

Citrus is one of Arizona's "Five C's"—(copper, cattle, cotton, citrus, and climate). The Buckhorn provided an abundant supply of two of the "C's" to its guests. An ideal climate was one; citrus the other. Alice, in casual garb, and young son Ted show off an armful of just-picked giant grapefruit, ready to be freshly served in the restaurant. The Buckhorn was a true family business, with everyone pitching in. Even with a hectic life, Ted and Alice always found time for their kids. (Courtesy MHM.)

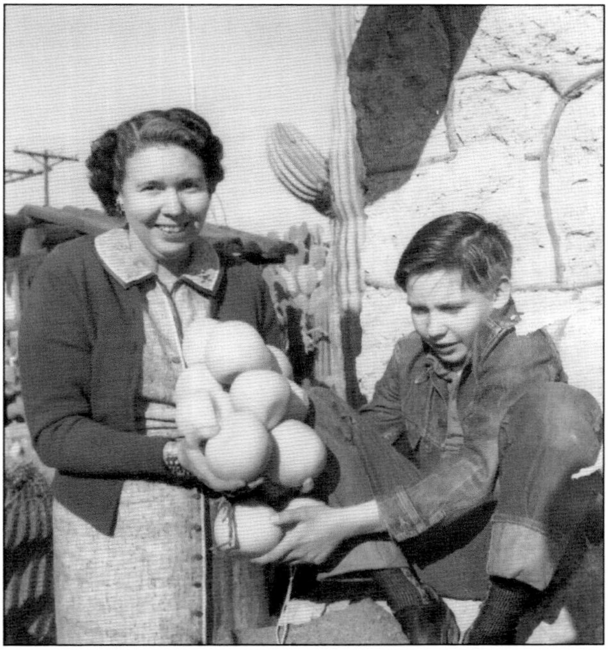

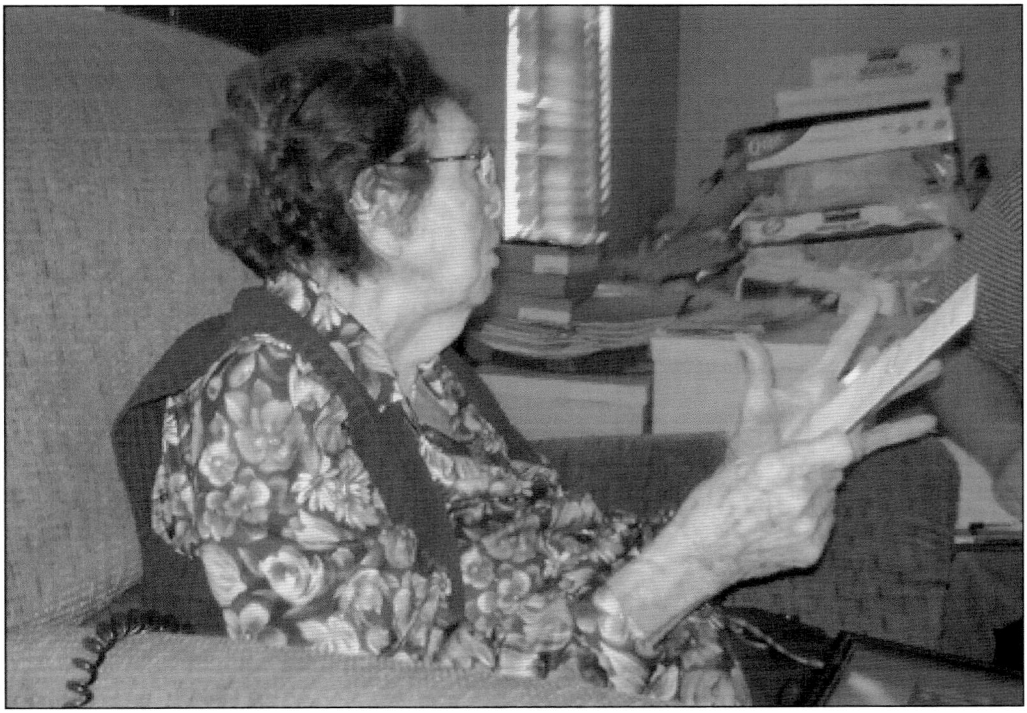

After Ted passed away in 1984, Alice continued running the Buckhorn. Finally, in 1999, at age 93, she closed the baths but kept the lodging units open until 2007. Even at age 101, when most people would be retired to a nursing home, Alice was at work every day, warmly greeting guests and overseeing the operation of the Buckhorn. Alice passed away in December 2010, a month shy of her 104th birthday.

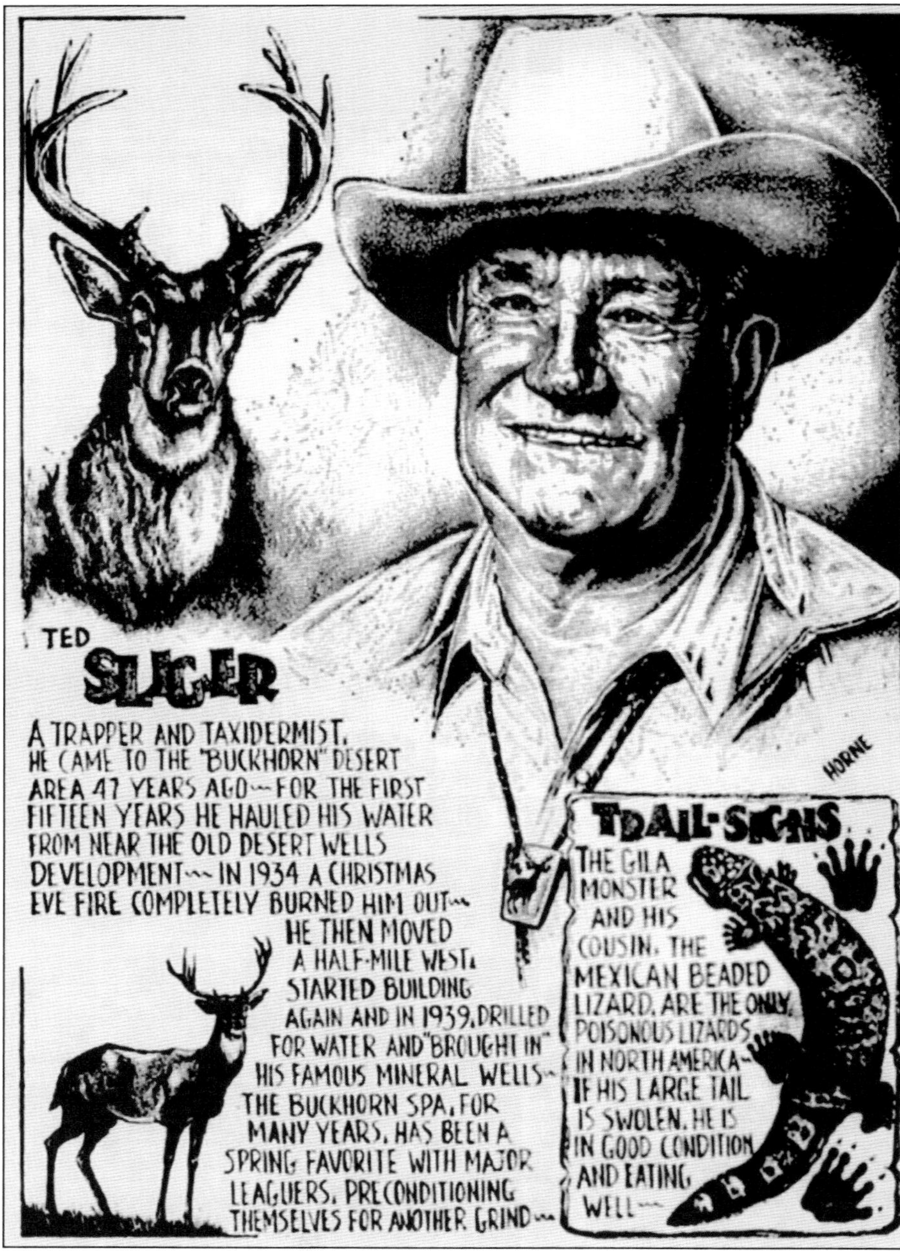

In 1966, nearly three decades after the Sligers opened their mineral baths, Ted had become a celebrity in his own right. John Horne, *Arizona Republic* outdoor cartoonist, featured Ted in one of his columns and included this wonderful sketch. Readers learned that Ted's renown reached far beyond the valley. Horne noted that Ted once mounted "an 'old cactus' buck with numerous points . . . (that) the great Ripley had featured in one of his 'Believe It Or Not' cartoons.' " Writing in March, Horne observed, "Spring coming to the Buckhorn, has nothing to do with robins or ground hogs. It arrives when major league baseball players appear and hit the mineral baths and rubbing tables to simmer off banquet circuit poundage and to condition themselves for the next pennant race." (Courtesy *Arizona Republic*.)

Two

From Fire to Empire

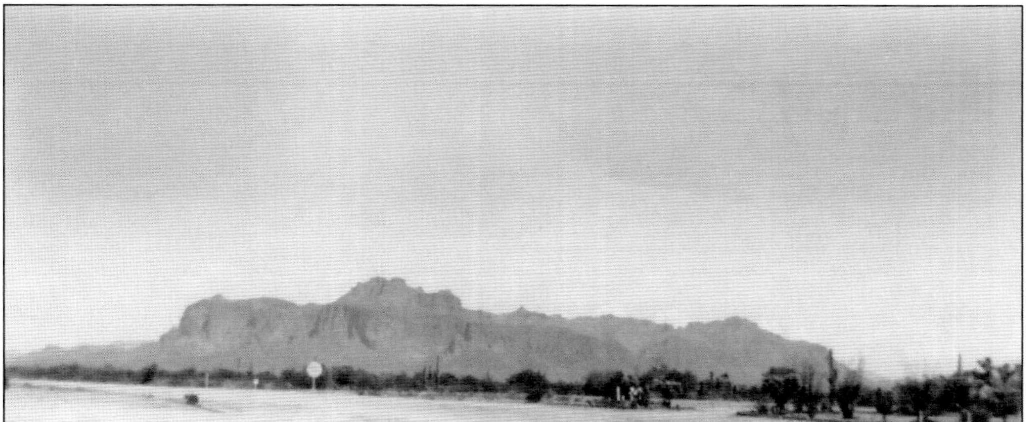

Christmas Eve 1935 was a devastating time for Ted and Alice Sliger. Married for only three months, the newlyweds were just building their business on the northwest corner of present-day Main Street and Power Road—a narrow two-lane route for US Highways 60, 70, 80, and 89. Then the unimaginable happened. While melting wax for his taxidermy work, a gasoline stove exploded. Ted received serious burns. The gas station was destroyed, but a small house they had recently moved to the property was undamaged. They could not know at the time that the tragedy would one day turn into triumph. Through pluck, luck, and determination, the pair would ultimately transform a barren piece of desert into a world-renowned oasis resort and spa. (Courtesy MHM.)

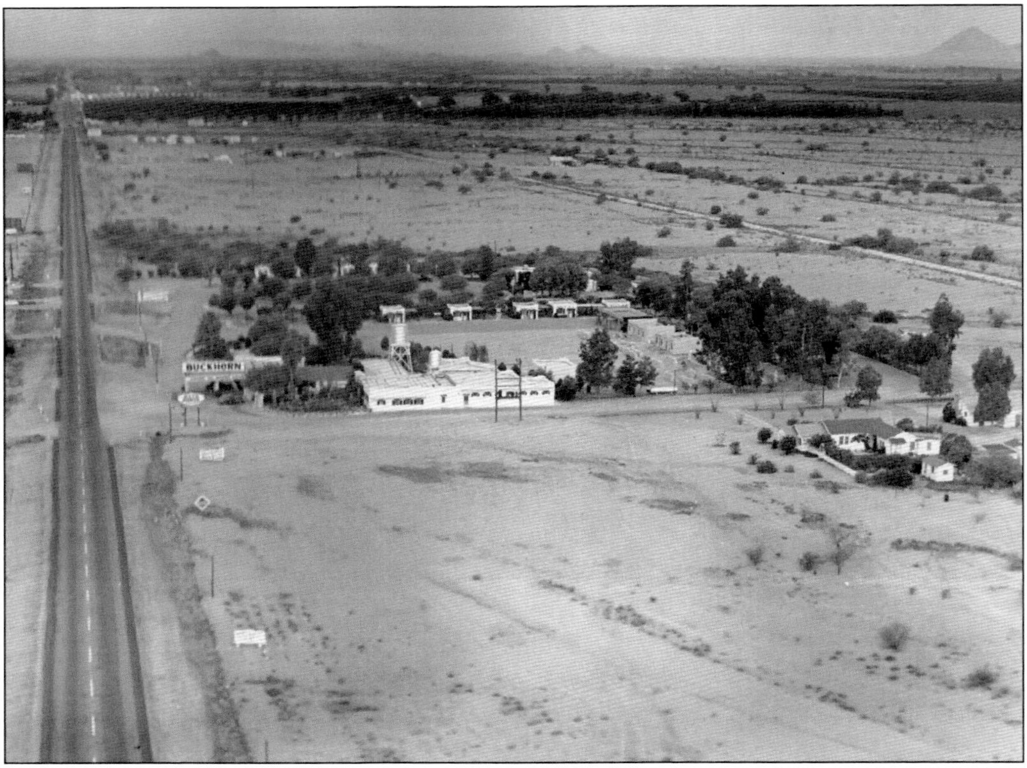

These mid-1940s aerial views clearly show an isolated Buckhorn surrounded more by desert than developments that were still two decades away. No doubt four federal highways passing by its front door helped boost business in the early years. As the popularity of the Buckhorn grew, the Sligers embarked on a program of expansion. There were some setbacks along the way. Major washes running across the site resulted in periodic flooding. And a rival motor court/spa immediately west of the Buckhorn caused tension between owners until the Sligers bought out their competition. (Above, courtesy MHM, below, courtesy Ted and Jerri Sliger.)

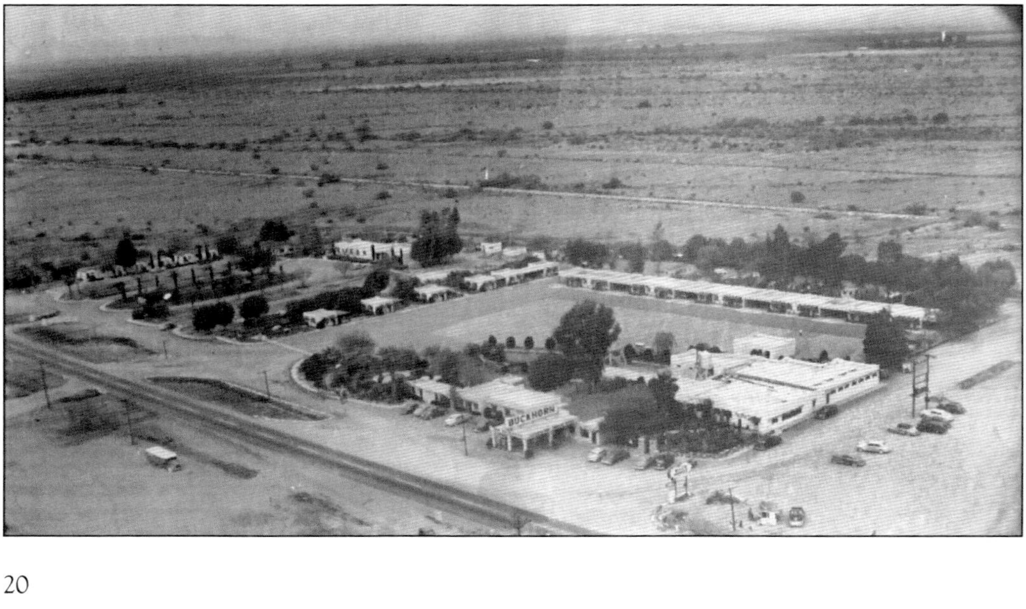

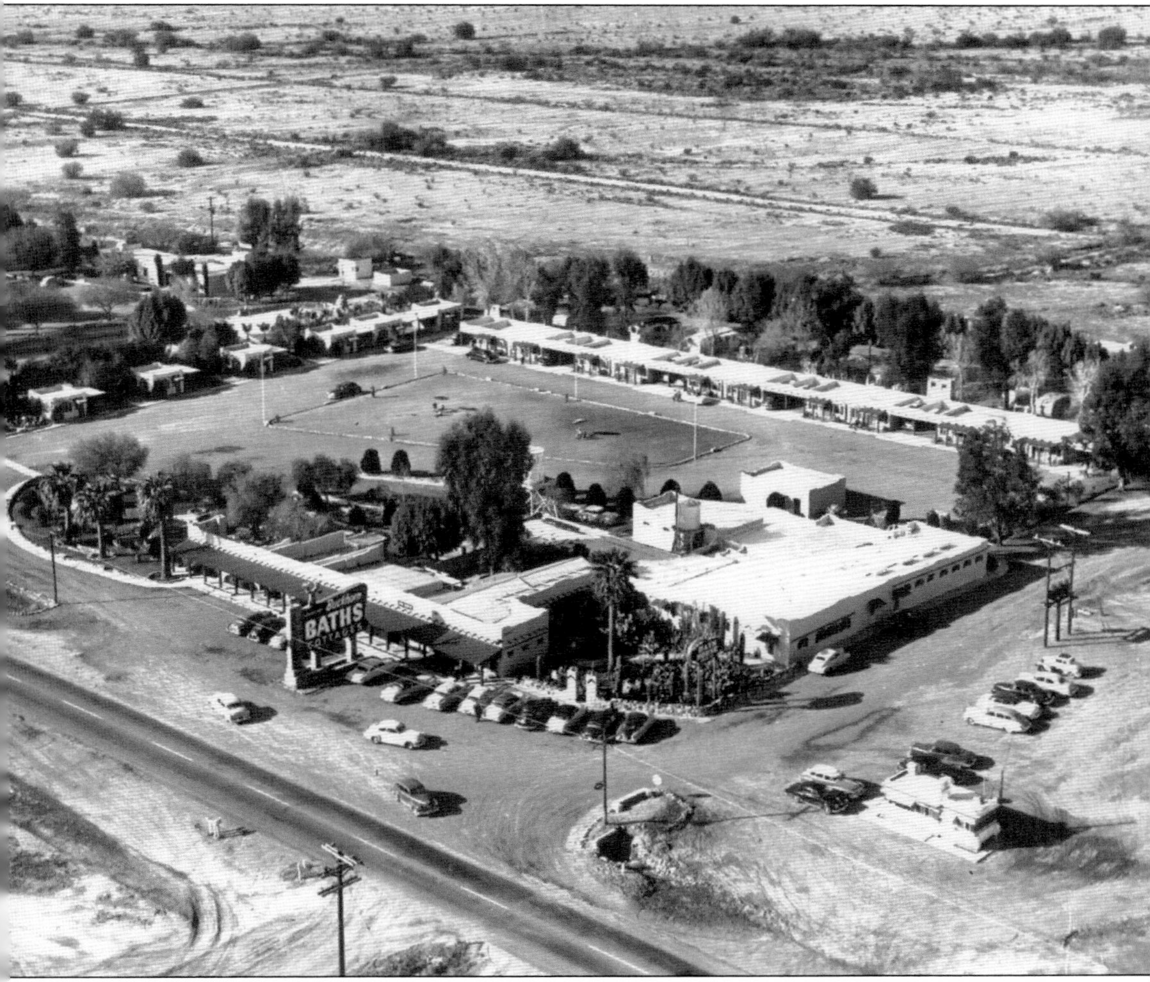

By 1949, when the old porte cochere and gas station were removed in favor of a new, monumental neon sign, the Buckhorn was a bustling place. Across present-day Recker Road (lower right), the independently owned Buckhorn Diner replaced the onsite restaurant. It was a time of continual growth and change. Business was booming in this mid-1950s aerial view. The rooftop of the casitas at right provided a deck for sunbathers. Accommodations were made for travel trailers (seen behind the casitas). Ted kept up the Southwestern theme in all of the additions. (Courtesy MHM.)

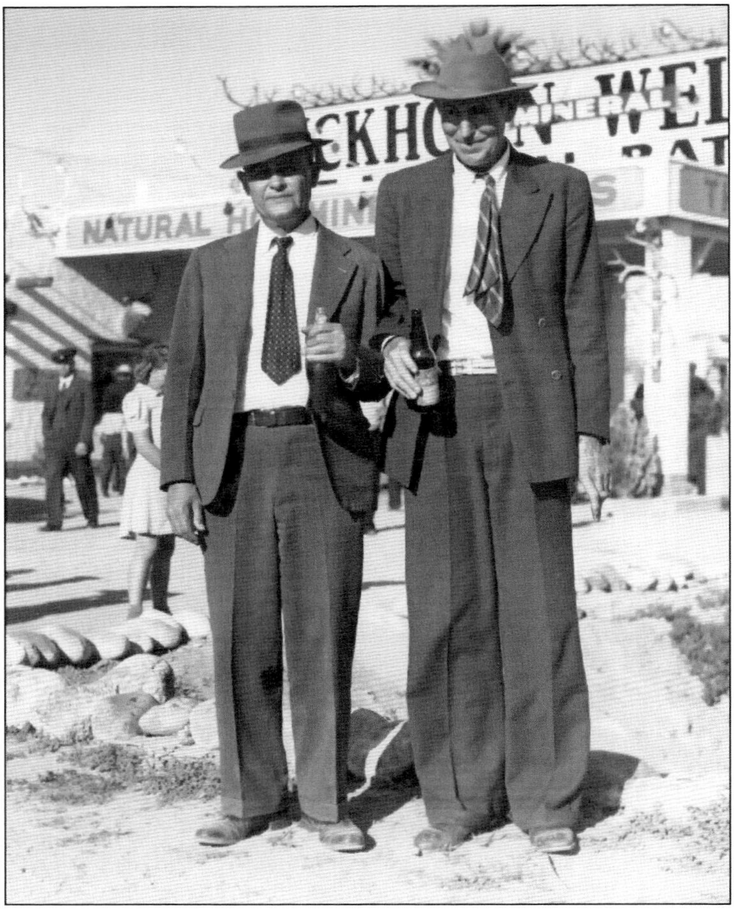

Guests were invited to stop by and say hi and enjoy a glass of water, soda, or beer. Hot baths with refreshing mineral water and Ted's collection of Arizona wildlife were the main attractions, but don't forget the famous Cactus Candy. (Courtesy MHM.)

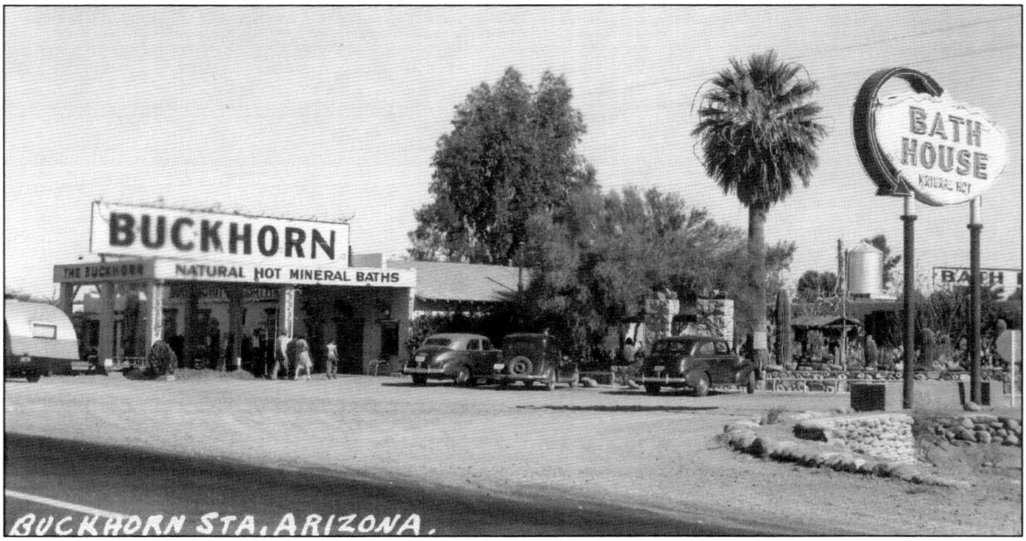

Prosperity is beginning to show, and a new neon "Bath House" sign points the way. Metate-embedded walls are in place around the cactus garden. Saunter in and make a wish at the wishing well.

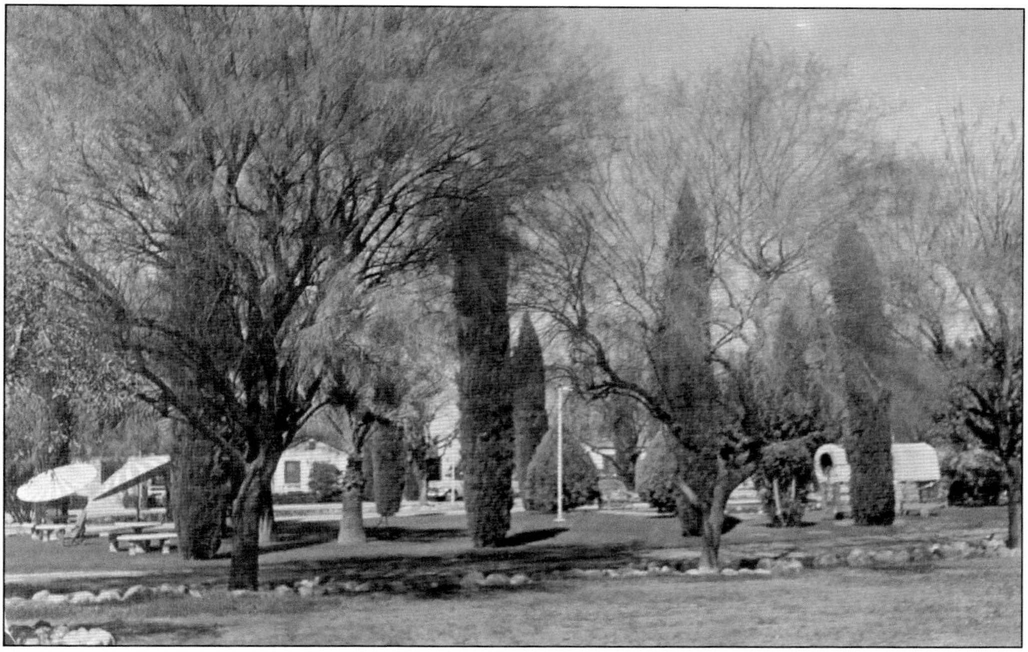

Little is known about the Buckhorn's competitor that opened right next door. In a 1997 interview, Alice recalled that she and Ted were very upset that the land had been bought without their knowledge. Larger and more successful, the Sligers would later buy out their rivals and incorporate that business into the Buckhorn. The grounds had a central green area with a reflecting pool and abundant landscaping. (Courtesy MHM.)

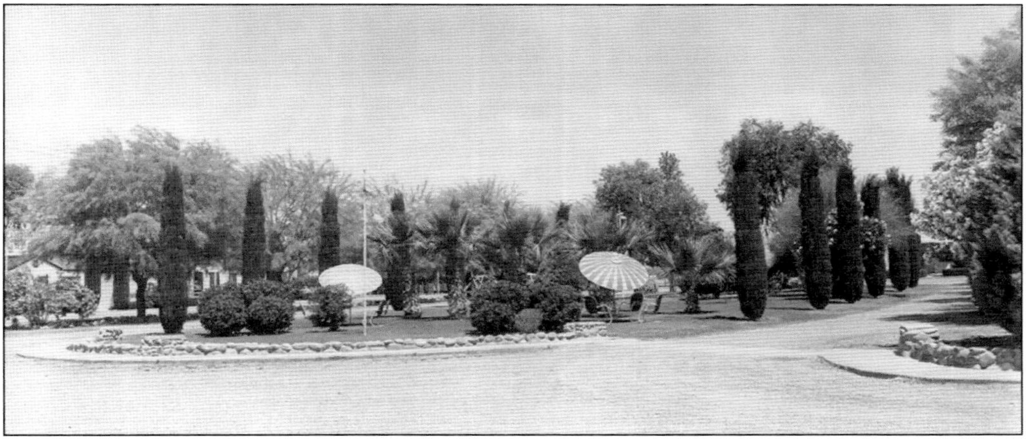

Believed to be the El Maro Hot Mineral Baths, the short-lived competitor did its best to duplicate the Buckhorn's lush, oasis-like look. (Courtesy MHM.)

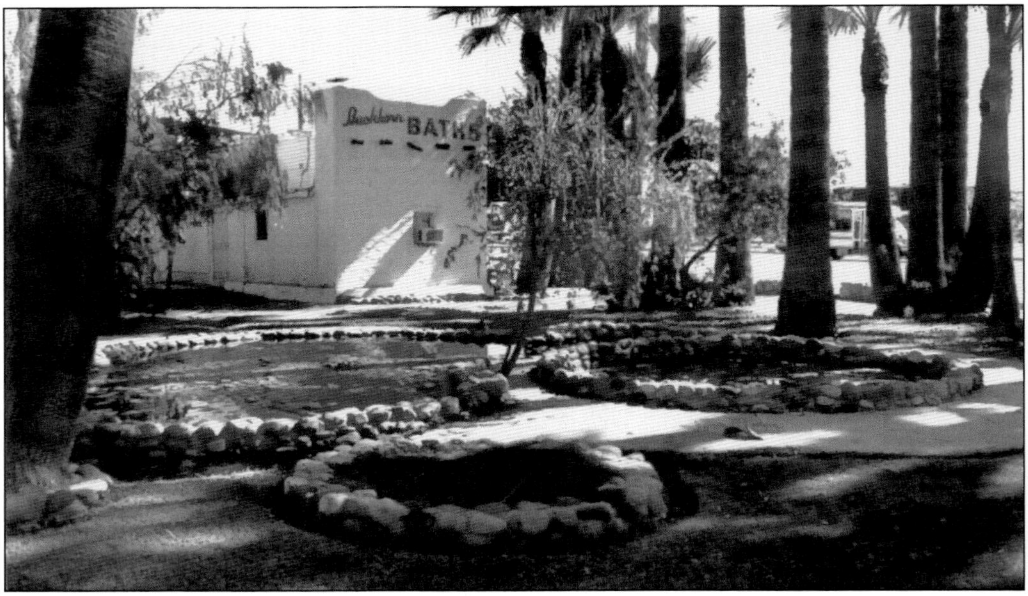

The Sligers quickly began turning the once scrub brush–covered desert into an inviting, lush oasis with numerous water features. Guests could relax and enjoy warm Arizona winter days strolling in the shade of large trees.

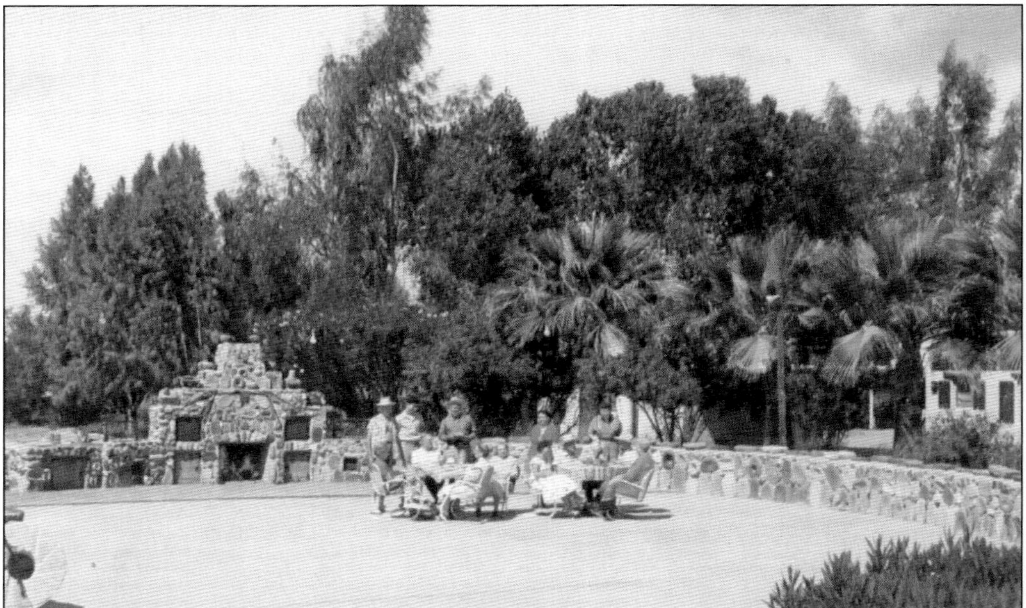

One of the most popular places at the Buckhorn was the expansive barbecue area. Hundreds of people at a time attended the numerous barbecues hosted by the Sligers. Fish fries featured catches brought back from trips to Mexico and wild pigs shot by patrons out in the area surrounding the Buckhorn. Alice later lamented that the barbecues stopped when baseball players left town and people had become too busy for long picnics. Ted once admitted he "liked the good old days" when men like cattleman Bernard Hughes, Tex Barkley, Boss Chilson, and Frank Colcord, "the lion hunter," would drop by. What a time was had at those Buckhorn feasts.

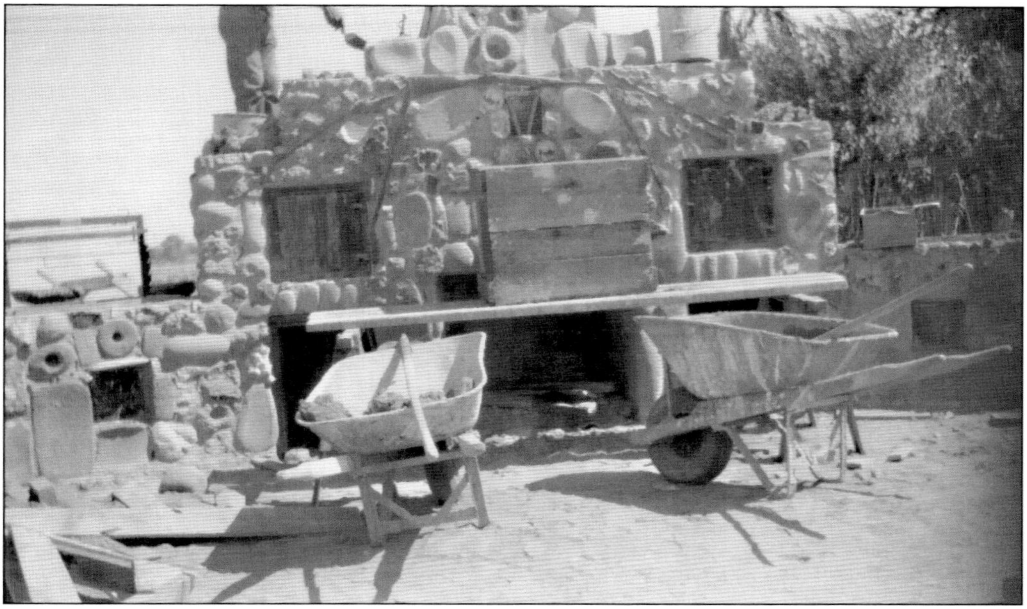

When he began building an elaborate barbecue area in the early 1940s, Ted did not want for material. Rocks were abundant—along with an ample supply of metates, axe heads, minerals, and other artifacts that were at hand to incorporate into the walls and fireplace. Looking carefully at all its elements, a visitor could easily spot rifle barrels, pistols, and all sorts of other Western memorabilia. Hidden amongst the embedded memorabilia are even ancient petroglyphs. Up by the chimney, a worker can be seen placing metates. (Courtesy MHM.)

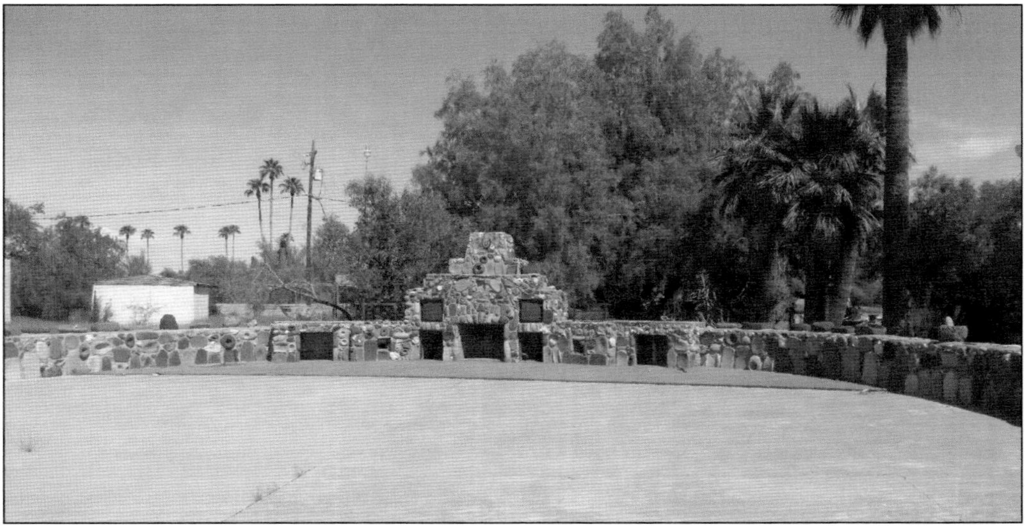

How many baseball and Hollywood stars and famous businessmen enjoyed wild pig smoked at the barbecue, one can only guess. Silent today, one can almost hear the voices of guests sitting at long tables filled with food and drink and country-and-western music filling the air, sometimes provided by the guests themselves. More than six decades after it was constructed, the rock masterpiece still survives to this day, although some of the historic and archeological artifacts have been taken by vandals or treasure hunters.

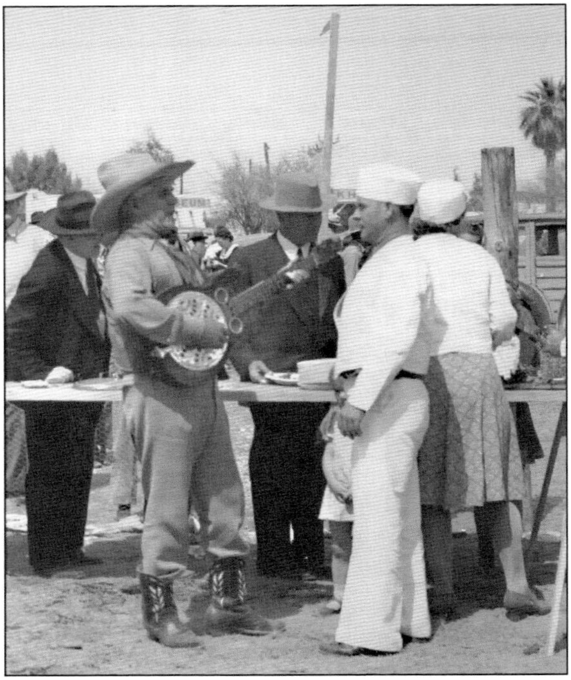

Buckhorn barbecues were the resort's signature activity, often attended by celebrity guests. While some may have been fully dressed in out-of-place business suits and ties, a decidedly Western theme always prevailed—right down to a popular local favorite, banjo-playing cowboy "Powder Jack" Lee. (Courtesy MHM.)

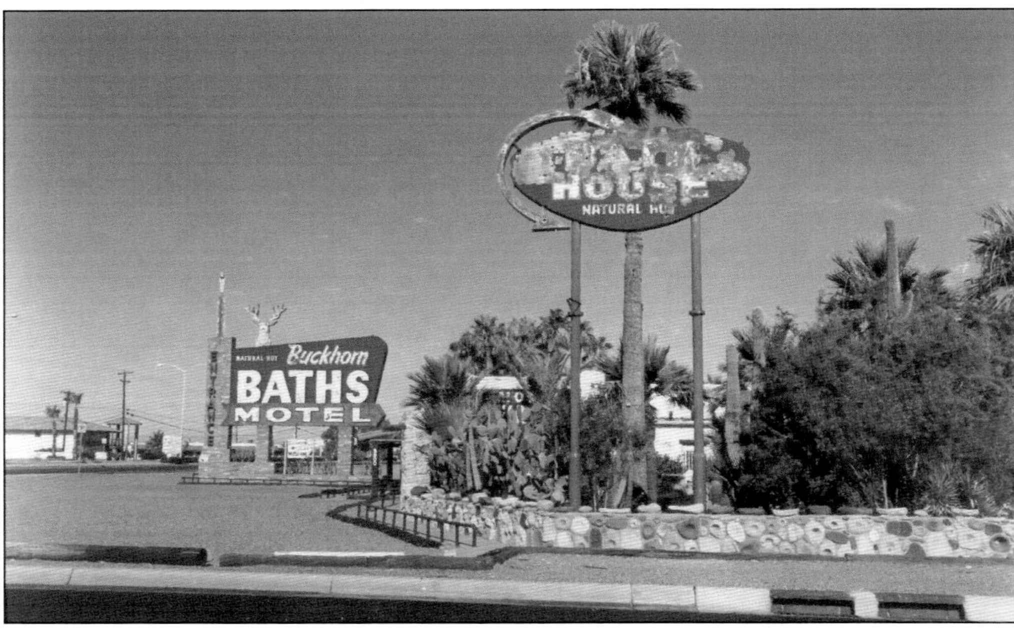

Approaching Mesa out of the darkness, the first thing a motorist saw on a journey down US Highways 60, 70, and 80 was a giant neon sign with a huge stag on top. Bright neon letters announced the "Buckhorn Baths Cottages." The Sligers understood the importance of an imposing sign, which is why they hired Paul Millet, the valley's premier sign maker, to create the biggest and best. The Buckhorn facade has experienced subtle changes over time, like the addition of a unifying tile-covered portal. And the sign that once read "cottages" was changed to the more modern term "motel." But the water always remained the same, "hot and full of minerals and wellness."

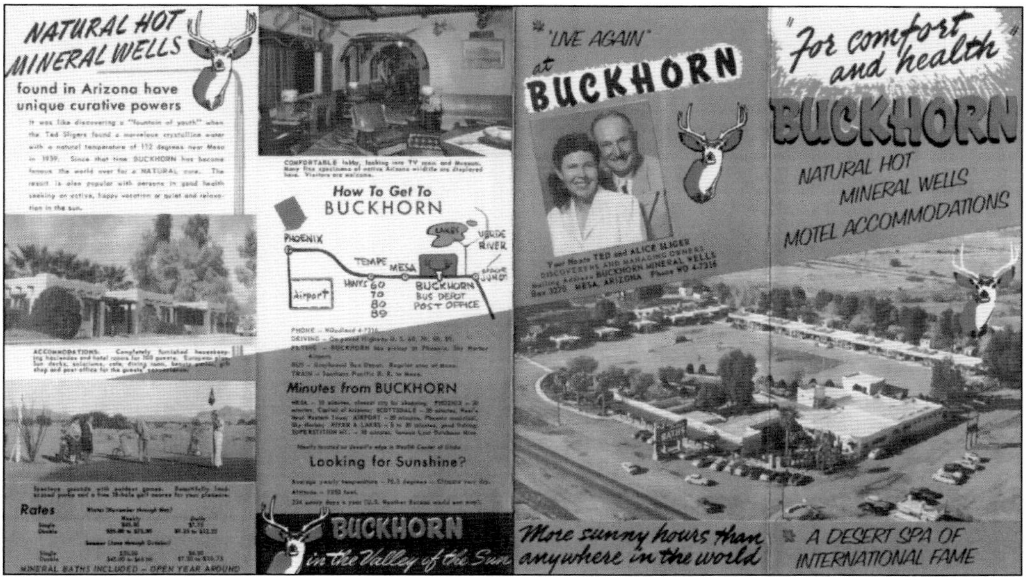

Colorful four-fold brochures were one of the Buckhorn's best promotional tools. One of the earliest was published in the late 1940s shortly after the New York Giants began coming to the resort prior to spring training. Not shy of using superlatives, the Sligers' pamphlet proclaims the Buckhorn as "A Desert Spa of International Fame." Who could argue with the claim "More sunny hours than anywhere in the world." All this for a single winter daily rate of $7.75 or $45 weekly.

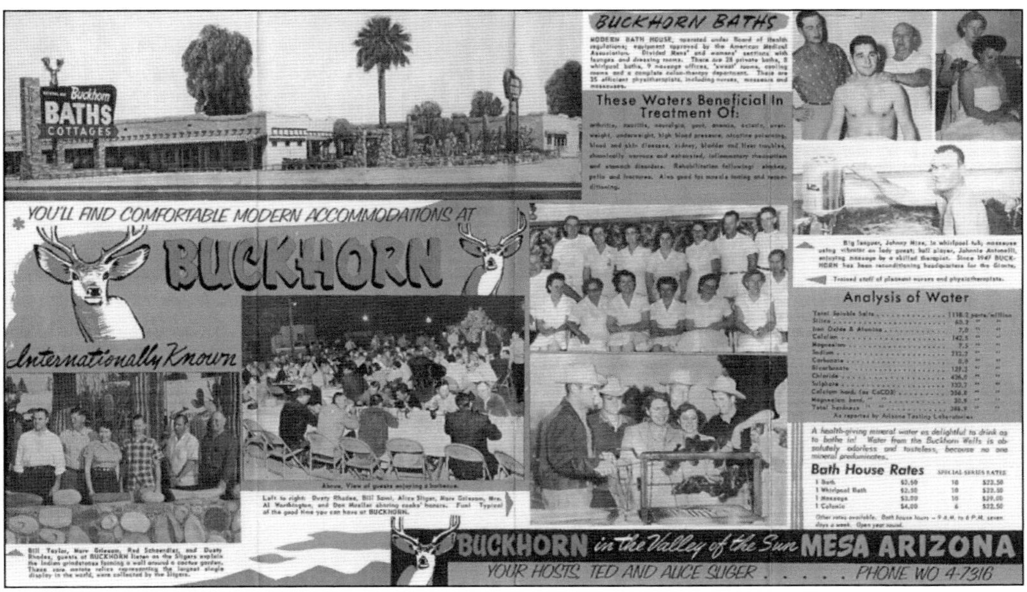

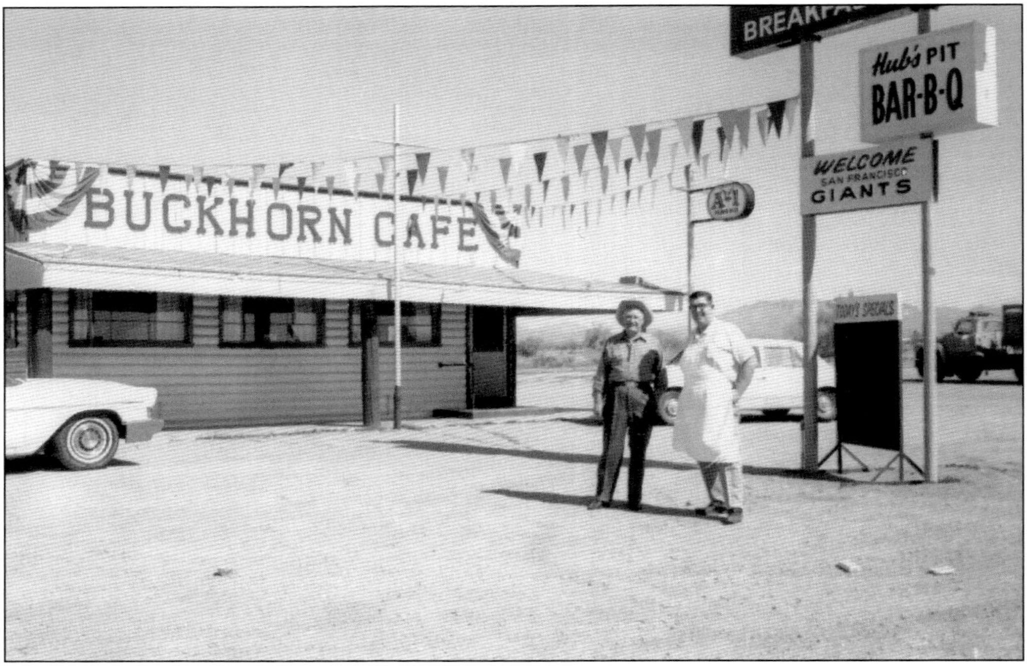

An early feature of the Buckhorn was a small café that the Sligers later closed to make room for a contract post office. Sometime after, the entrepreneurial couple helped set up a new restaurant across what is today Recker Road. The Buckhorn Café featured Hub's Pit Bar-B-Q. Under a sign welcoming the Giants, Ted Sliger poses with Hub in front of the new restaurant. (Courtesy MHM.)

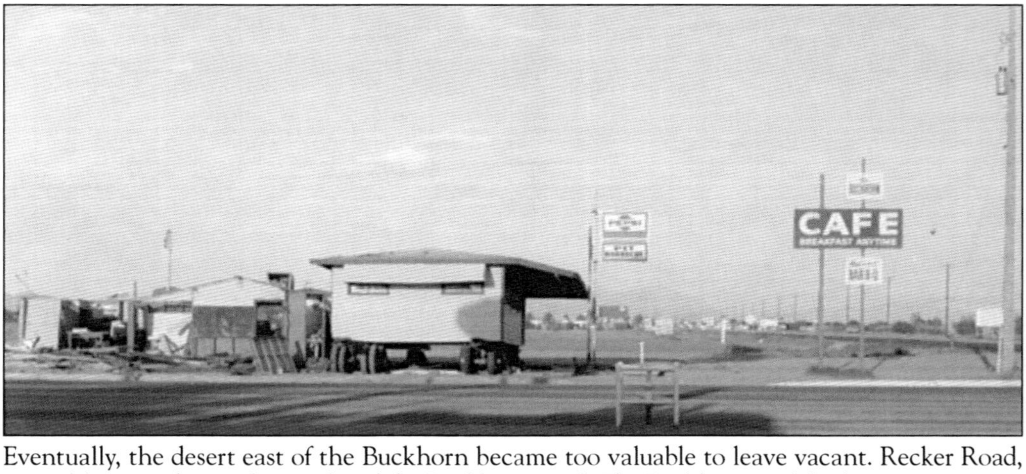

Eventually, the desert east of the Buckhorn became too valuable to leave vacant. Recker Road, named for a nearby rancher, replaced the Buckhorn Trail. The Buckhorn Café had to go. A carriage was placed underneath, and the building was unceremoniously moved north on Recker Road to a new location. A Walgreens parking lot occupies the site today. (Courtesy MHM.)

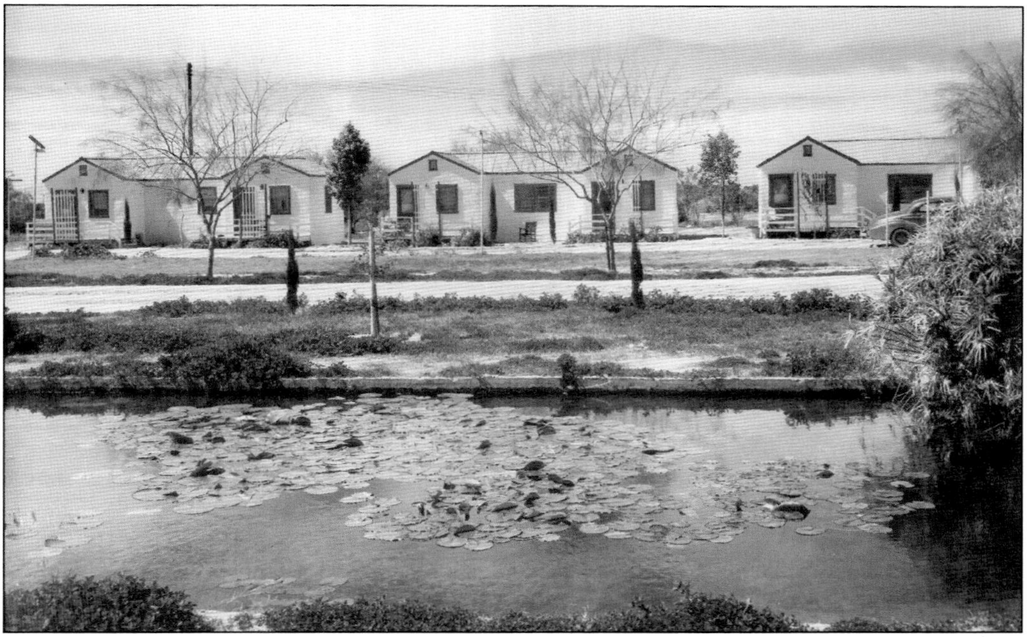

When Ted first tapped into the fissure that produced hot, mineral-laden water, he knew others would probably soon find it too. One of the Buckhorn's early competitors turned up right next door, where three war surplus wood-framed duplex cottages, a four-bath spa, a caretaker's residence, and some limited outdoor amenities were quickly erected. Like many early motor courts, it was an inexpensively built mom-and-pop operation. Virtually all that was needed was a piece of "desert" and a few thousand dollars. The secondhand cottages were poorly constructed, and the block bathhouse had only four hot mineral baths. Four attached motel units made 10 total rental units. In a 1997 interview, Alice stated that she believed the wood cottages had been relocated from nearby Falcon Field after the war, but that claim has not been verified. Following the Sligers' acquisition of the property, the bathhouse was converted into a restaurant. Today, the site is badly deteriorated. (Courtesy MHM.)

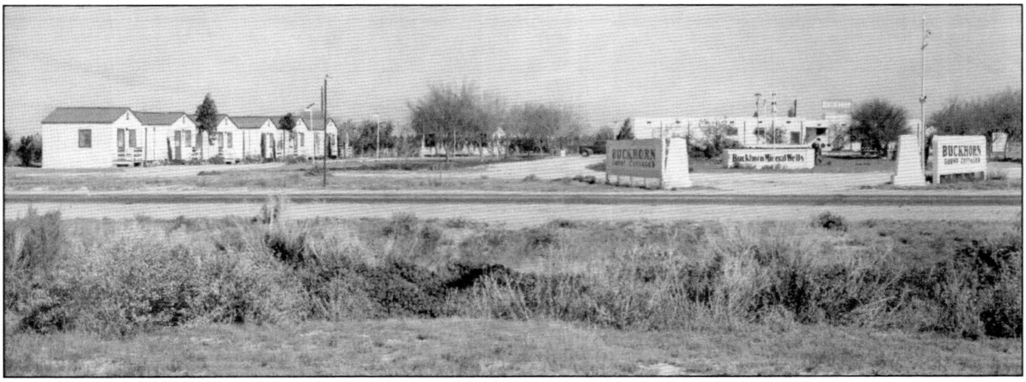

At first, dropping in for a dip at the Buckhorn Baths was a neighborly pastime. But it did not take long for the Sligers to turn the spa into a profitable enterprise. With success came competition nipping at their heels. One of the first was El Maro, an unwelcome neighbor immediately to the west. But it could not steal away much of the Buckhorn business. The Sligers soon bought out their rivals. El Maro was so short-lived that no photographs of it in operation are known to exist. (Courtesy MHM.)

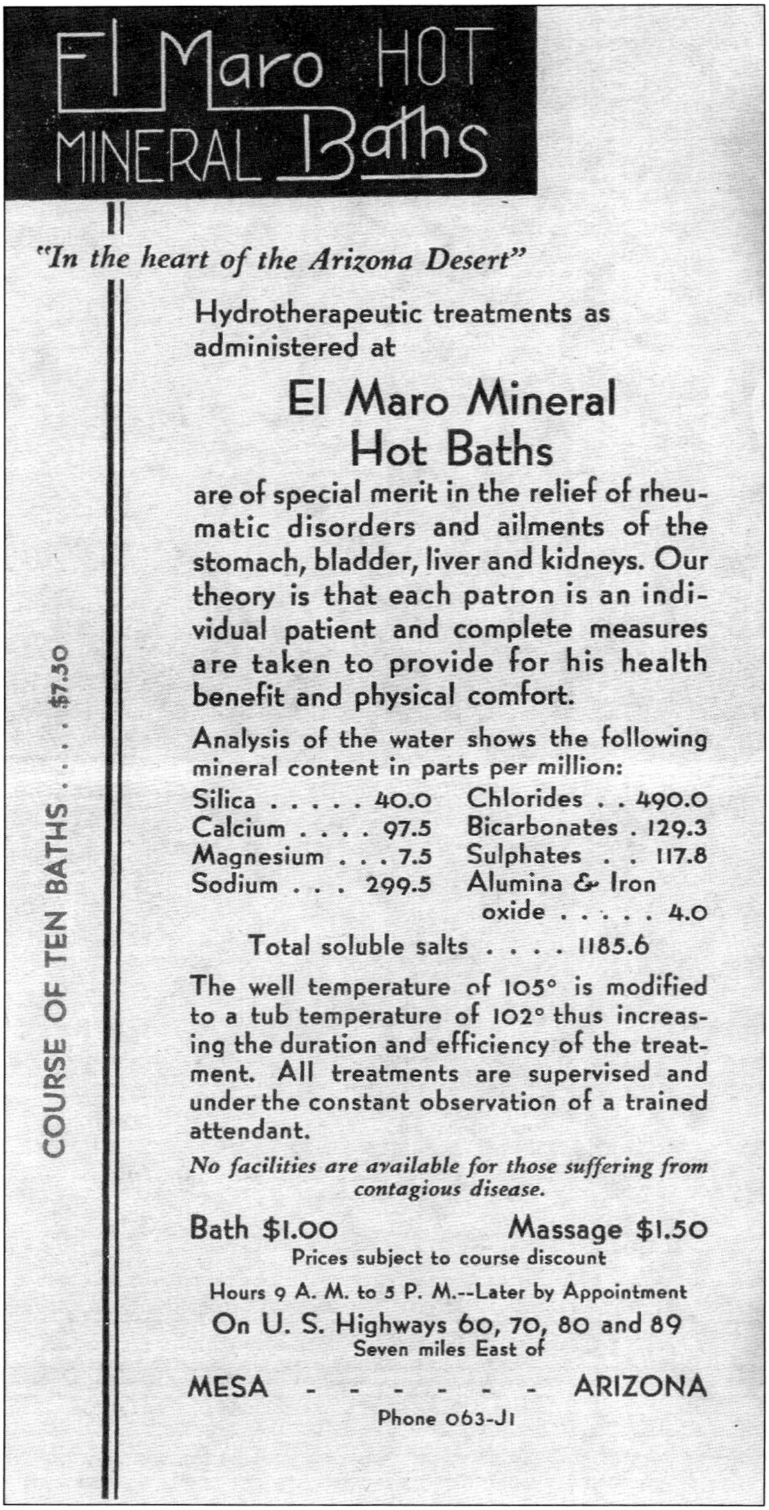

Success always leads to competition. And the Buckhorn was not without its challengers; however, none achieved the resort's fame or outlasted it. Less than two years after the first guest stepped into a Buckhorn hot tub, the El Maro had tapped into the hot springs and began offering its own mineral baths. Short-lived, El Maro advertisements disappeared after 1942. (Courtesy Ted and Jerri Sliger.)

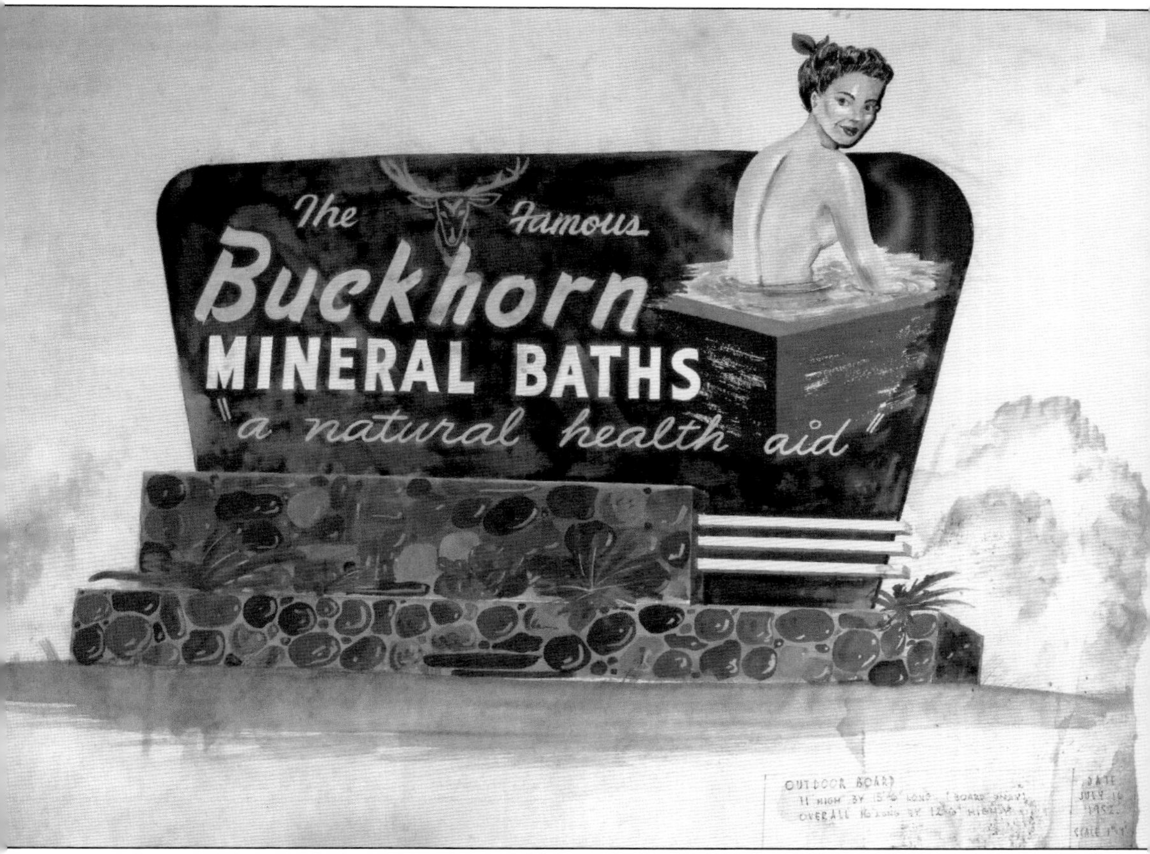

The sign that never was. Many questions surround this recently discovered watercolor rendering by an unidentified artist for a proposed new Buckhorn sign. It was created in 1952. Its most prominent feature was a somewhat risqué bather enjoying a soak in a hot tub. Decidedly Mid-Century Modern, it also incorporated Buckhorn design elements like the iconic stag head and landscaping walls with the base featuring the use of river rock, as opposed to flagstone in the earlier sign. Smaller than the current Buckhorn sign, this one measured 11 feet in height by 15.5 feet in length. Was it meant to replace the existing sign or to be placed in another position on the long frontage road? That is still to be determined. Whatever the full story, the Sligers rejected the design. (Courtesy Ted and Jerri Sliger.)

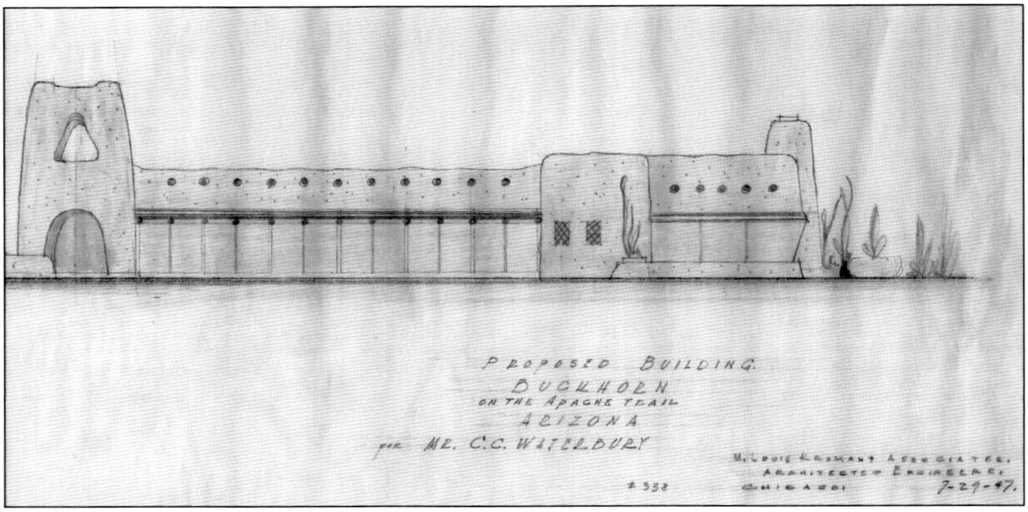

The charm of the Buckhorn is how it evolved organically in the mind of Ted Sliger. He eschewed professional architects, preferring to build what he imagined—all without formal training. That did not stop friend and frequent guest Carl C. "Doc" Waterbury from hiring Chicago architects M. Louis Kroman + Associates in 1947 to create a new, Pueblo-style design and floor plan to replace the front buildings Ted began erecting in 1936. In this scheme, the museum was moved to the east end of the building where the lobby is today. Like the risqué sign design, these plans were rejected, too.

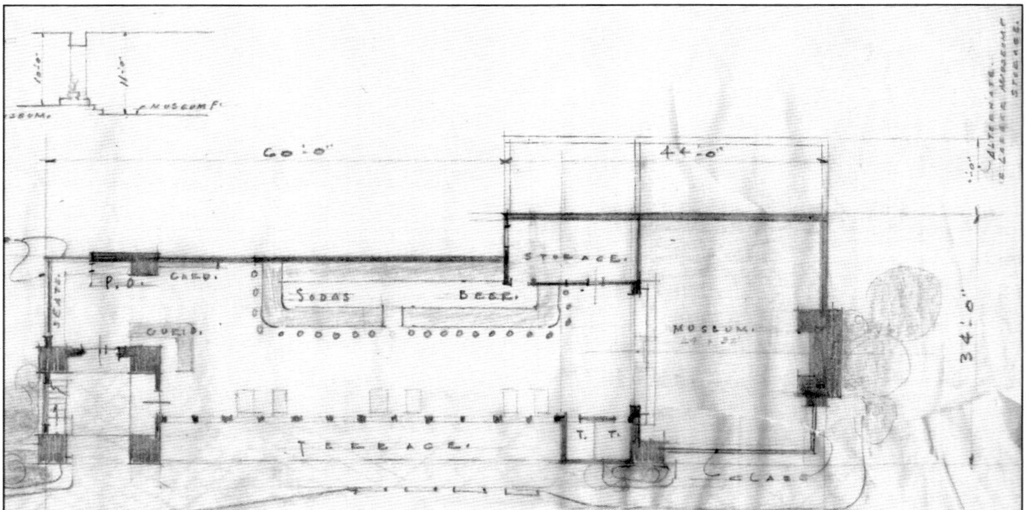

Three

Building a Business One Metate at a Time

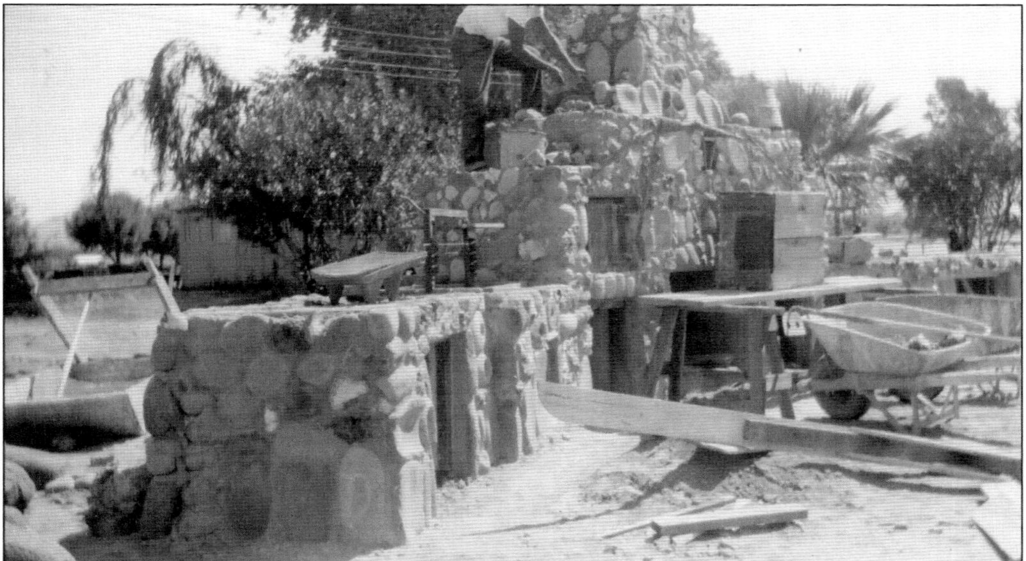

Metate is a stone with a shallow concave surface for grinding corn with a *mano*. Mano (Spanish for "hand") is a small stone used for grinding grain in a metate. Ad hoc is the best way to describe how the Buckhorn evolved—not from some elaborate master plan, but in response to growth and changing needs. In an era free of building codes and permits, Ted Sliger was able to construct whatever he could imagine. Often recycling materials and employing local labor and hands, Ted and Alice economically expanded their continually escalating business in a decidedly distinctive and eclectic manner. (Courtesy MHM.)

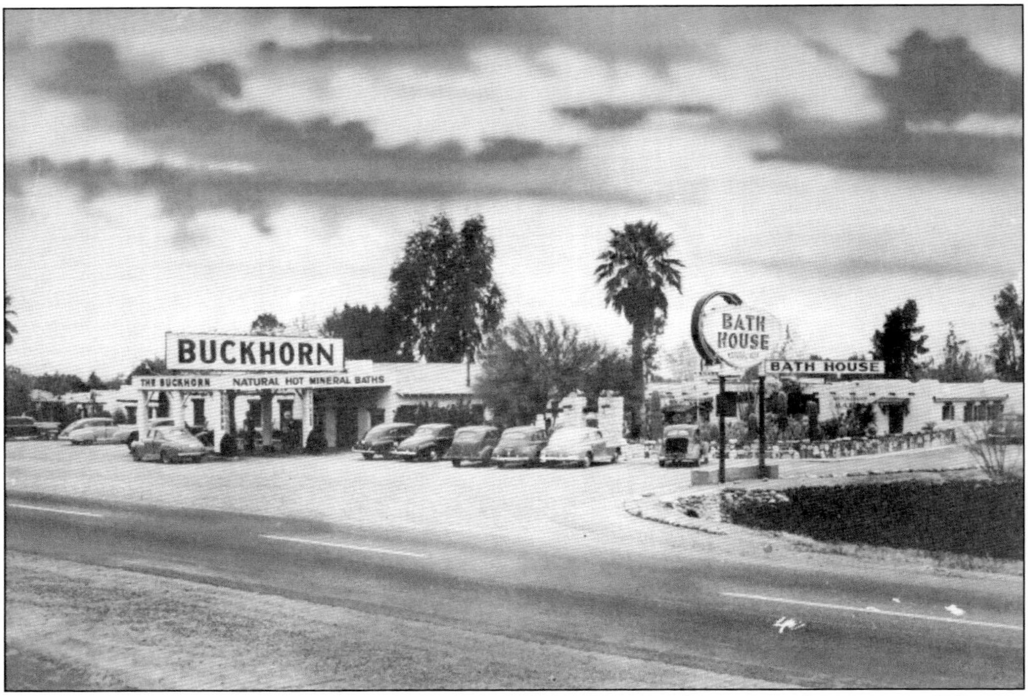

The Buckhorn began in 1936 as a gas station and tourist stop. A porte cochere covered the gas pumps and served as the entrance. After the discovery of hot, mineral-laden water three years later, the Buckhorn erected its first neon sign featuring an arrow brightly pointing the way to the newly opened four-tub bathhouse. From that small sign would come the generous use of more neon in signage and decorative banding throughout the campus.

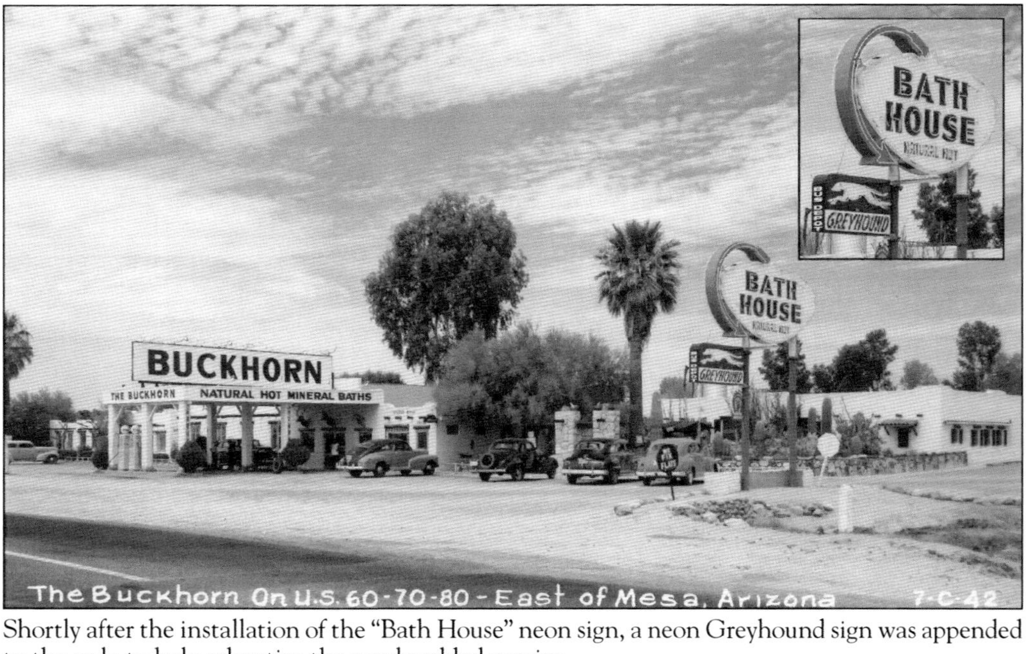

Shortly after the installation of the "Bath House" neon sign, a neon Greyhound sign was appended to the pole to help advertise the newly added service.

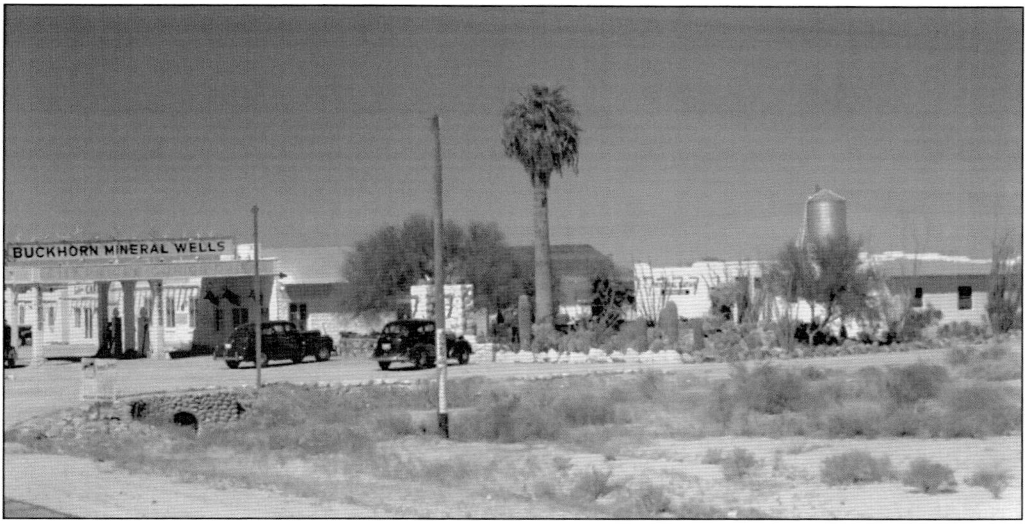

An abundance of early photographs and postcards help document the progress of the Buckhorn's growth. These two postcards detail subtle changes in a short time. The long, horizontal, hand-painted Buckhorn Mineral Wells sign is replaced by a more readable block-letter sign. The cactus garden construction has just gotten under way in the above photograph, while below, the elaborate, inlaid landscape wall has been completed. The image below also shows the addition of the neon bathhouse sign with its distinctive arrow, and an expansion of the bathhouse can be seen. Along the roadside leading up to the Buckhorn is a quaint hand-painted sign touting "Arizona's Largest Wild Life Museum."

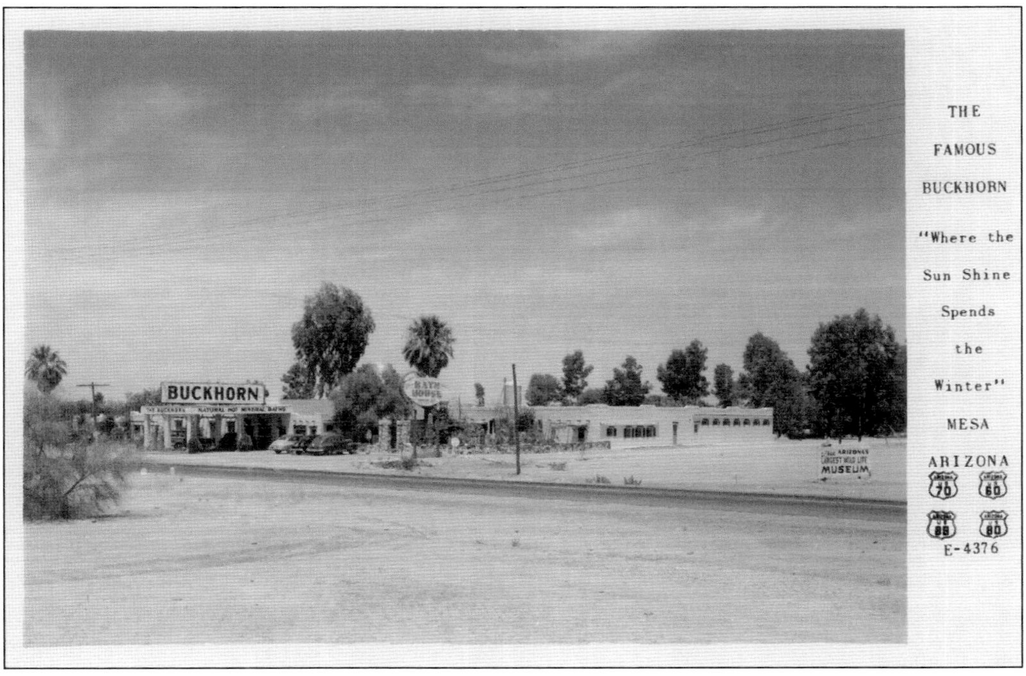

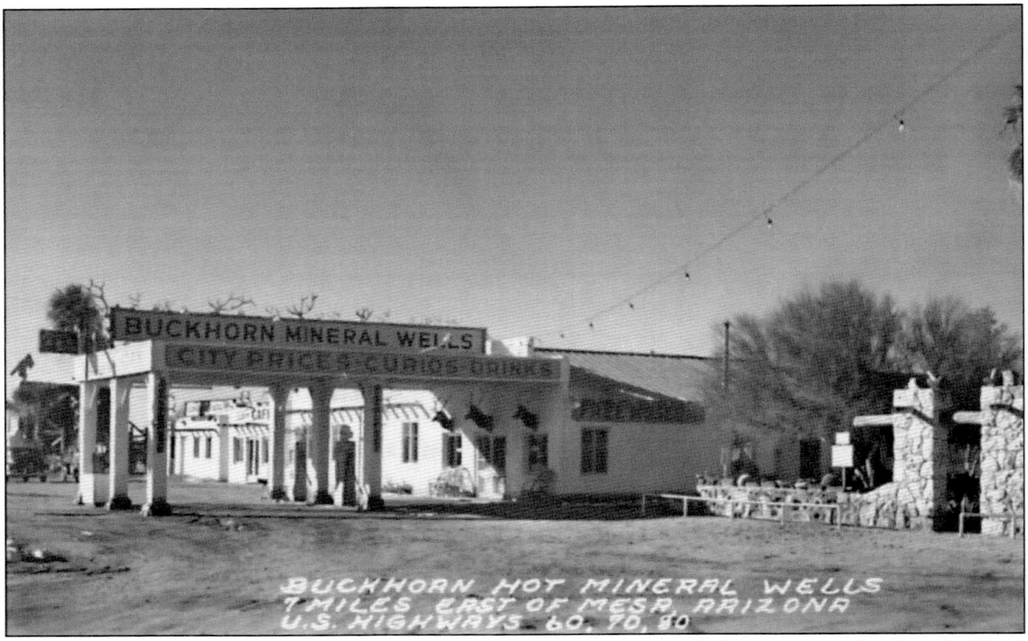

In its earliest years, the Buckhorn more resembled the business Ted Sliger ran on the Apache Trail and Bush Highway before the 1935 Christmas Eve fire. Signage was typical of what was used to entice motorists to pull off the road—"City Prices–Curios–Drinks." A small ABC Beer sign at the front of the port cochere signals availability of the popular refreshment.

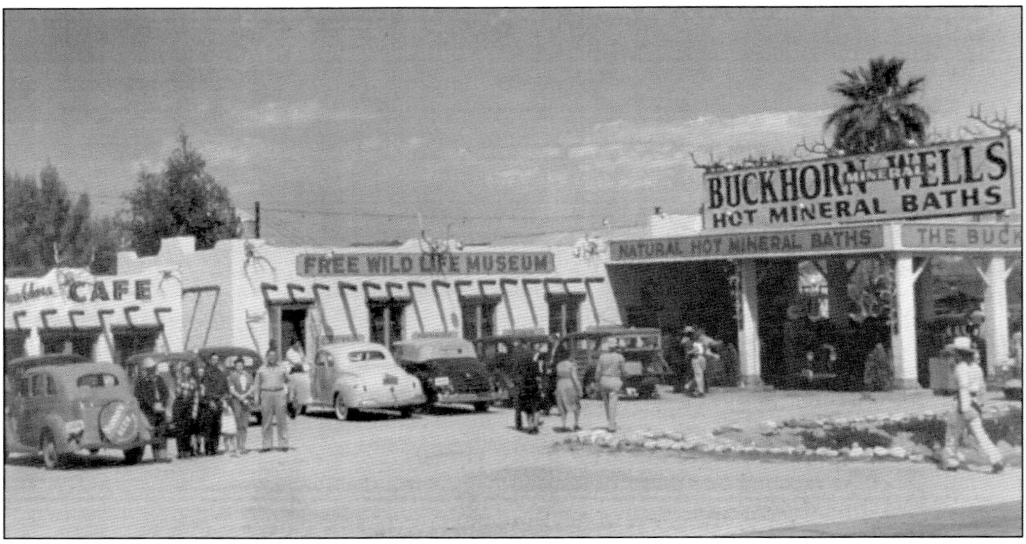

A couple of years later, Buckhorn signage was simplified and began emphasizing its most unique offering, the hot mineral baths. Every day, more and more travelers and tourists were discovering one of the most diverse and appealing attractions along the Apache Trail. A Ford Prefect "Woodie" station wagon (partially visible at right), manufactured between 1938 and 1941, helps date this postcard.

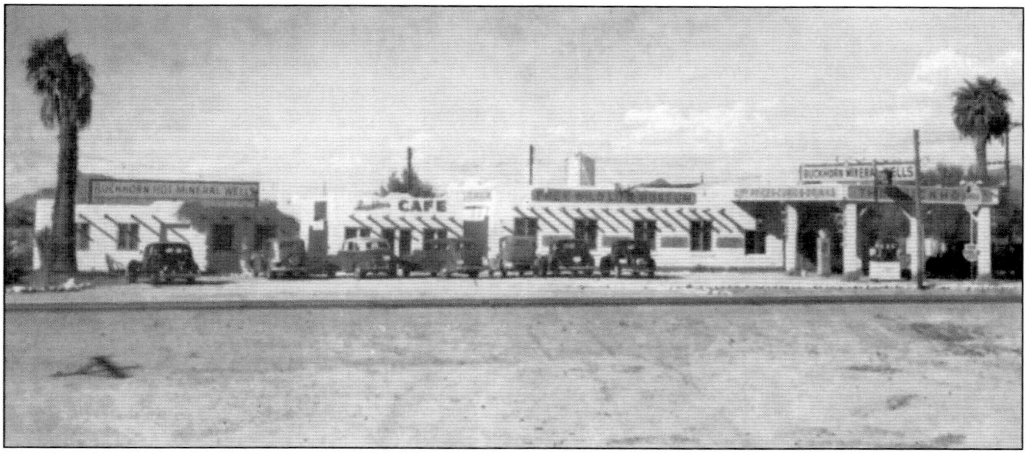

To accommodate a mushrooming empire, the Buckhorn expanded one building at a time, adding along its frontage a café, beauty shop, post office, and Greyhound bus stop. (See the map on page 44 for dates.) Seven miles east of Mesa, the Buckhorn was one of the first stops for road-weary travelers. That is why it did not take long for the resort to become the premier attraction along the Apache Trail.

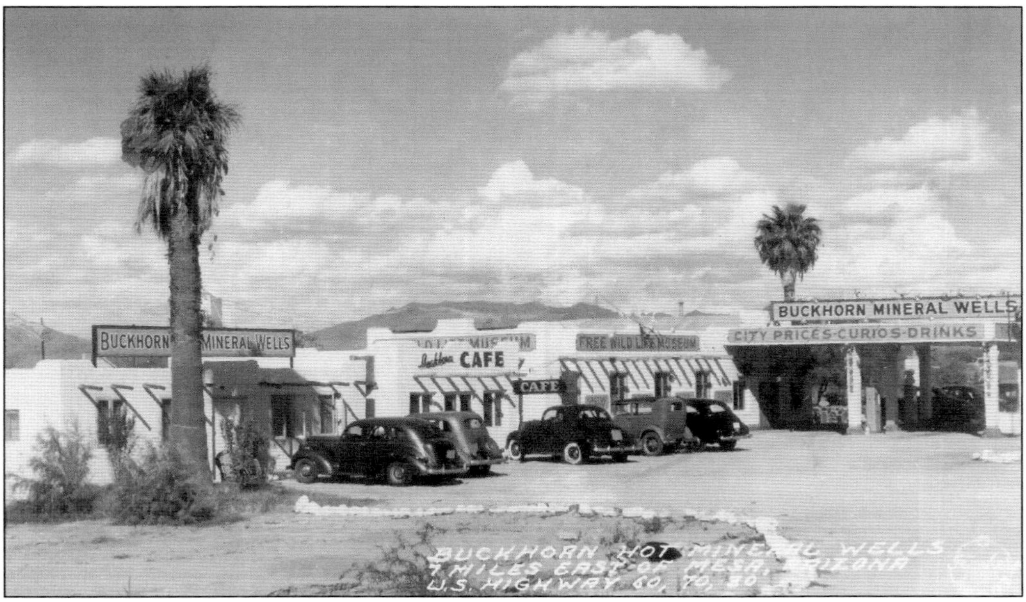

World War II restrictions slowed tourist traffic, but that was somewhat offset by military personnel training at nearby Williams and Falcon Airfields. Cars pulled in for food, gas, refreshments, the Wildlife Museum, and, of course, the mineral baths—sufficient to keep the Buckhorn growing though that troubled period.

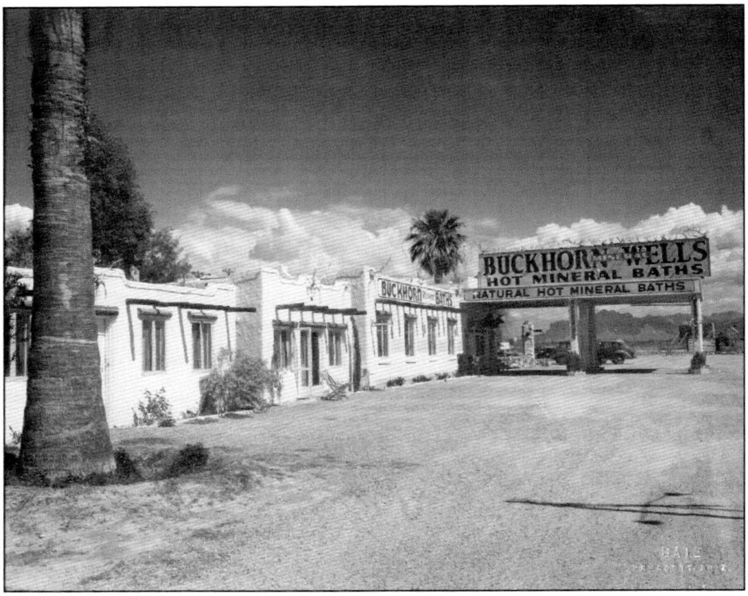

Recognized as art patrons, the Sligers always sought the best talent. They commissioned Prescott newspaper and portrait photographer Thomas Bate to take photographs of the Buckhorn. This early image is the only one known to exist from a series. (Courtesy MHM.)

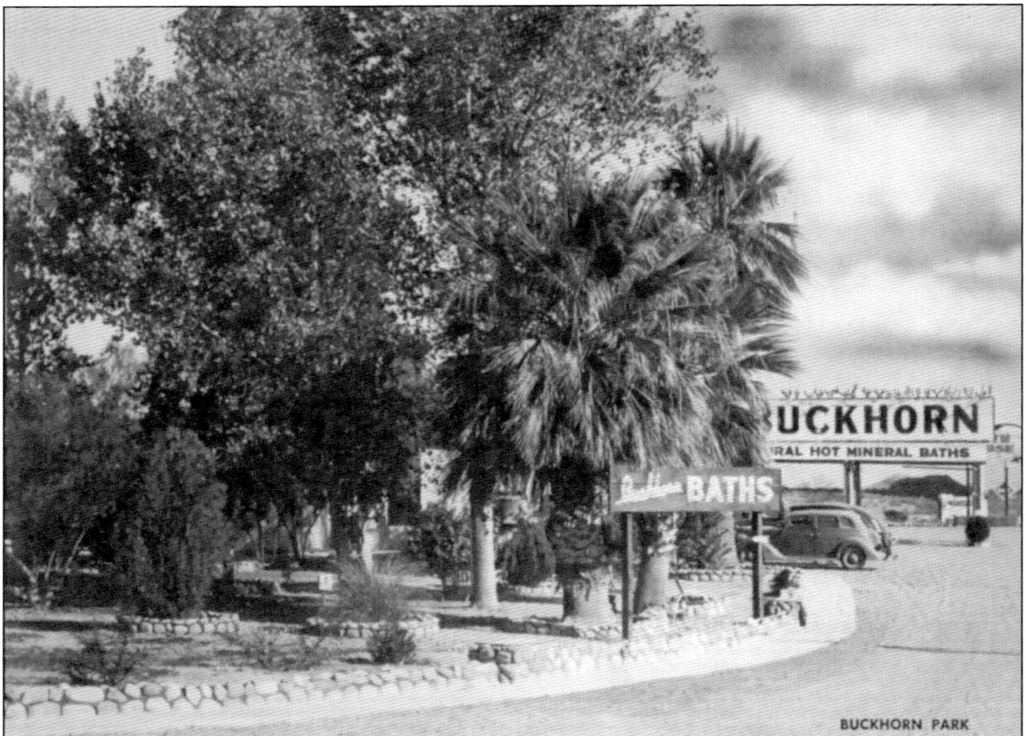

When the Sligers finally secured a reliable supply of well water on the property, they made sure the Buckhorn became a welcoming oasis for road-weary motorists. A hint of the lush Buckhorn Park is shown on this postcard.

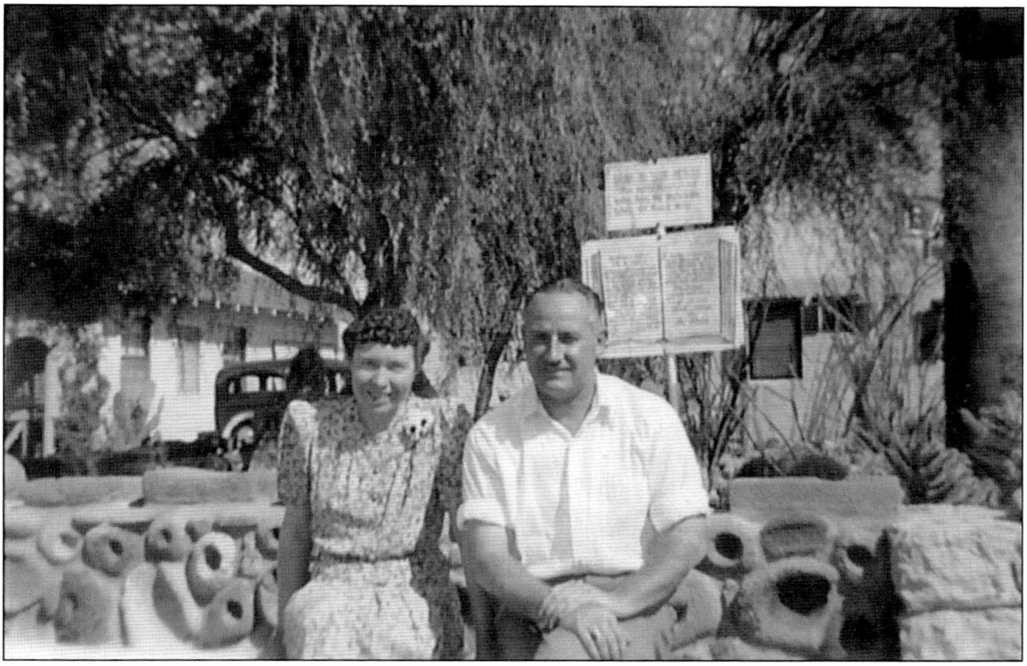

Ted and Alice pose in front of their newly completed cactus garden wall, with their small home at left in the background. A sign behind the couple proclaims the wall contains "the world's largest collection of Indian grindstones (metates)." Another describes how and why the wall was built. (Courtesy Ted and Jerri Sliger.)

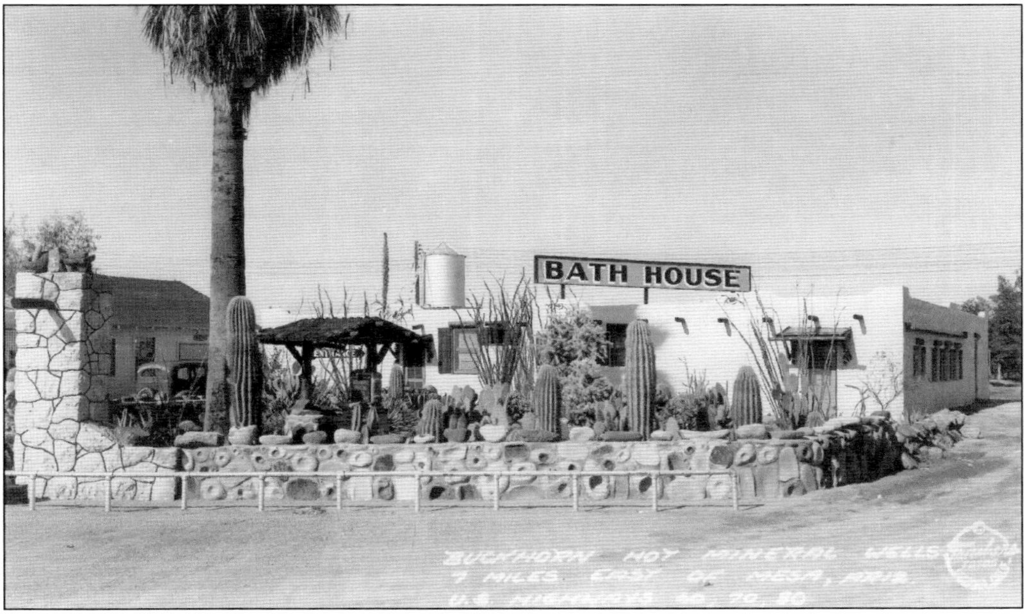

The Buckhorn cactus garden, with its metates embedded into the walls, was one of Ted Sliger's earliest constructed features. Varieties of cacti were planted. When a wishing well was added, guests could drop coins in it.

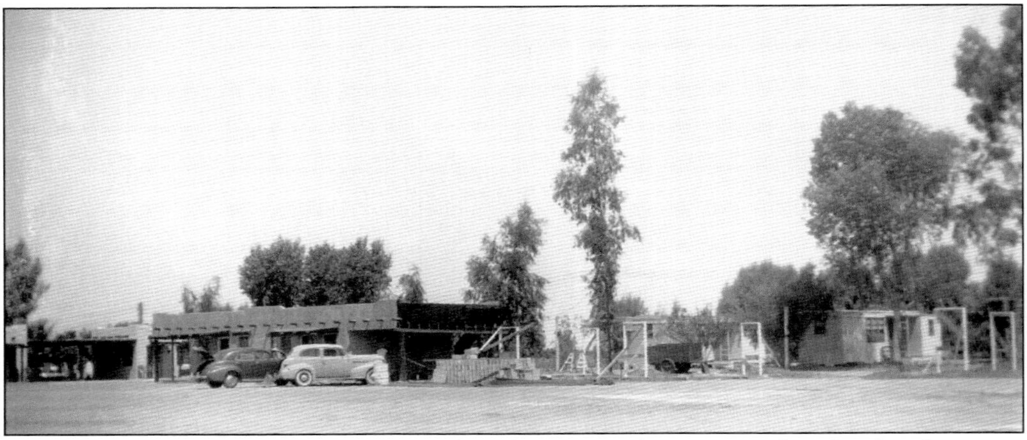

Of the thousands of Buckhorn photographs Alice amassed over seven decades, few document how it was built. A handful of images taken during the construction of the northern motel units in 1949 have recently surfaced. Here, two completed units sit next to others undergoing framing, while cement blocks are stacked up. (Courtesy Ted and Jerri Sliger.)

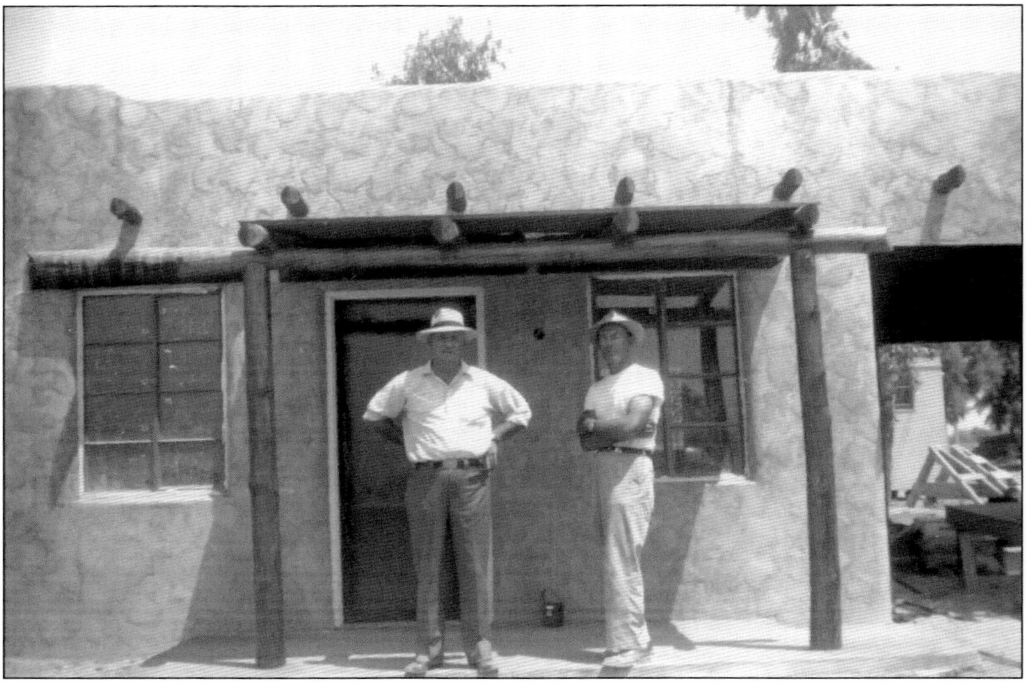

In a rare 1949 photograph, Ted Sliger (left) stands with an unidentified builder in front of a newly completed and freshly stuccoed motel unit. In building the new rooms to supplement the older cottages, the Sligers were acknowledging postwar traveler's changing tastes. (Courtesy Ted and Jerri Sliger.)

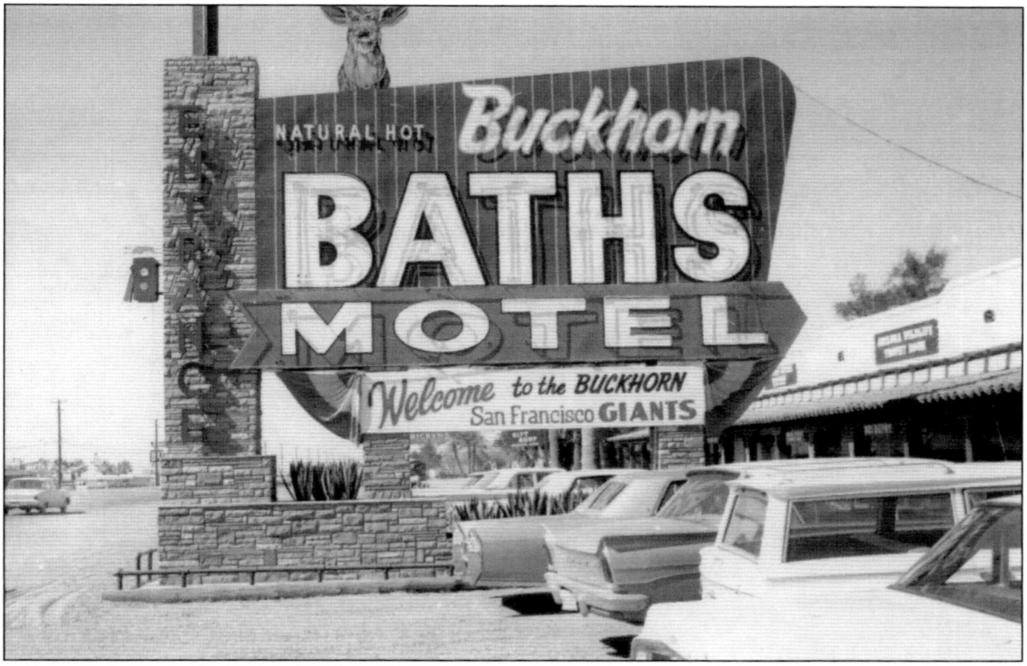

In 1949, after nearly a decade of successfully running their health spa, the Sligers gave up selling gas and demolished the old porte cochere, replacing it with a monumental neon sign designed by graphic artist Glen Guyette and built by master sign maker Paul Millett. For travelers along Highways 60, 70, 80, or 89, there was no missing the sign with the giant stag on top, day or night.

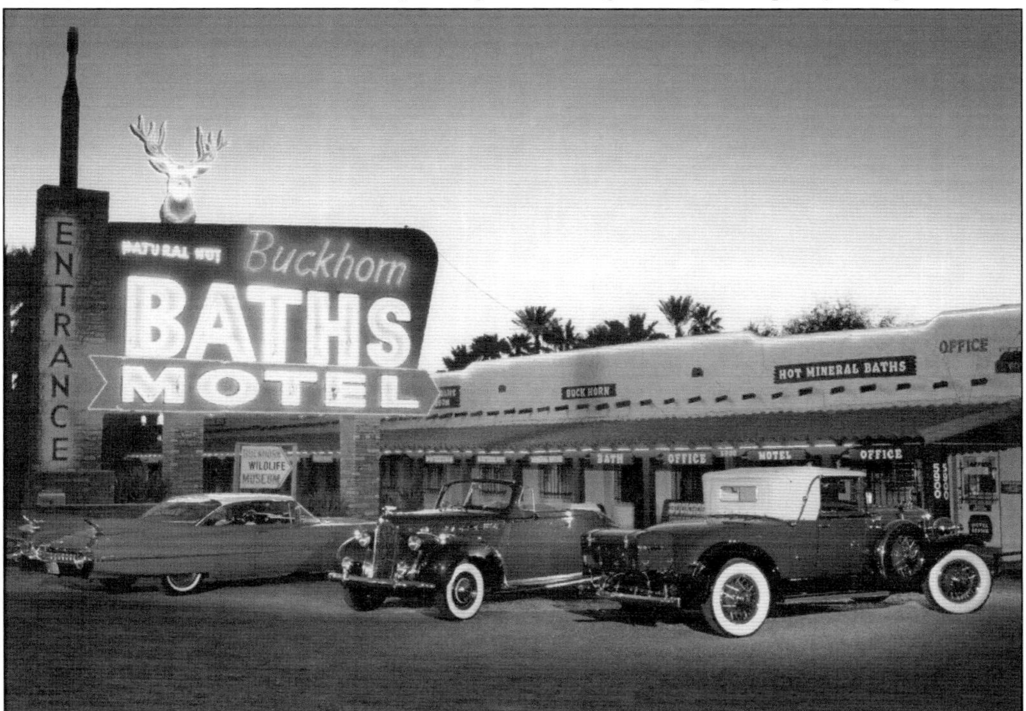

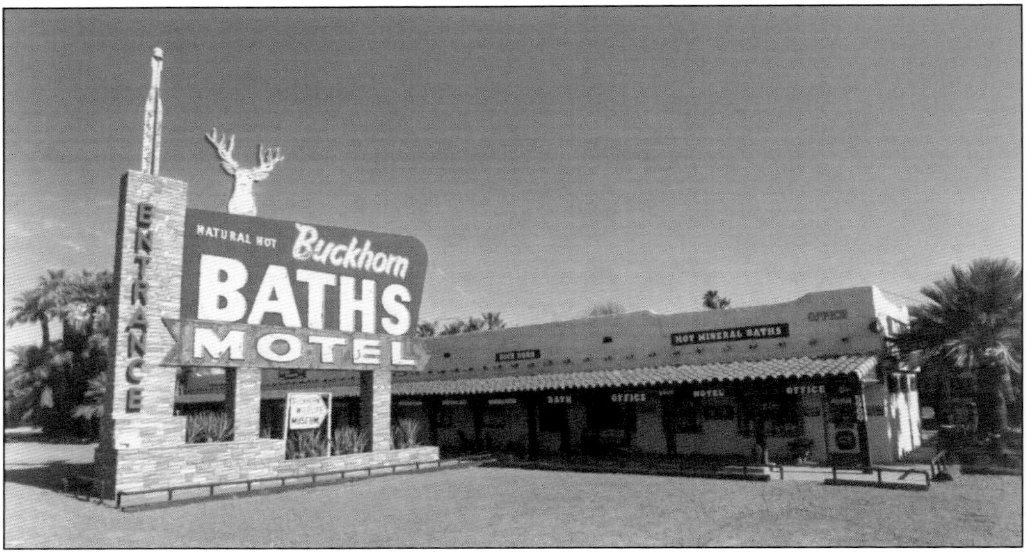

Although subtle alterations were made to it over the years, there is no argument that the most recognizable feature of the Buckhorn is its imposing and towering neon sign. Regrettably, no receipts exist to tell how much the Sligers paid for the masterpiece. It is safe to conclude, however, that when it was installed about 1949, it was the single most expensive investment they had made in the business to date. With its bright, colorful neon lighting up the night sky and its giant size attracting daytime attention, they no doubt agreed it was well worth the price.

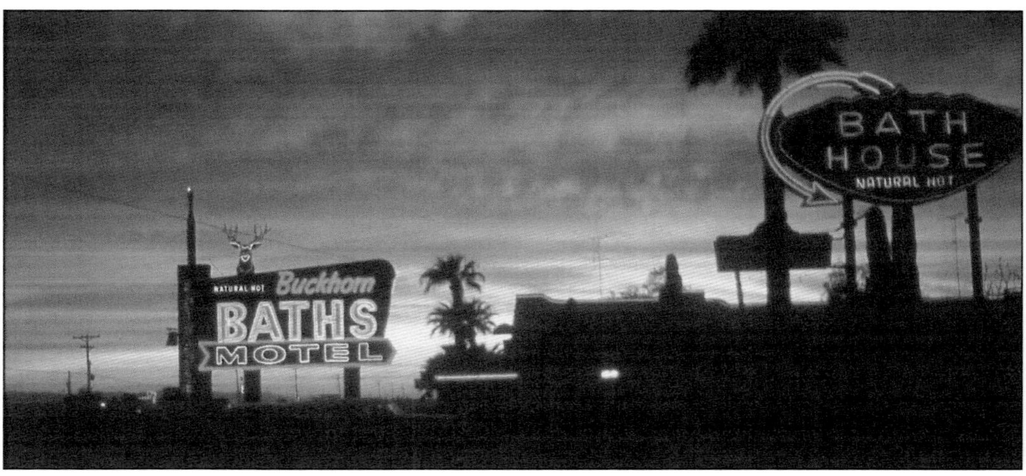

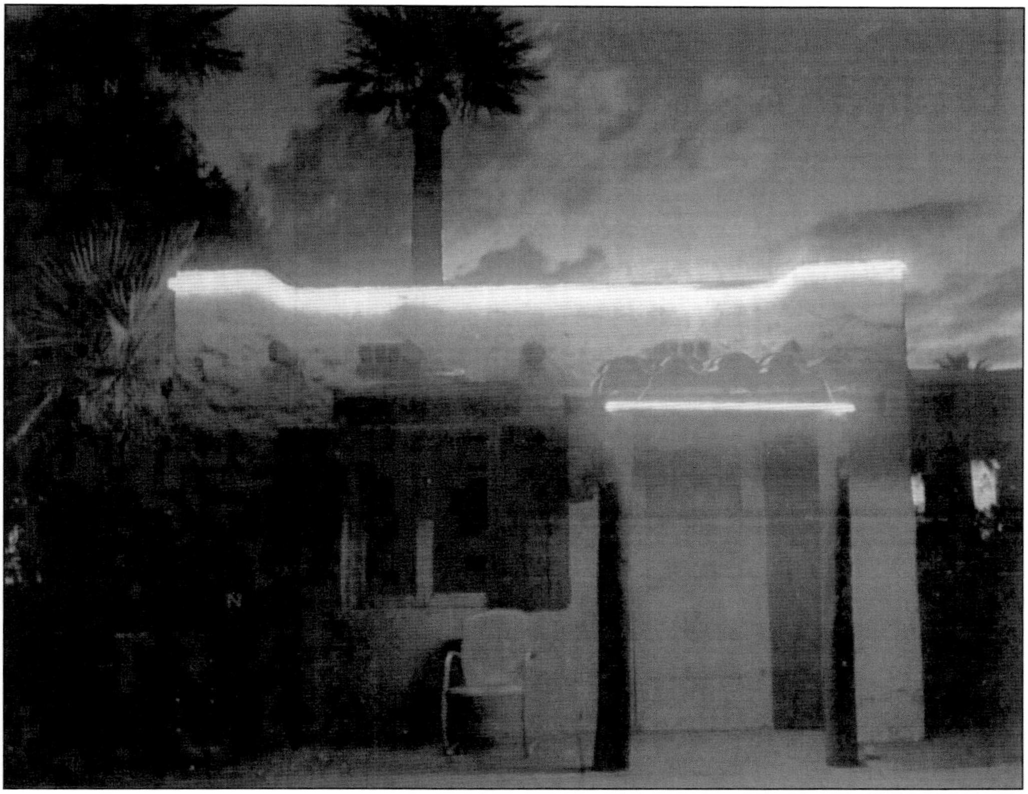

The Buckhorn was pioneering in its recognition of the value of incorporating neon into roadside signage and architecture. The resort may very well have had more lineal footage of neon than any other business on Main Street. Along with more than a dozen neon signs large and small, all building rooflines were outlined with colorful neon. All that neon created a glow around the Buckhorn that could be seen from a considerable distance by motorists traveling the dark two-lane highway. (Courtesy MHM.)

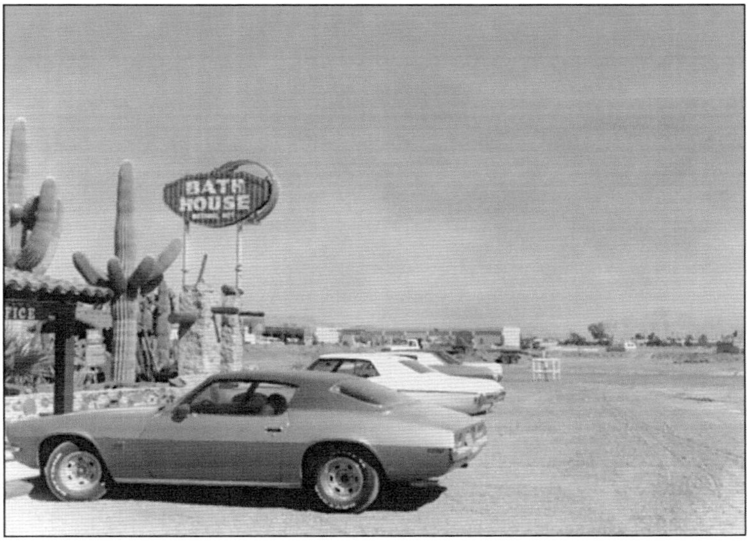

By the 1970s, Mesa's growth had expanded all the way to the Buckhorn and beyond. The once open desert just east of the resort was being cleared for an automobile-oriented strip shopping center. The first neon sign, erected shortly after the baths opened to the public, was still maintained—its large, arcing arrow pointing the way to the bathhouse. (Courtesy MHM.)

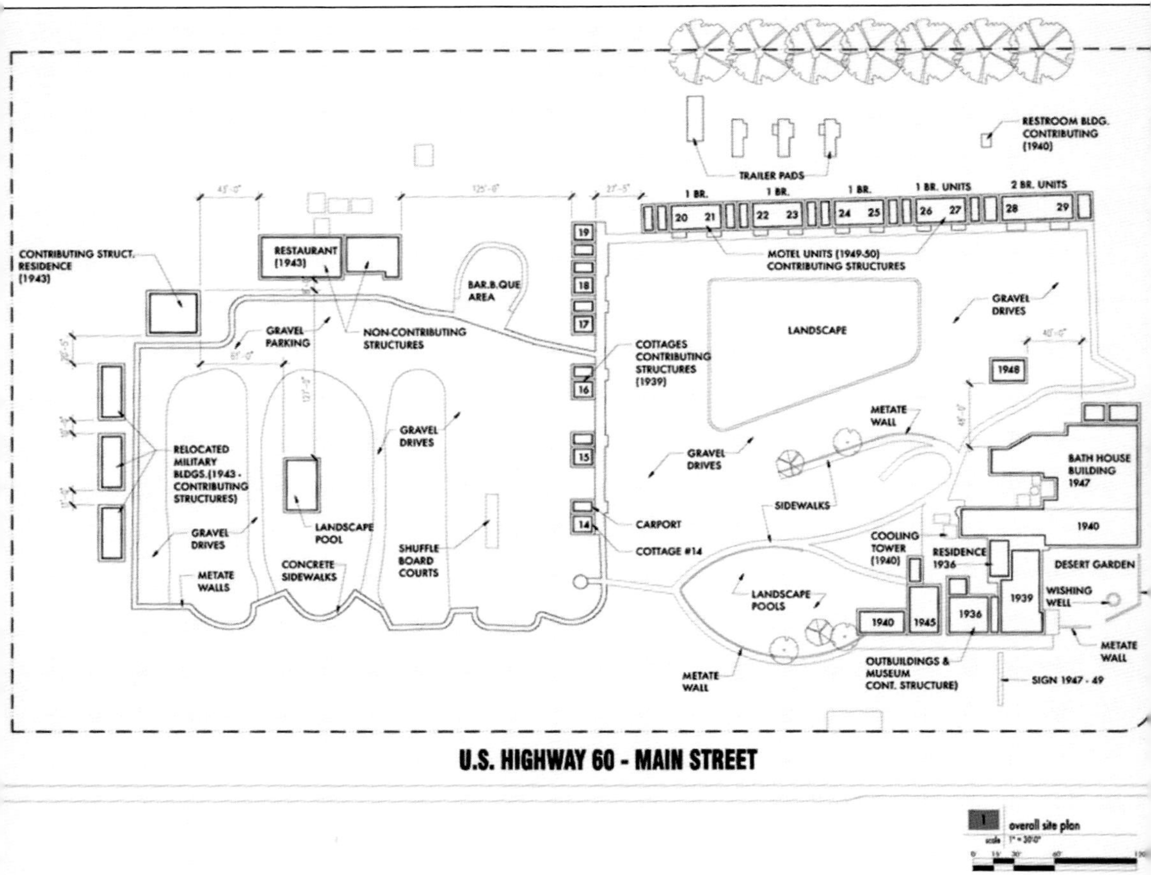

Following the progress of the Buckhorn's growth has always been a challenge. Considerable research went into the preparation of this detailed site plan. After the New York Giants introduced baseball to the Buckhorn in 1947, a flurry of building activity began, including the addition of an enlarged bathhouse and more motel rooms. Evidence indicates that most major construction was completed by the 1950s, with only minor modifications afterward, mostly for maintenance. In helping to provide dates, Alice Sliger could not completely vouch for their accuracy, saying in 1998, "Well it's the best I can do. After all I'm 92 years old and my memory is not what it used to be." Some have been verified through dated photographs and documents. As time took its toll on the buildings, fewer people stayed in the cottages or motel. Caretakers took up residence, and other structures were sealed for protection. Alice closed the baths in 1999. The motel and Buckhorn were entirely shuttered to the public in 2007. (Courtesy of HistoricStreetscapes Architects.)

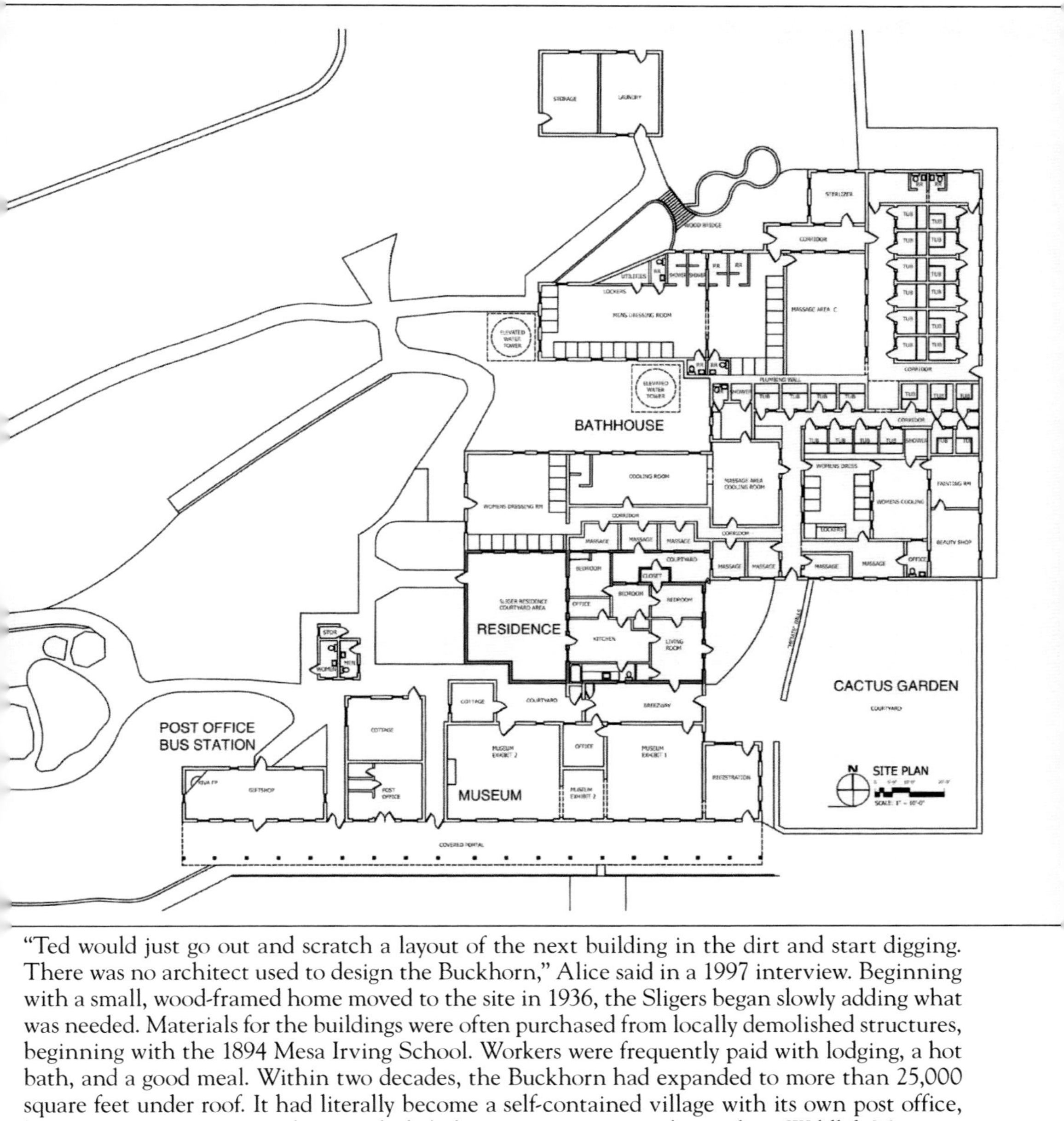

"Ted would just go out and scratch a layout of the next building in the dirt and start digging. There was no architect used to design the Buckhorn," Alice said in a 1997 interview. Beginning with a small, wood-framed home moved to the site in 1936, the Sligers began slowly adding what was needed. Materials for the buildings were often purchased from locally demolished structures, beginning with the 1894 Mesa Irving School. Workers were frequently paid with lodging, a hot bath, and a good meal. Within two decades, the Buckhorn had expanded to more than 25,000 square feet under roof. It had literally become a self-contained village with its own post office, bus stop, gas station, curio shop, roadside lodging, restaurant, taxidermy shop, Wildlife Museum, 27-bath mineral spa, and even a beauty shop. (Courtesy of HistoricStreetscapes Architects.)

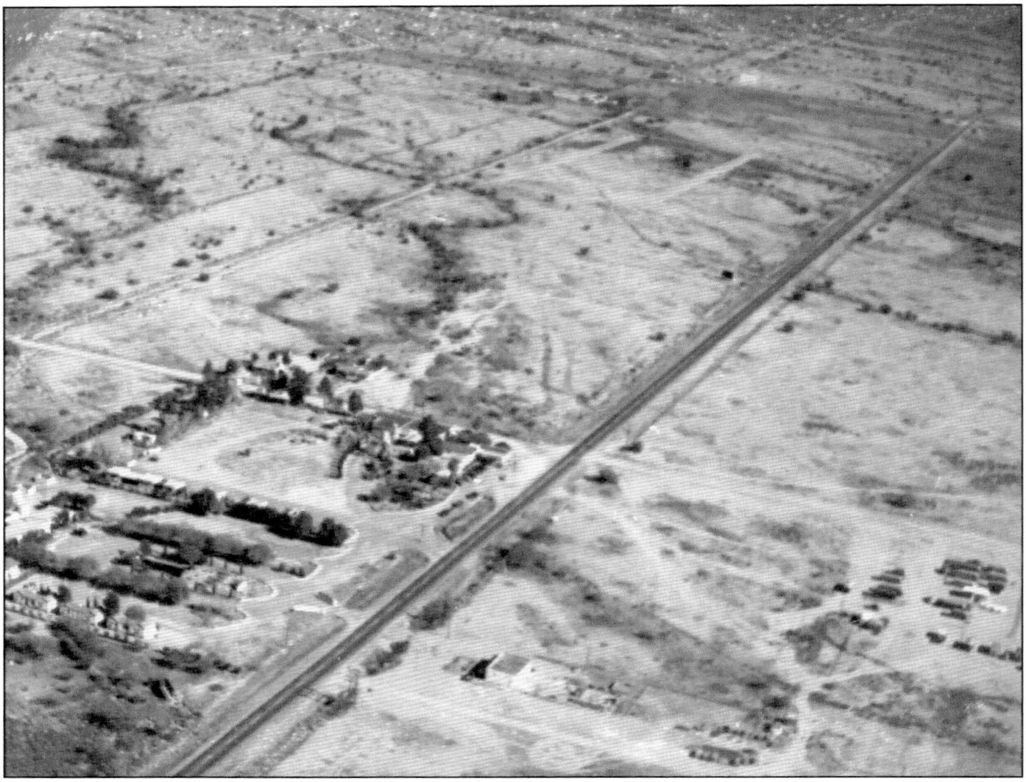

Aerial views help illustrate the evolution of the Buckhorn while revealing how isolated it was in the beginning. The earliest photograph (above), looking to the northeast, shows the first cottages and the competing El Maro in full operation to the west.

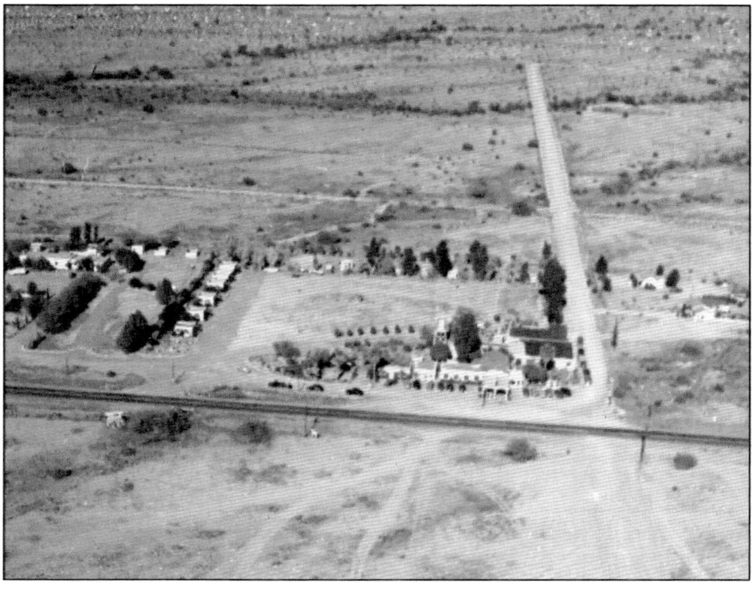

An early aerial view looking north reveals the two-lane Apache Trail. What would become Recker Road runs north into the desert. Today on the brush-covered ground across Recker Road is the Buckhorn Shopping Center.

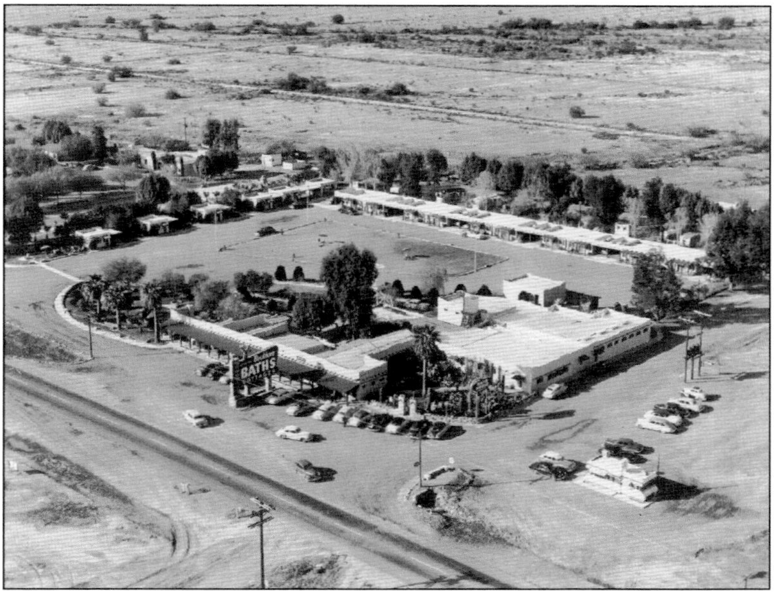

By 1949, the Buckhorn sign advertising "cottages" had been erected, along with the motel units on the northern edge of the property. Larger than the original café in the frontage building, a newly contracted Buckhorn diner, across Recker Road, is seen in the lower right corner. (Courtesy MHM.)

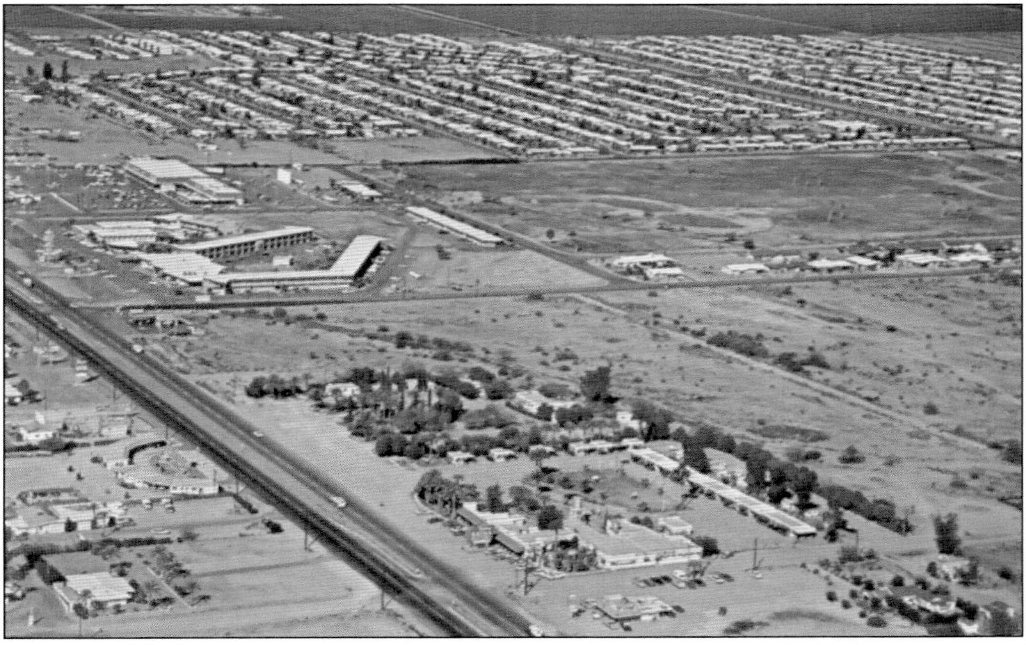

After acquiring the initial five acres, the Sligers over time purchased all of Charles Mitten's 160-acre homestead. Around 1958, the couple sold off part of the land (at center left) to Joe Farnsworth for his Dreamland Villa, a pioneering seniors' development. (Courtesy MHM.)

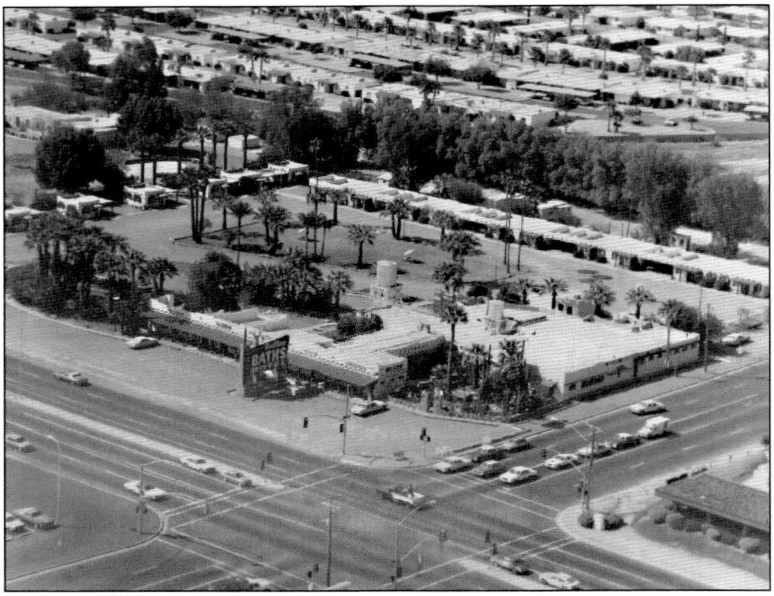

A half-century after first opening its doors on an isolated patch of desert, the Buckhorn was fully surrounded by development. The two-lane Apache Trail grew into a six-lane divided highway. Separated only by a canal, Dreamland Villa's hundreds of homes to the north encroached on and overwhelmed the Buckhorn. (Courtesy MHM.)

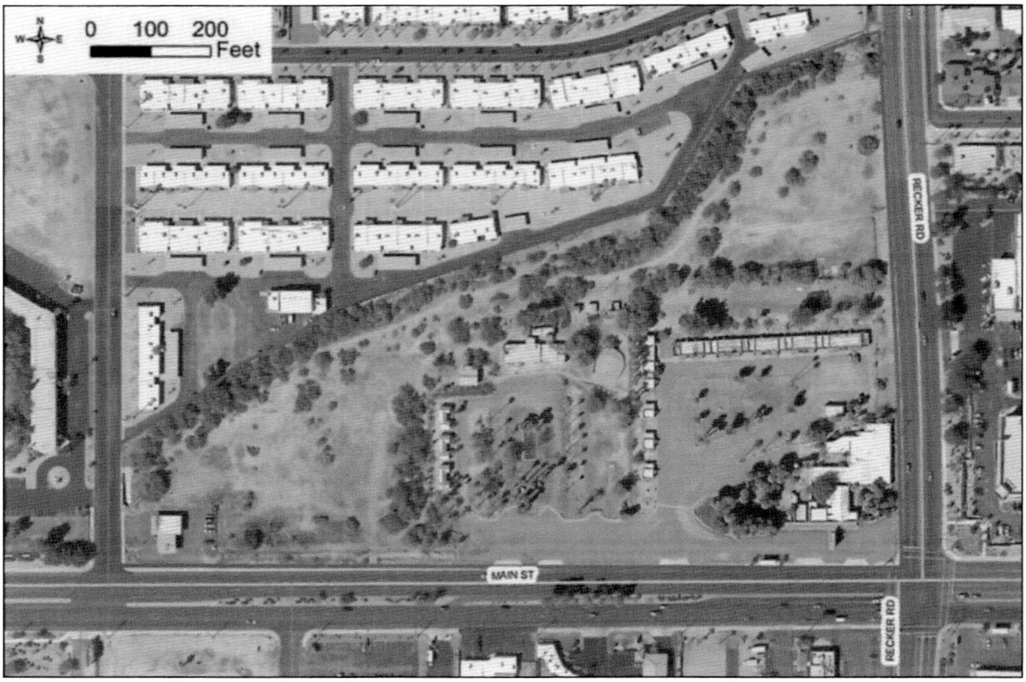

Today, the Buckhorn property is the largest remaining expanse of open desert along Main Street. This modern aerial view shows the entire property. (Courtesy City of Mesa.)

Four

Getting into Hot Water

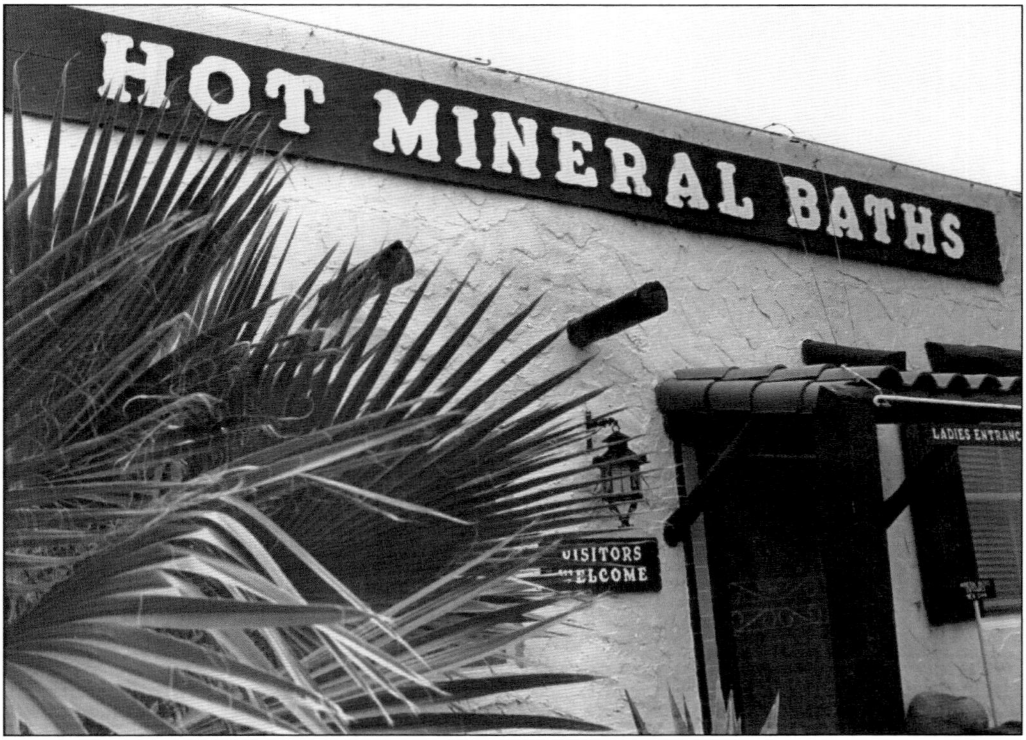

"We get you in hot water—for your own good!" That is how the Buckhorn publicized its therapeutic mineral hot baths. What better endorsement than "For a new lease on life—to feel better, to look better, and to do better—take a tip from Baseball's Major Leaguers!" Never planned, the baths were the result of a serendipitous discovery in October 1939. Drilling for cool, potable water, Ted Sliger instead tapped a gusher of hot mineral-laden water. And so, a spa was born with just four baths.

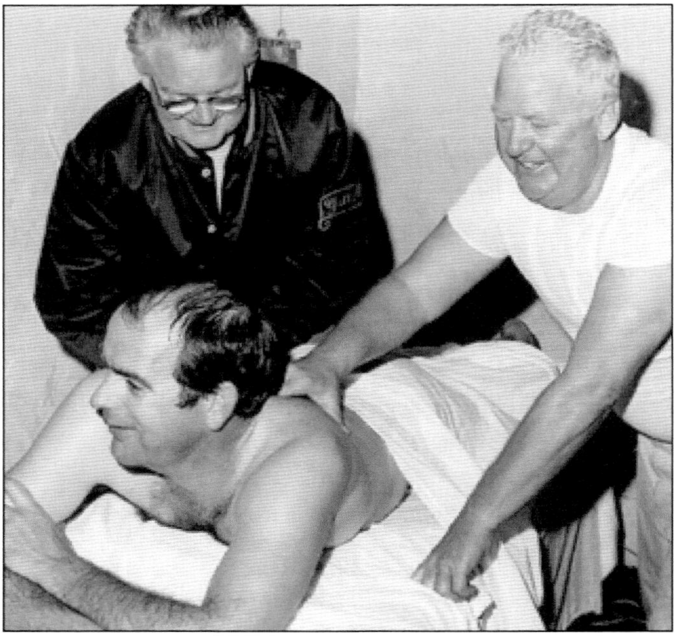

At the peak of activities, the Buckhorn Baths featured a staff of more than 25 professionals—nurses, physiotherapists, and masseurs and masseuses. Although considered and advertised as healthful, the spa never made any medical claims. Generally, a patient's diagnosis was performed before arriving at the Buckhorn. Invalid patients were required to provide their own nurse or companion. Baseball players were especially pampered. Here, Giants pitcher Gaylord Perry gets a rubdown from Buckhorn masseuse Ed Nordquist (right) and trainer Harry Jordon. (Courtesy MHM.)

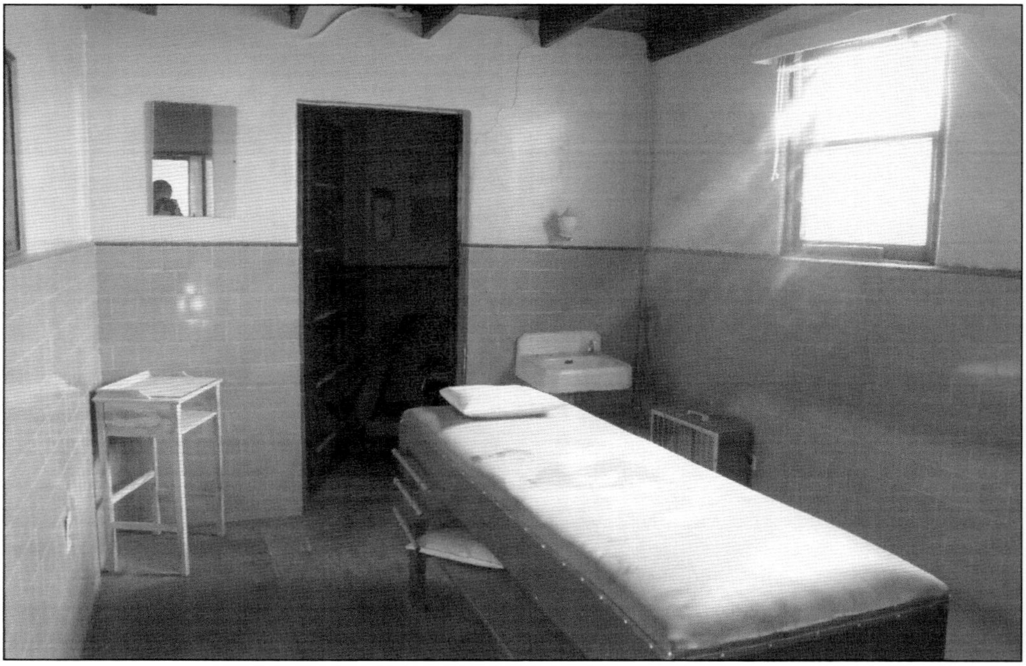

The Sligers boasted that their mineral waters were determined to be most beneficial for arthritic guests, which made up over 60 percent of the clientele. Beyond those who came for the spa's therapeutics, the resort and its amenities were also very popular with persons in good health who were just seeking a relaxing vacation in the Valley of the Sun. More than 100 guests could be accommodated in furnished cottages, apartments, and motel units. Additional space for visitors arriving with travel trailers was also available. Solariums and sun decks were located on the roofs of the motel units and the bathhouse. (Courtesy MHM.)

Throughout the bathhouse is evidence of where one phase started and the next began. Former exterior walls and walkways became interior spaces. In its prime, with thousands of guests per year coming through the facility, all finishes were intended to be easily maintained. Exterior veneers are stucco over concrete block walls. The roof is flat and surrounded by parapet walls. Initially, evaporative coolers and fans helped keep the humid building tolerable.

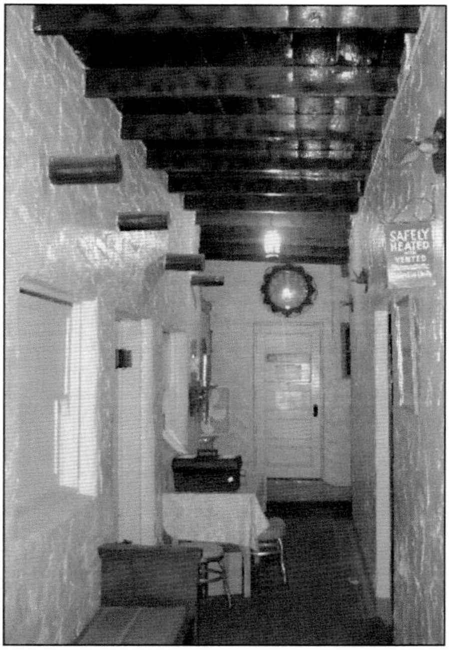

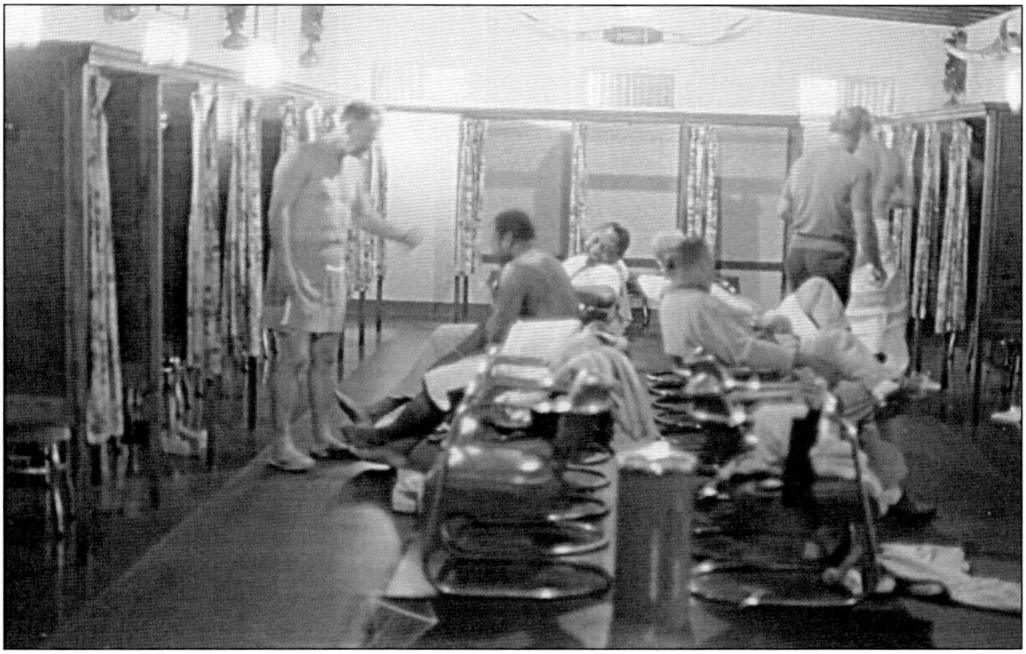

"Following your hot mineral bath you go into a cooling room for a rest period. Blankets are provided to induce generous perspiration, a further aid in weight reduction or the elimination of poisons. Swedish massages are available. Finish off with a shower, dress and relax in one of the resorts attractive dressing rooms, and go forth with a glorious sense of rejuvenation." That is how a 1980s brochure described the spa experience. In addition to the healthful treatment was the opportunity for a chance locker room encounter with a celebrity. Guests might just find themselves having a conversation with Ty Cobb or Joe E. Brown. (Courtesy MHM.)

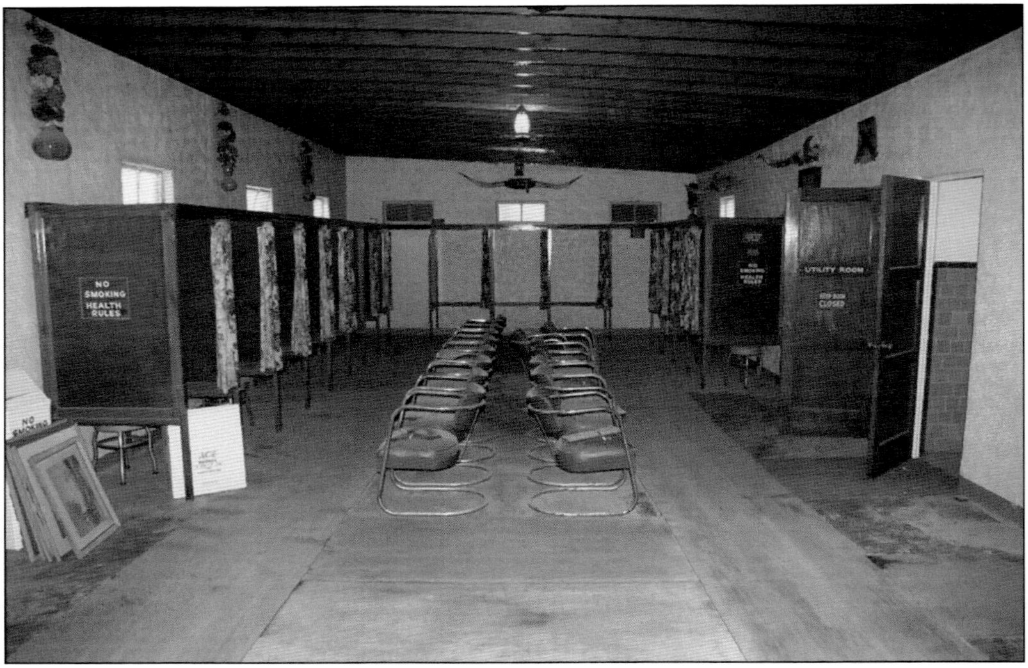

As the Buckhorn grew, so did its bathhouse, from an original four tubs to 27, ultimately evolving into a confusing rabbit warren of corridors and rooms. Visitors began their spa experience in the changing room (above). From there it was on to a hot mineral bath, followed by a cooldown in the cooling room (below). Topped off with an optional Swedish massage, a guest came out fully refreshed. (Both, courtesy AZMNH.)

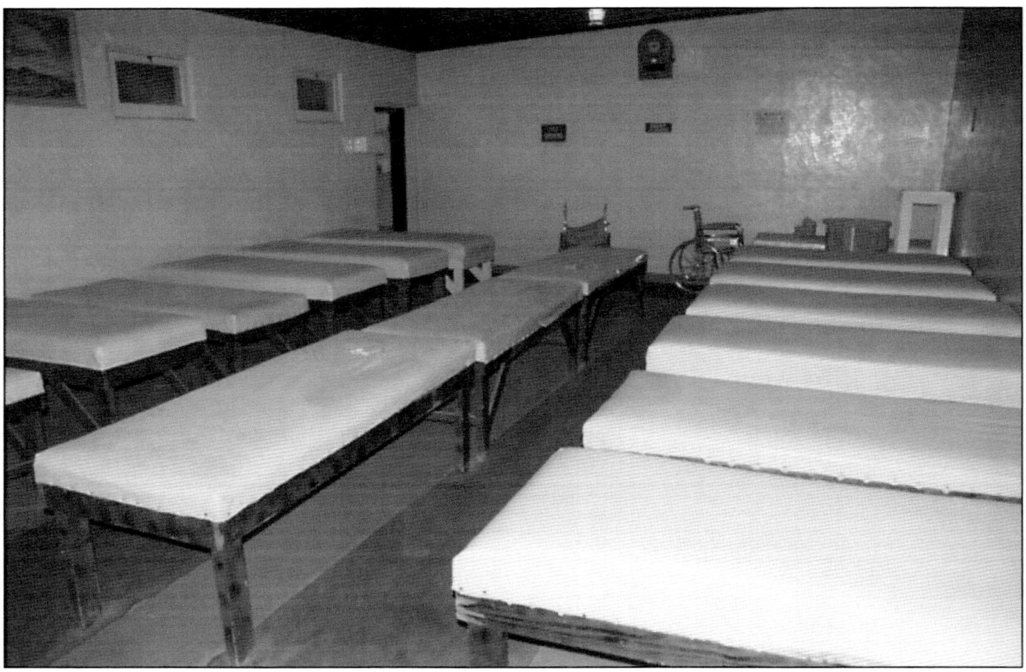

Topped by ever-present steer horns and original art, lockers with hand-painted numbers provided bathhouse guests a safe place to store their belongings.

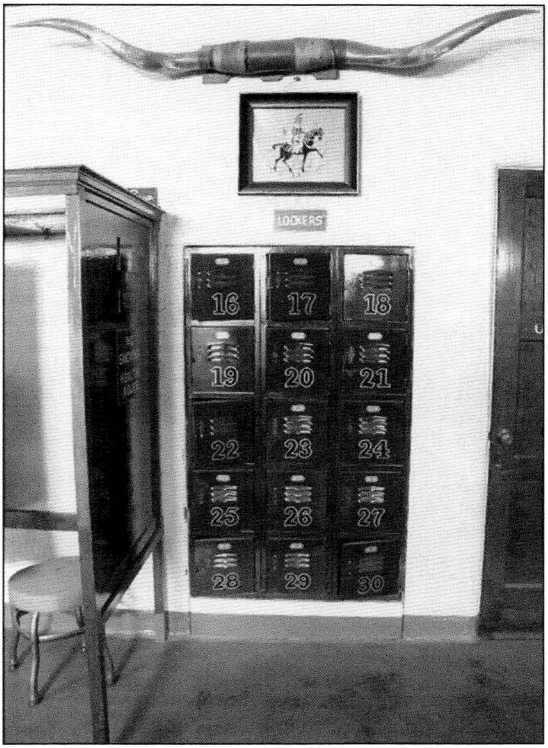

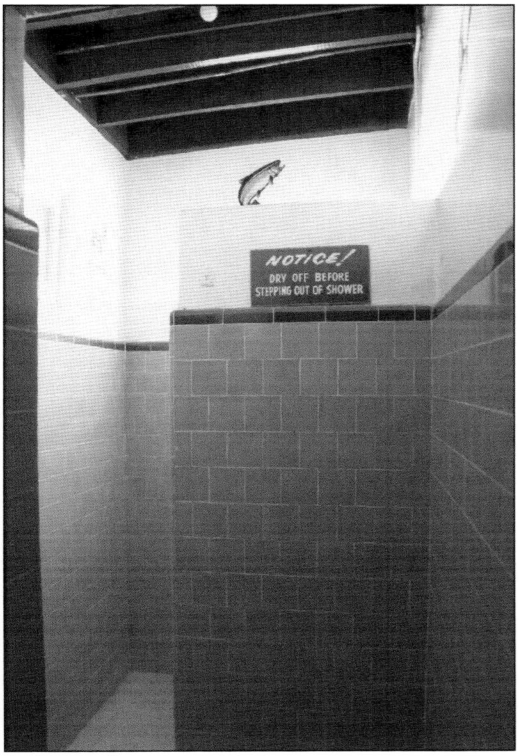

No place in the bathhouse was without a hand-painted sign, not even the showers. Here, guests were advised to "dry off before stepping out of the shower."

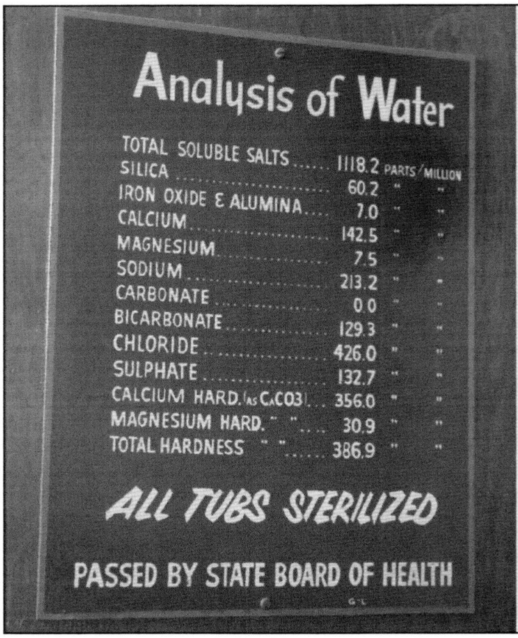

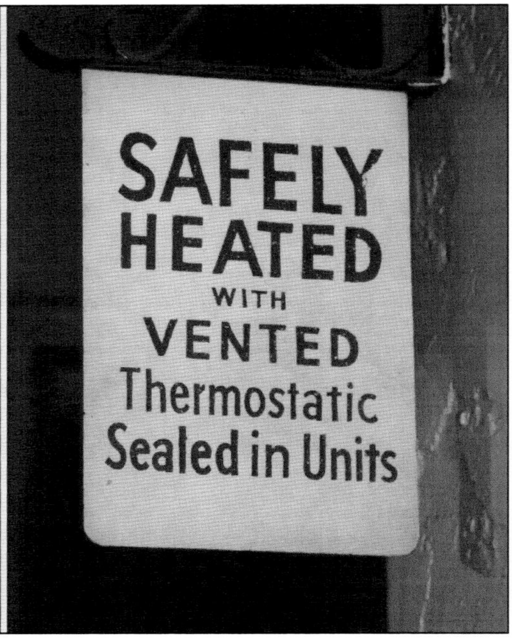

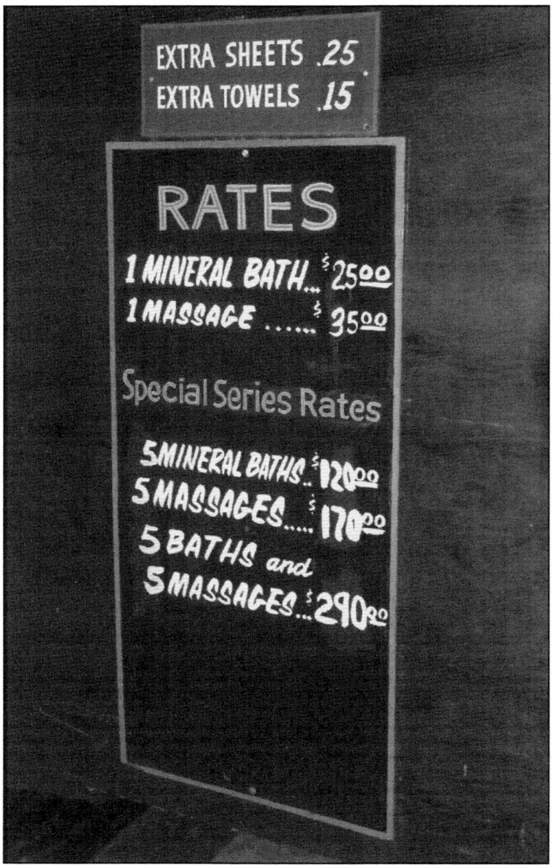

Healthful vacation retreats and mineral springs were popular destinations. Medical science may have debunked most of their outlandish claims of miracle cures, but nonetheless, millions of visitors flocked to spas to be pampered, relax, and maybe be cured. Signs were abundant at the Buckhorn. They were everywhere—and all were hand-painted. Round a corner and there was another sign telling guests where they were, or what was in the water, or how hot the water was, or that their towels were "sanitized." And of course, there were signs reminding guests of the various charges. In the maze-like bathhouse, signs also proved invaluable for navigation.

For privacy and to keep the room warm, each bath featured a door. A hand-painted sign informed bathers of the mineral content of the hot waters in which they soaked.

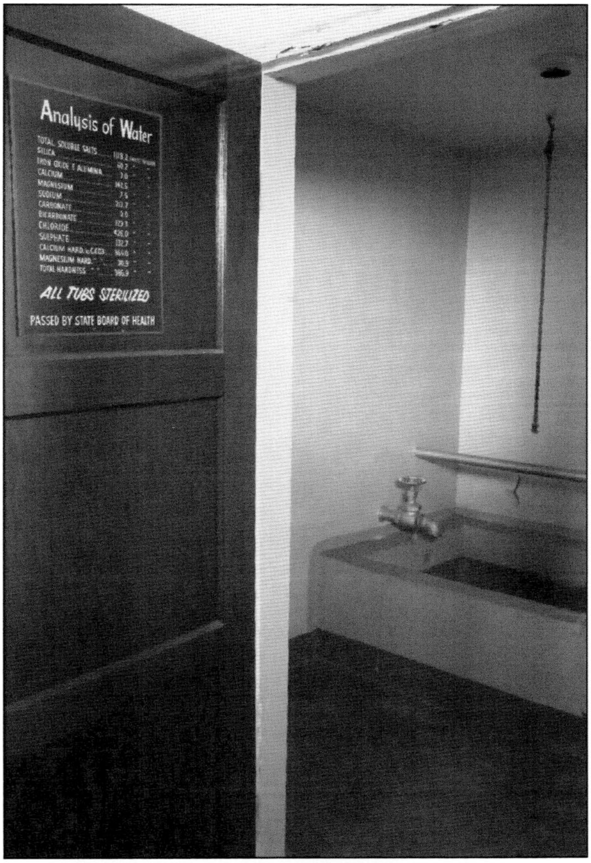

In the beginning, a soak in a hot tub cost $2. At its peak, the Buckhorn featured 27 baths, ranging from 75-gallon tubs to 750-gallon pools. More than 25 staff members pampered guests. Alice Sliger, writing in 1995, acknowledged her loyal and capable staff: "I would like to thank the fine and devoted people who have helped us over the years here at the Buckhorn. Elna Sowder worked side by side with Ted and me in the office for 35 years. Myrtis Gann [second from right] has taken care of the bathers in our bathhouse since 1958. Wilma McCain Shape was another devoted employee for many years, as was Nettie Nicholson, Agnes Jenson, and Eddie Nordquist. Jose Chavez came in 1969 and is still with us. Dorothy Farr joined us in 1992. Miguel Jimenez started in 1972. Silvia Chavez and her mother, Maria have worked faithfully here since 1981."

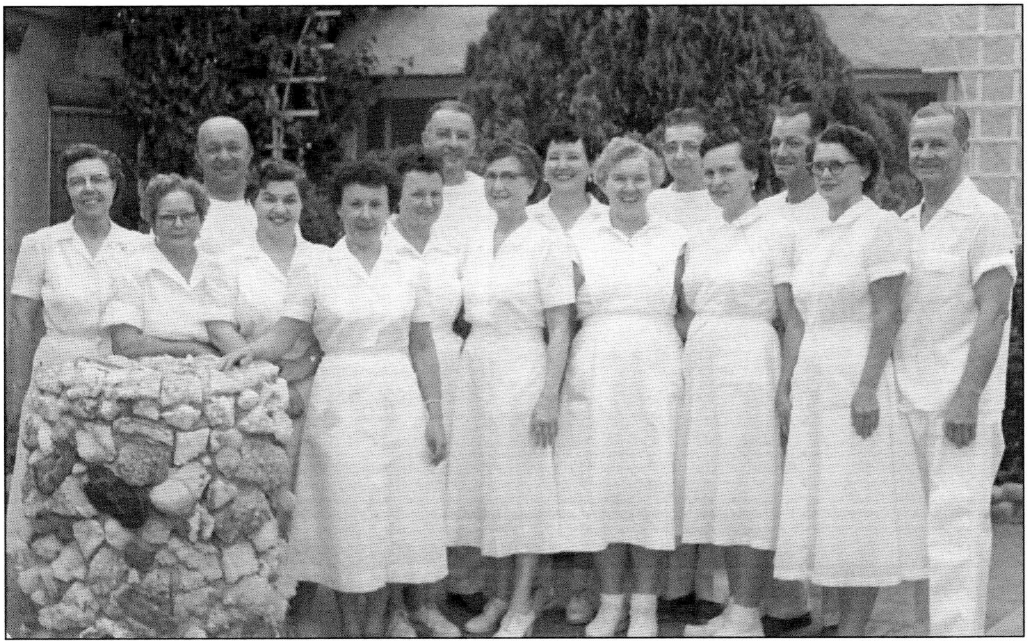

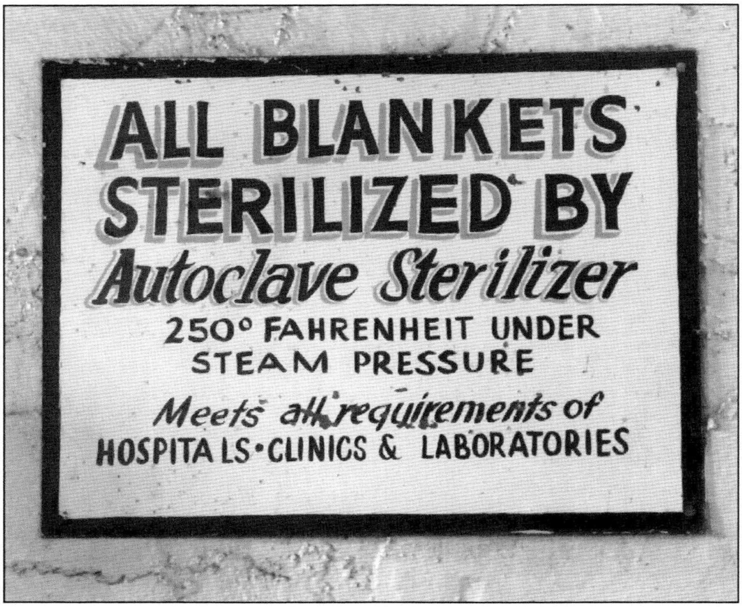

Overseen by state health regulations and federal guidelines, the Buckhorn contained everything necessary for a therapeutic spa and maintained the bathhouse to the highest standards. With the introduction of antibiotics and other medications, health resorts began to decline in Arizona and around the nation. Penicillin treated many of the diseases and ailments that once brought health-seekers to the baths.

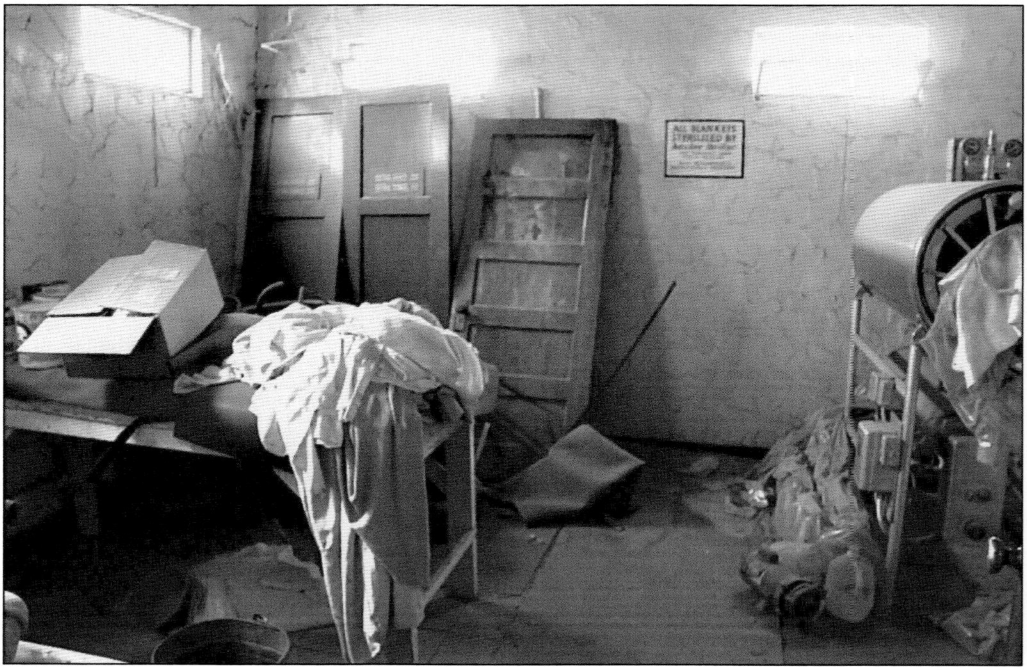

A Buckhorn brochure said the "mineral water is as delightful to drink as it is to bathe in." But universal refrigeration and a carefully monitored food supply nipped chronic dyspepsia in the bud, reducing the need for dosing one's innards with mineral water or wrapping up in a sterilized blanket to induce perspiration and get rid of all the poisons. Today, the once pristine sterilizing room has become a dusty catchall for various bathhouse materials.

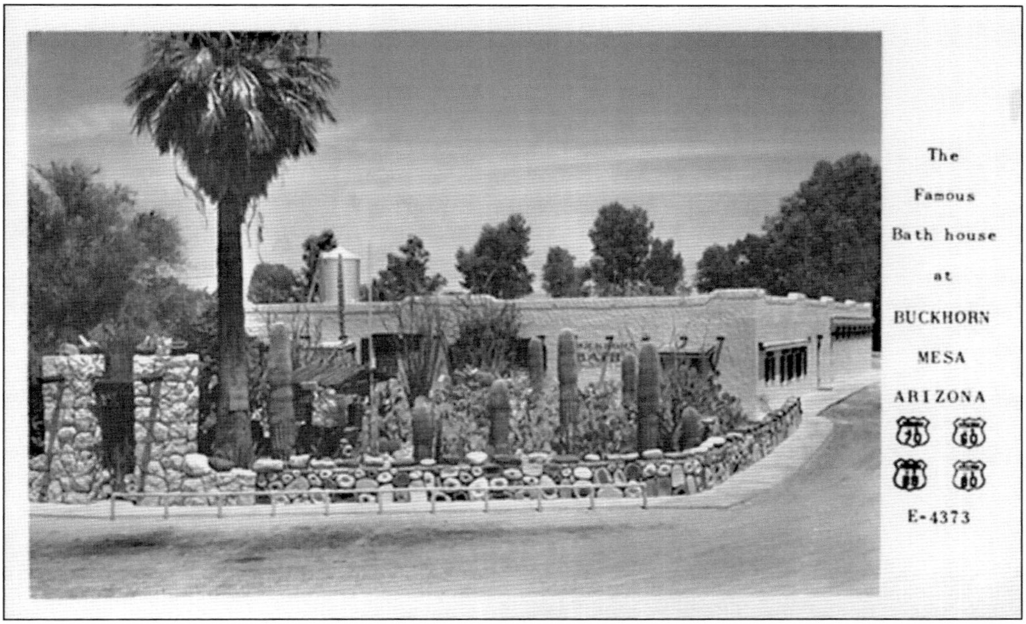

Vernacular Pueblo-style architecture was featured throughout the Buckhorn campus, except for the early bungalow-style cabins that were moved, according to Alice Sliger, to the site from nearby Falcon Field around 1945. The rest of the structures were constructed from 1936 to 1949. Alice asserted that the plans for all the structures were created in Ted Sliger's mind and laid out on the ground by foot or stick. The original brick building, now covered with stucco, was constructed by a local bricklayer looking for work. He happened by when he saw a pile of bricks lying on the property. Over the years, Ted hired local contractors to do most of the remaining construction. A four-percent $50,000 government loan was used to finance construction of the motel units. While individual buildings are difficult to date, a 1949 aerial photograph shows all the major construction in place. By 1950, only minor modifications were made to Buckhorn buildings. No major additions were made thereafter.

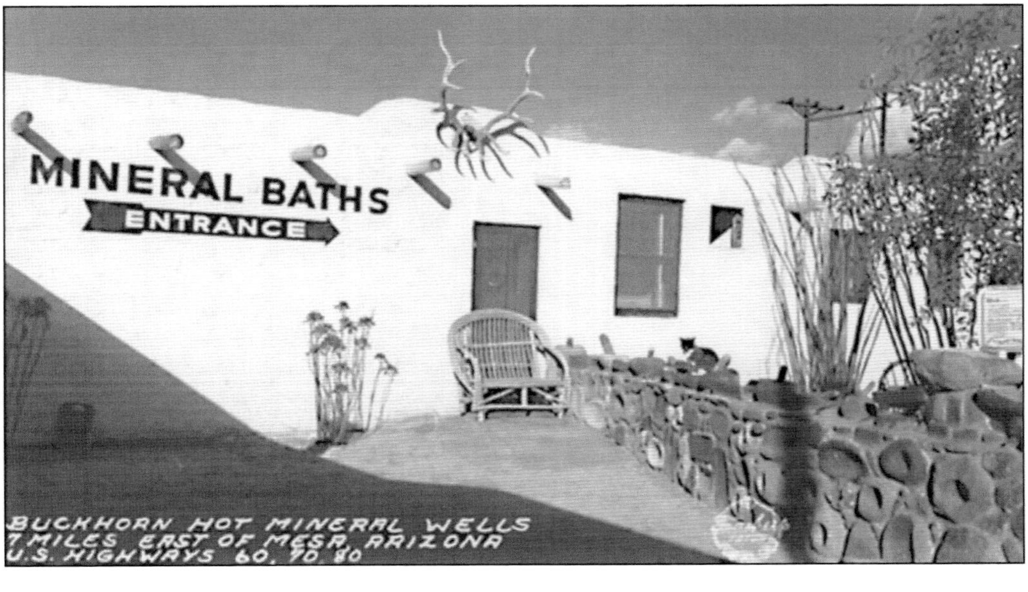

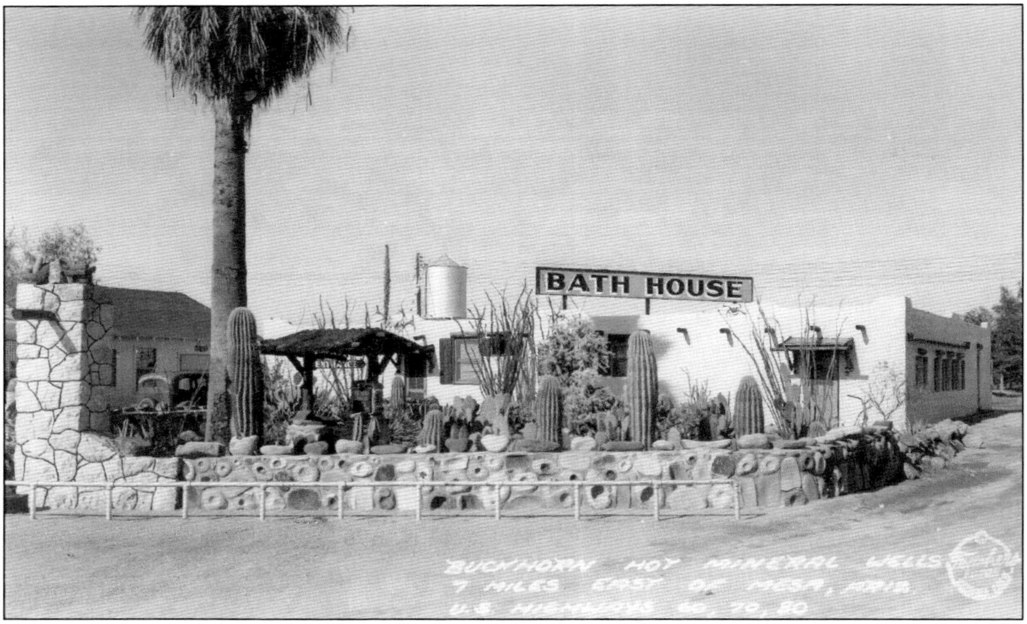

After three years of hauling water to the site, Ted hired George Peterson in 1939 to drill a well on the property, reaching water at 225 feet. Unfortunately, it was hot (112 degrees) and full of minerals. Eventually, five wells were dug. The deepest went to 1,100 feet, where the water was even hotter—130 degrees. A cooling tower to lower the temperature to 106 degrees was erected. Water was lifted with a gasoline pump. Later, a Delco generating system was installed. When the Salt River Project first provided electricity to the Buckhorn, it was only 25 cycle. Eventually, 60-cycle power became available. (Both, courtesy MHM.)

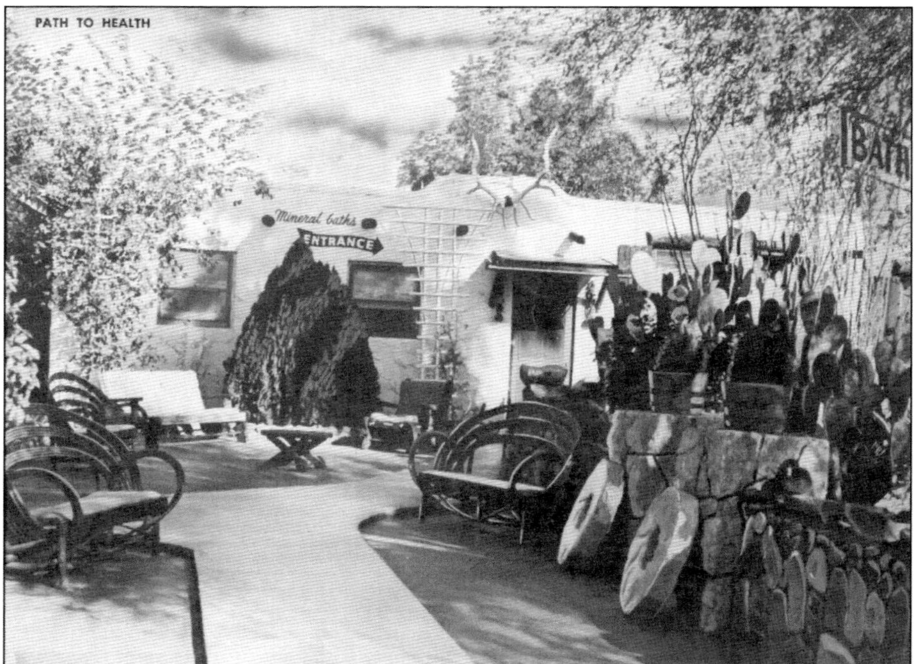

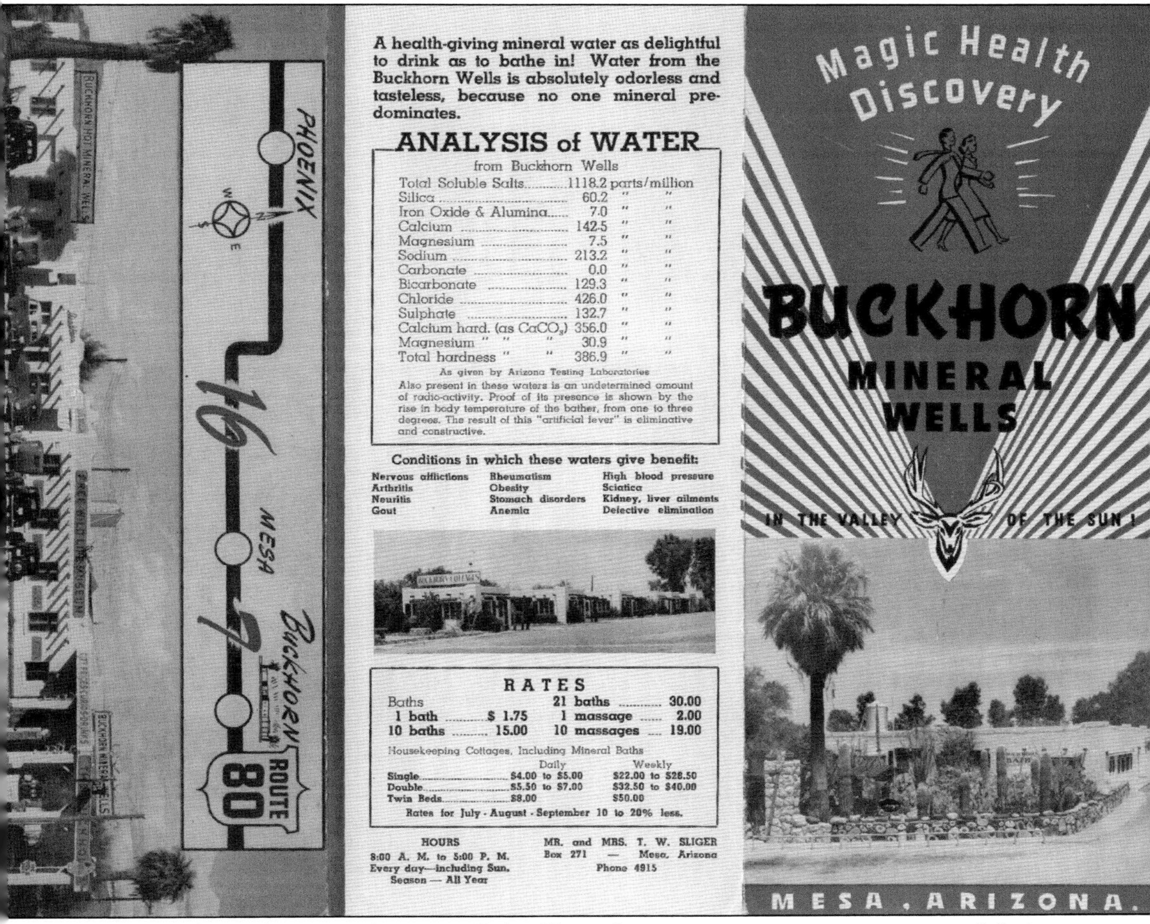

Magic Health Discovery

BUCKHORN MINERAL WELLS

IN THE VALLEY OF THE SUN!

MESA, ARIZONA.

A health-giving mineral water as delightful to drink as to bathe in! Water from the Buckhorn Wells is absolutely odorless and tasteless, because no one mineral predominates.

ANALYSIS of WATER

from Buckhorn Wells

Total Soluble Salts	1118.2	parts/million
Silica	60.2	" "
Iron Oxide & Alumina	7.0	" "
Calcium	142.5	" "
Magnesium	7.5	" "
Sodium	213.2	" "
Carbonate	0.0	" "
Bicarbonate	129.3	" "
Chloride	426.0	" "
Sulphate	132.7	" "
Calcium hard. (as $CaCO_3$)	356.0	" "
Magnesium " " "	30.9	" "
Total hardness " "	386.9	" "

As given by Arizona Testing Laboratories

Also present in these waters is an undetermined amount of radio-activity. Proof of its presence is shown by the rise in body temperature of the bather, from one to three degrees. The result of this "artificial fever" is eliminative and constructive.

Conditions in which these waters give benefit:

Nervous afflictions	Rheumatism	High blood pressure
Arthritis	Obesity	Sciatica
Neuritis	Stomach disorders	Kidney, liver ailments
Gout	Anemia	Defective elimination

RATES

Baths			
1 bath	$ 1.75	21 baths	30.00
10 baths	15.00	1 massage	2.00
		10 massages	19.00

Housekeeping Cottages, Including Mineral Baths

	Daily	Weekly
Single	$4.00 to $5.00	$22.00 to $28.50
Double	$5.50 to $7.00	$32.50 to $40.00
Twin Beds	$8.00	$50.00

Rates for July - August - September 10 to 20% less.

HOURS
8:00 A. M. to 5:00 P. M.
Every day—including Sun.
Season — All Year

MR. and MRS. T. W. SLIGER
Box 271 — Mesa, Arizona
Phone 4915

PHOENIX
16
MESA
7
Buckhorn
ROUTE 80

Once they got themselves "into hot water," the Sligers became consummate promoters of their unique enterprise. This early trifold brochure provided, along with rates, the mineral makeup of the water. One paragraph stands out: "Also present in these waters is an undetermined amount of radio-activity. Proof of its presence is shown by the rise in body temperature of the bather, from one to three degrees. The result of this 'artificial fever' is eliminative and constructive."

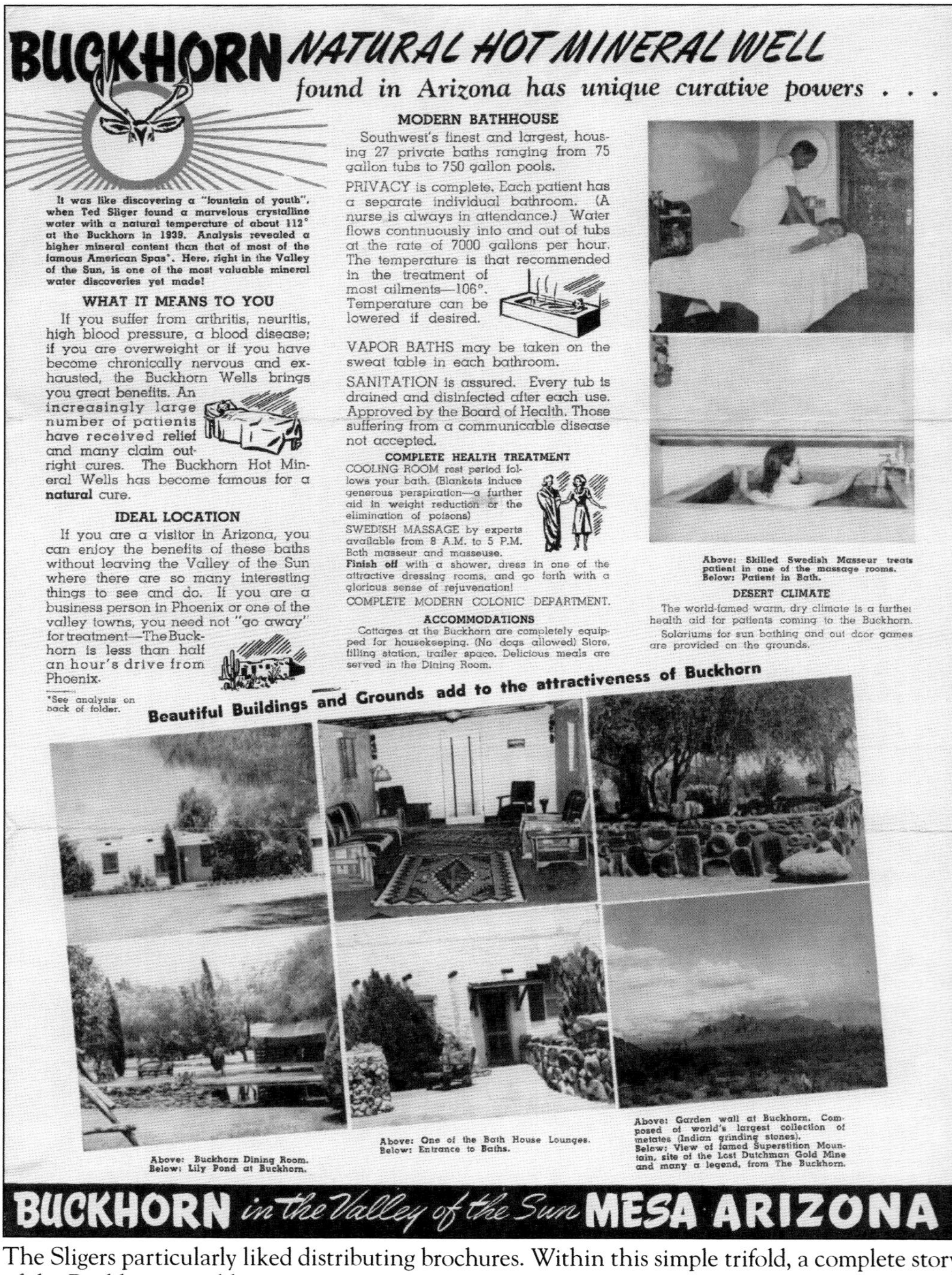

BUCKHORN NATURAL HOT MINERAL WELL found in Arizona has unique curative powers . . .

It was like discovering a "fountain of youth", when Ted Sliger found a marvelous crystalline water with a natural temperature of about 112° at the Buckhorn in 1939. Analysis revealed a higher mineral content than that of most of the famous American Spas*. Here, right in the Valley of the Sun, is one of the most valuable mineral water discoveries yet made!

WHAT IT MEANS TO YOU

If you suffer from arthritis, neuritis, high blood pressure, a blood disease; if you are overweight or if you have become chronically nervous and exhausted, the Buckhorn Wells brings you great benefits. An increasingly large number of patients have received relief and many claim outright cures. The Buckhorn Hot Mineral Wells has become famous for a **natural** cure.

IDEAL LOCATION

If you are a visitor in Arizona, you can enjoy the benefits of these baths without leaving the Valley of the Sun where there are so many interesting things to see and do. If you are a business person in Phoenix or one of the valley towns, you need not "go away" for treatment—The Buckhorn is less than half an hour's drive from Phoenix.

*See analysis on back of folder.

MODERN BATHHOUSE

Southwest's finest and largest, housing 27 private baths ranging from 75 gallon tubs to 750 gallon pools.

PRIVACY is complete. Each patient has a separate individual bathroom. (A nurse is always in attendance.) Water flows continuously into and out of tubs at the rate of 7000 gallons per hour. The temperature is that recommended in the treatment of most ailments—106°. Temperature can be lowered if desired.

VAPOR BATHS may be taken on the sweat table in each bathroom.

SANITATION is assured. Every tub is drained and disinfected after each use. Approved by the Board of Health. Those suffering from a communicable disease not accepted.

COMPLETE HEALTH TREATMENT

COOLING ROOM rest period follows your bath. (Blankets induce generous perspiration—a further aid in weight reduction or the elimination of poisons)

SWEDISH MASSAGE by experts available from 8 A.M. to 5 P.M. Both masseur and masseuse.

Finish off with a shower, dress in one of the attractive dressing rooms, and go forth with a glorious sense of rejuvenation!

COMPLETE MODERN COLONIC DEPARTMENT.

ACCOMMODATIONS

Cottages at the Buckhorn are completely equipped for housekeeping. (No dogs allowed) Store, filling station, trailer space. Delicious meals are served in the Dining Room.

Above: Skilled Swedish Masseur treats patient in one of the massage rooms. Below: Patient in Bath.

DESERT CLIMATE

The world-famed warm, dry climate is a further health aid for patients coming to the Buckhorn.

Solariums for sun bathing and out door games are provided on the grounds.

Beautiful Buildings and Grounds add to the attractiveness of Buckhorn

Above: Buckhorn Dining Room. Below: Lily Pond at Buckhorn.

Above: One of the Bath House Lounges. Below: Entrance to Baths.

Above: Garden wall at Buckhorn. Composed of world's largest collection of metates (Indian grinding stones). Below: View of famed Superstition Mountain, site of the Lost Dutchman Gold Mine and many a legend, from The Buckhorn.

BUCKHORN in the Valley of the Sun MESA ARIZONA

The Sligers particularly liked distributing brochures. Within this simple trifold, a complete story of the Buckhorn is told.

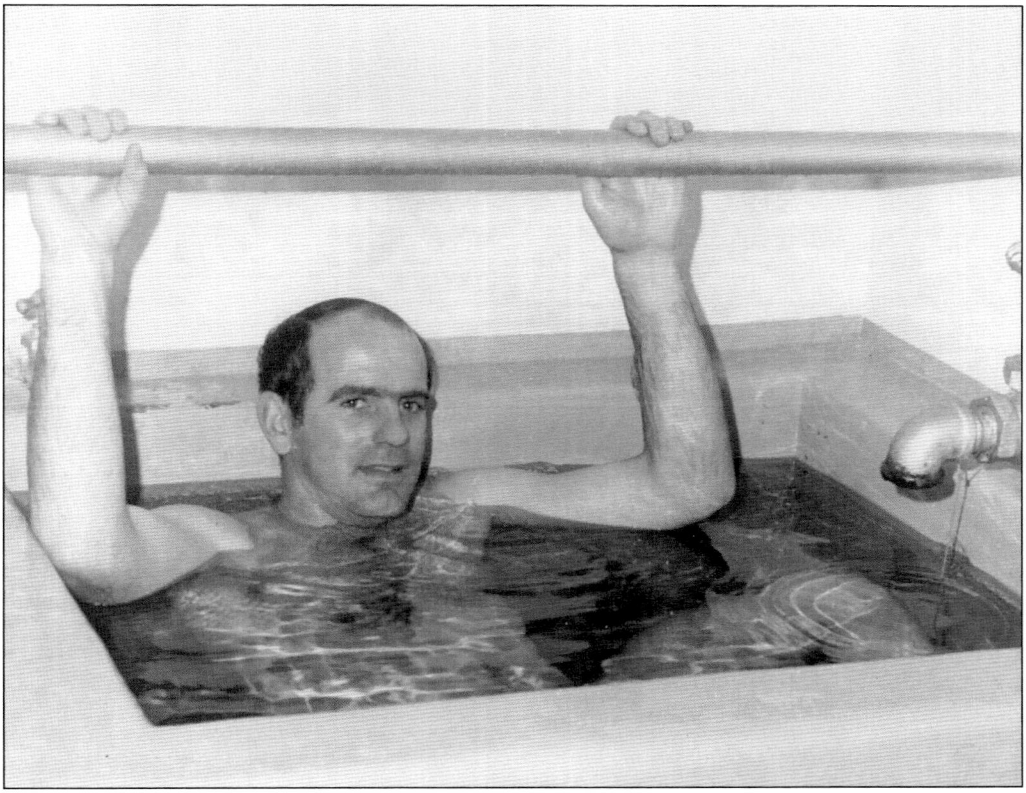

Of the hundreds of baseball players who signed the Buckhorn's guest register, legendary spitball pitcher Gaylord Perry may have been the resort's most frequent and popular visitor. Even after retiring from baseball, Perry continued returning to the Buckhorn, not only for its soothing baths, but more importantly, to see his good friend Alice Sliger. (Courtesy MHM.)

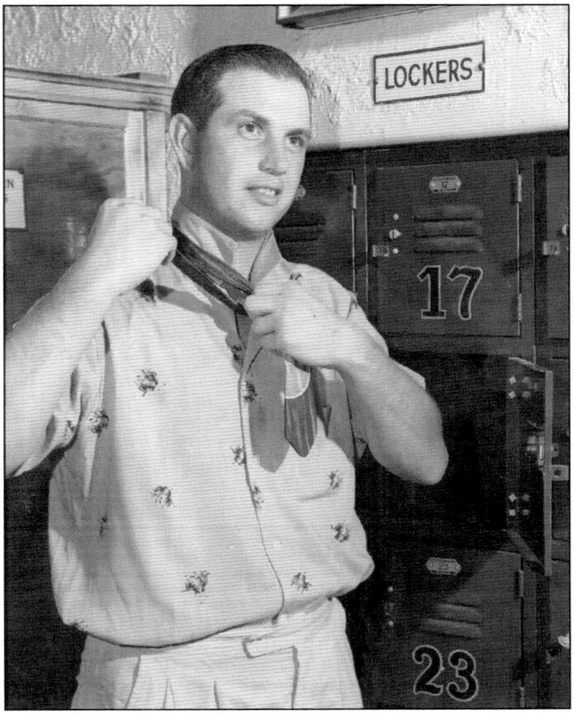

Out of respect for the status of their big-league baseball player guests, the Buckhorn reserved a special locker room for just the team. In that space, they could relax apart from the other guests. Here, Hoyt Wilhem, a star San Francisco Giants pitcher nicknamed "Old Sarge," clad in a casual shirt, dons a Western necktie after another medicinal soak in the mineral baths. (Courtesy MHM.)

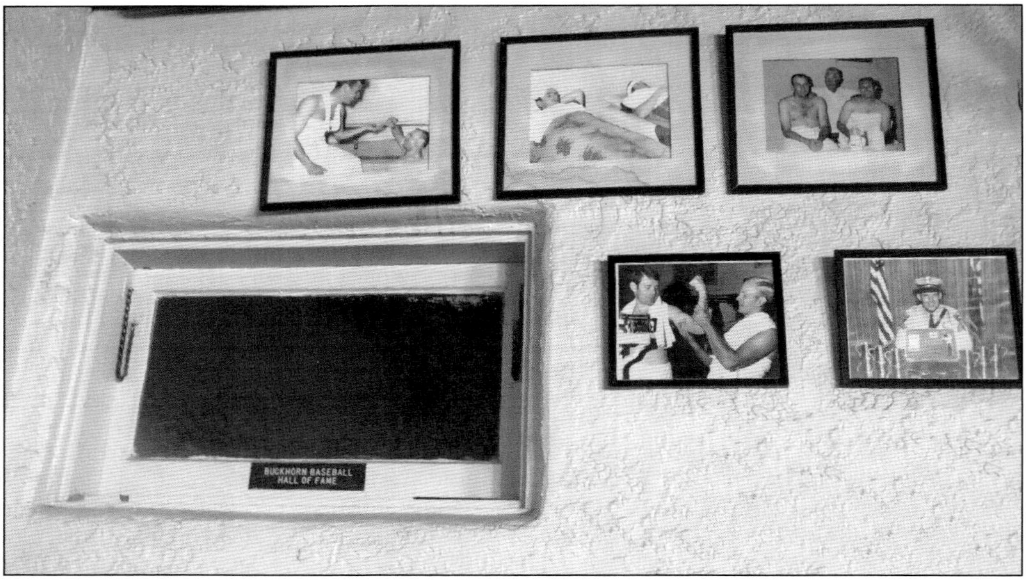

Judging by the number of photographs of ballplayers posed in various bathhouse activities that ultimately wound up adorning the locker-room walls, they never seemed shy in front of a camera.

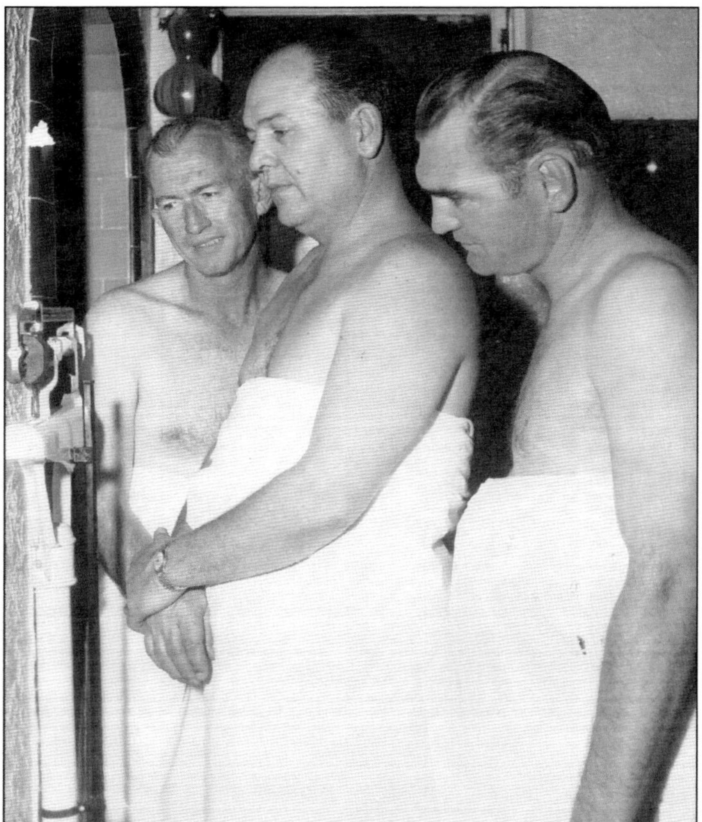

In the huge collection of Buckhorn baseball images, players were photographed in the bathhouse room more than anywhere else. This 1958 photograph shows, from left to right, San Francisco Giants players Bill Rigney, Herman Franks, and Dusty Rhodes weighing in. (Courtesy MHM.)

Five

Buckhorn's Artistic Side

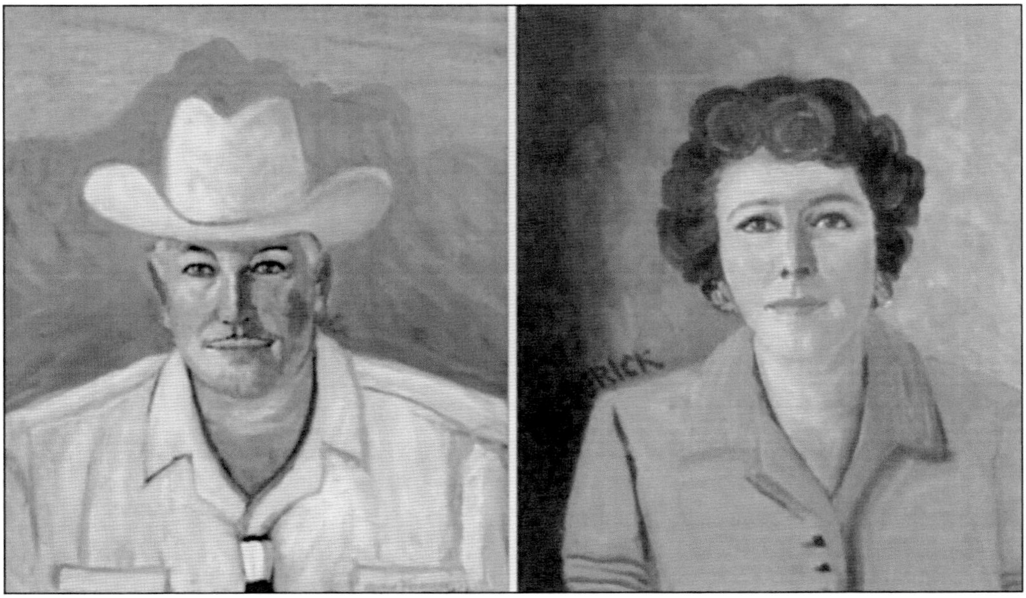

The fact that Ted and Alice Sliger were the self-trained, sole designers of everything Buckhorn demonstrated their innate artistic sensibilities. Maybe that is why they both shared a passion for the arts that is apparent throughout the Buckhorn, from the innovative use of indigenous materials and artifacts in its construction, to the enormous number of hand-painted signs that covered all areas of the campus, to the proliferation of works by visiting artists and guests themselves, to commissioned original paintings by artists-in-residence like these 1960 portraits of the Sligers by George Frederick. (Courtesy MHM.)

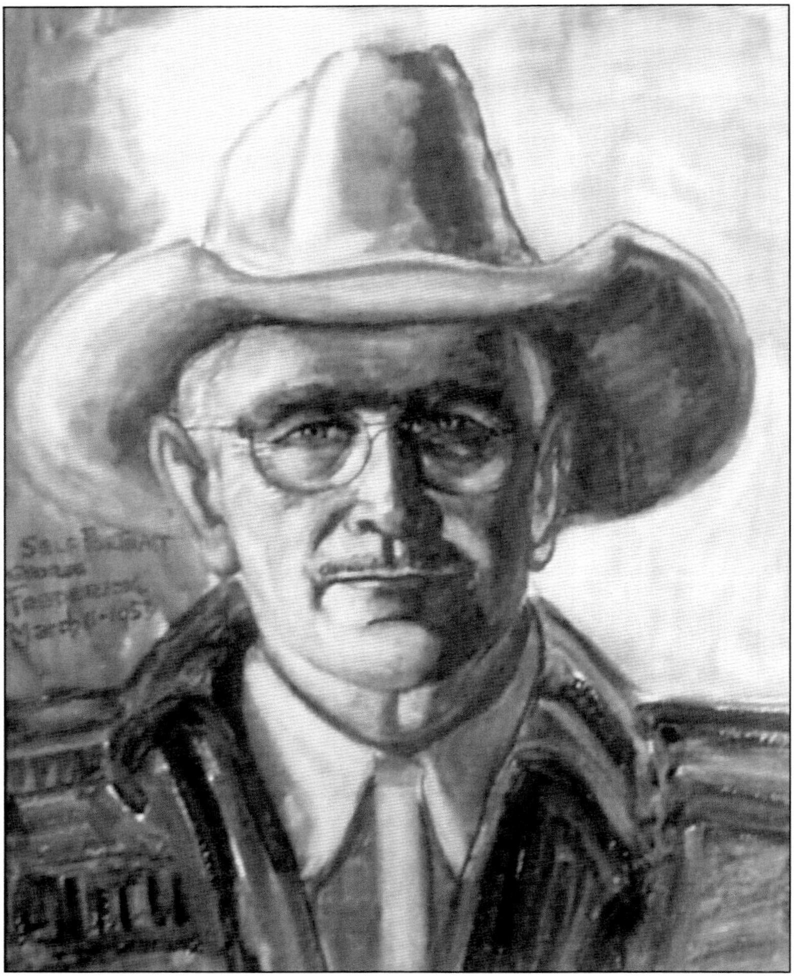

George Frederick (1889–1964), pictured here in a self-portrait dated March 11, 1953, emerged as the Buckhorn's most prolific artist, creating dozens of paintings and sketches, including a 1940 pen-and-ink rendering considered the earliest image of Buckhorn. Born George Gleich in 1889 in Germany, he traveled extensively before making his way to Arizona, first to Tucson, and then in 1940 to Mesa, where he fell in love with the majesty of the Superstition Mountains. (Courtesy MHM.)

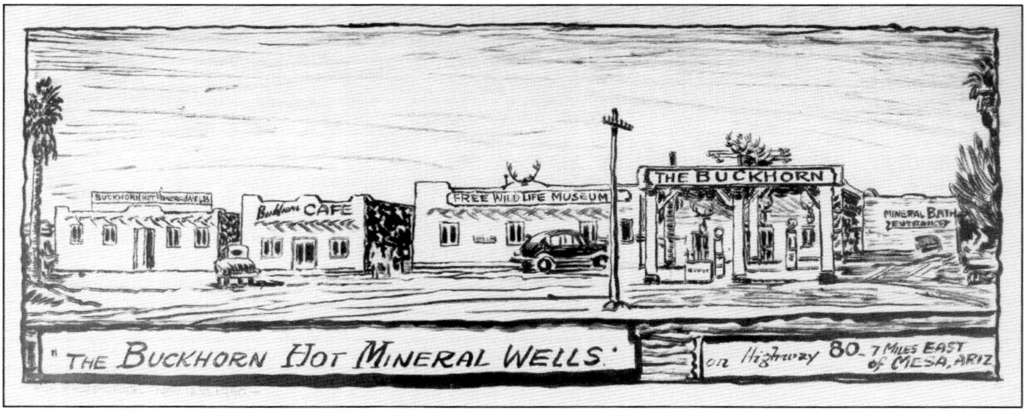

Frederick arrived at the Buckhorn at the perfect moment. One of his first drawings for Ted and Alice Sliger was this detailed panoramic pen-and-ink sketch dated 1940. It represents the earliest known image of the Buckhorn, with its gas pumps, porte cochere topped with stag horns, Wildlife Museum, café, and newly opened mineral baths. (Courtesy MHM.)

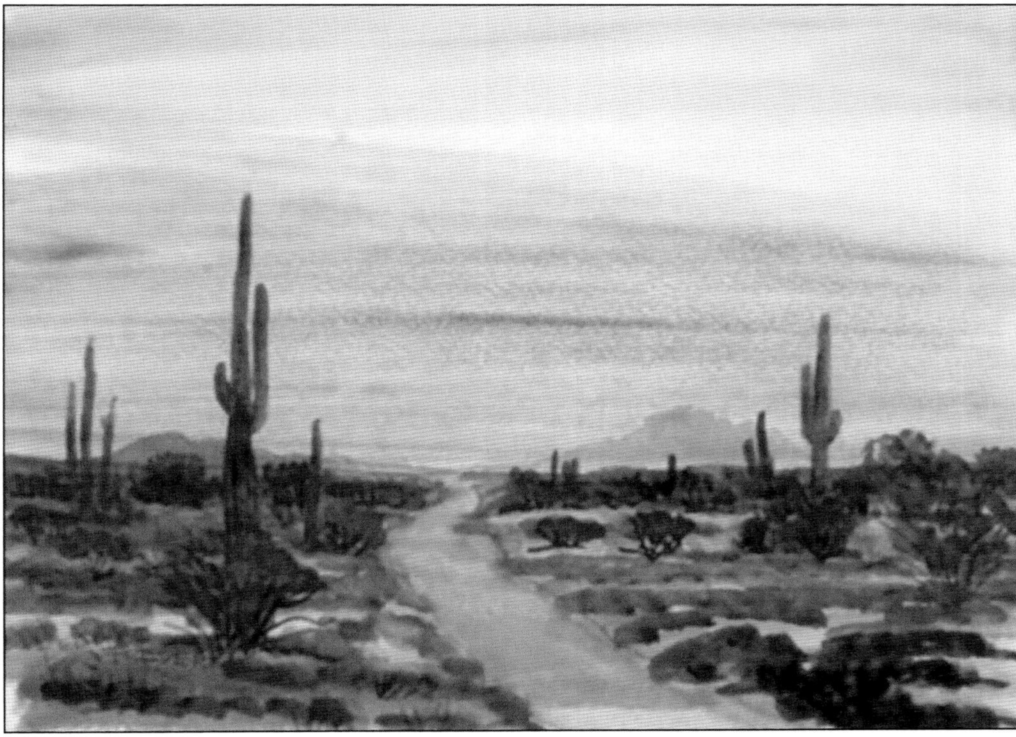

With east Mesa sparsely populated, it did not take long for Frederick to meet Ted and Alice Sliger and form a strong and lasting friendship that continued until Frederick's death. The Sligers found something irresistible in his work, such as this early painting of the Superstition Mountains. It was just one of many that would be added to the Sligers' growing collection of his work. (Courtesy MHM.)

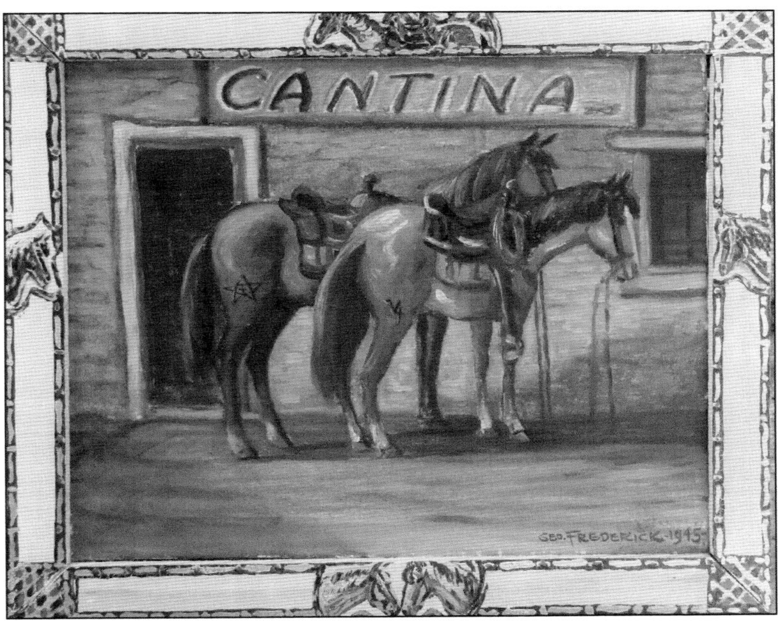

George Fredrick painted *Cantina* in 1945, one of his many works that adorned the Buckhorn's walls. Frederick's custom-made, hand-painted frame further evoked the West's Mexican heritage. (Courtesy MHM.)

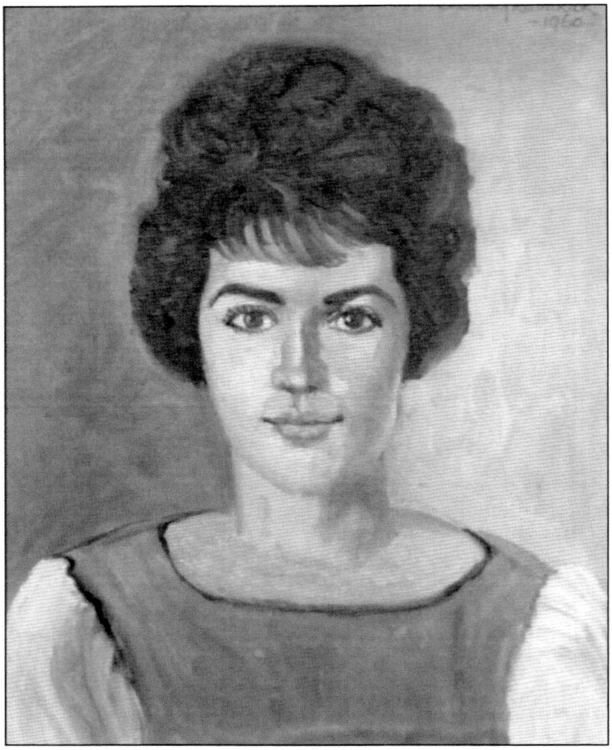

A prolific landscape painter, Frederick also found time for portraits, including his patrons and their children. In 1960, twenty years after he first met the Sligers, Frederick took time to capture on canvas the image of 15-year-old daughter Marilyn. (Courtesy MHM.)

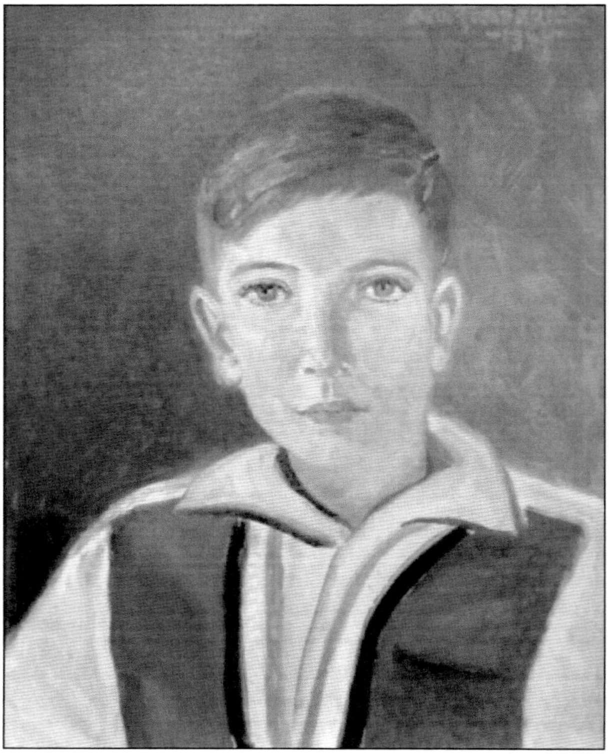

That same year, Frederick painted the Sligers' 12-year-old son Ted Newton. Four years later, George Frederick, nicknamed "Smoke Tree George," passed away peacefully at the Buckhorn, leaving a substantial body of work that was continually displayed until the resort closed. (Courtesy MHM.)

George Frederick's sketchbook shows how elaborately the artist studied his subjects with detailed notes and drawings before committing them to canvas. After his passing, the Sligers found Frederick's sketchbook and kept it as an important record of how this artist worked. (Courtesy MHM.)

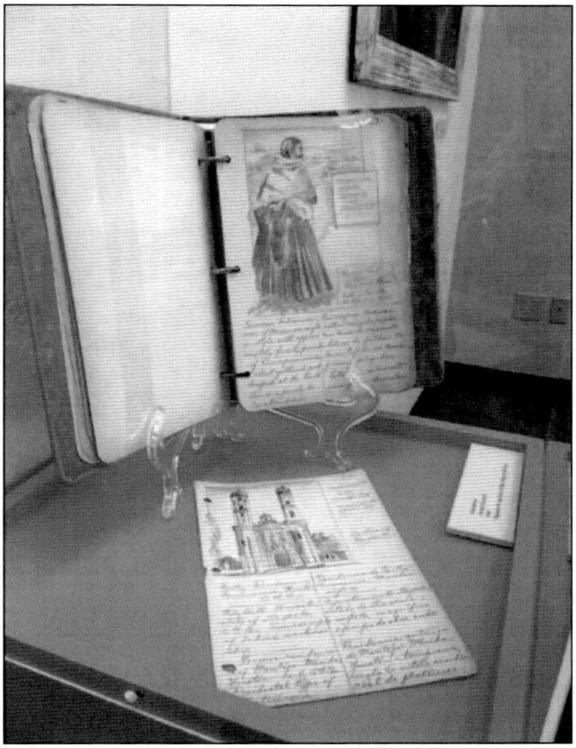

George Frederick split his time between painting portraits and landscapes. Camelback Mountain with the iconic "Praying Monk" is depicted here. (Courtesy MHM.)

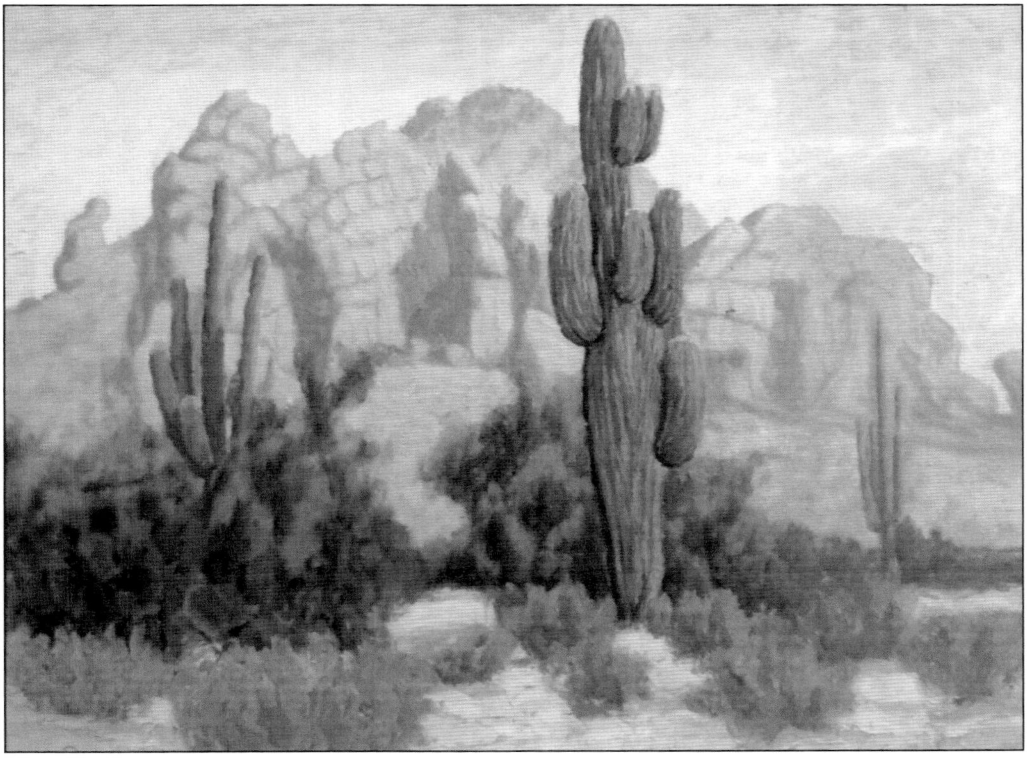

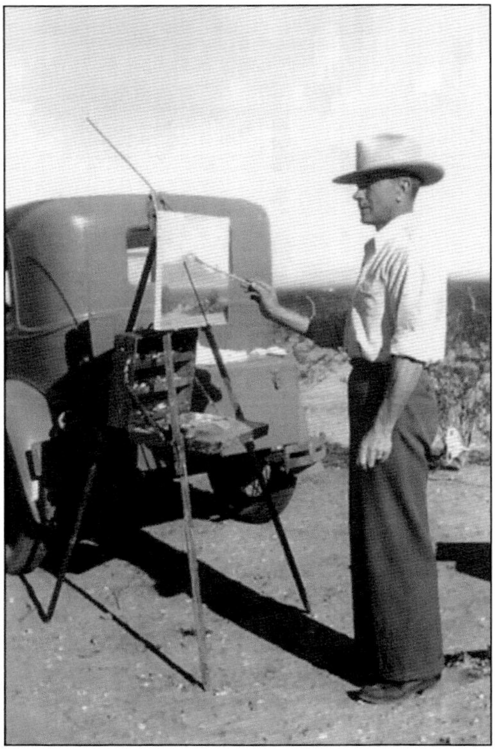

Arnold Otto Krug (1896–1942) was another Buckhorn artist-in-residence, considered by some a more accomplished painter than Frederick. Born in Forest, Wisconsin, Krug was a self-taught artist who discovered Arizona in the 1930s. He was immediately captivated by the desert's beauty. After meeting the Sligers, Krug was invited to become a Buckhorn artist-in-residence. Unlike the more outgoing Frederick, Arnold Krug was described as "a quiet and shy" type. (Courtesy MHM.)

Western scenes, particularly the imposing Superstition Mountains depicted here in a 1935 painting, were a favorite of Arnold Krug. Given more time, Krug could have left a larger body of work at the Buckhorn, but he succumbed to bronchial pneumonia in 1942. Reflecting on his untimely passing and referring to her own bout of undulant fever (bronchial pneumonia), Alice Sliger said Krug was "an artist friend . . . who lived in a small room here and spent lots of time with us, got undulant fever too, but he did not survive it." (Courtesy MHM.)

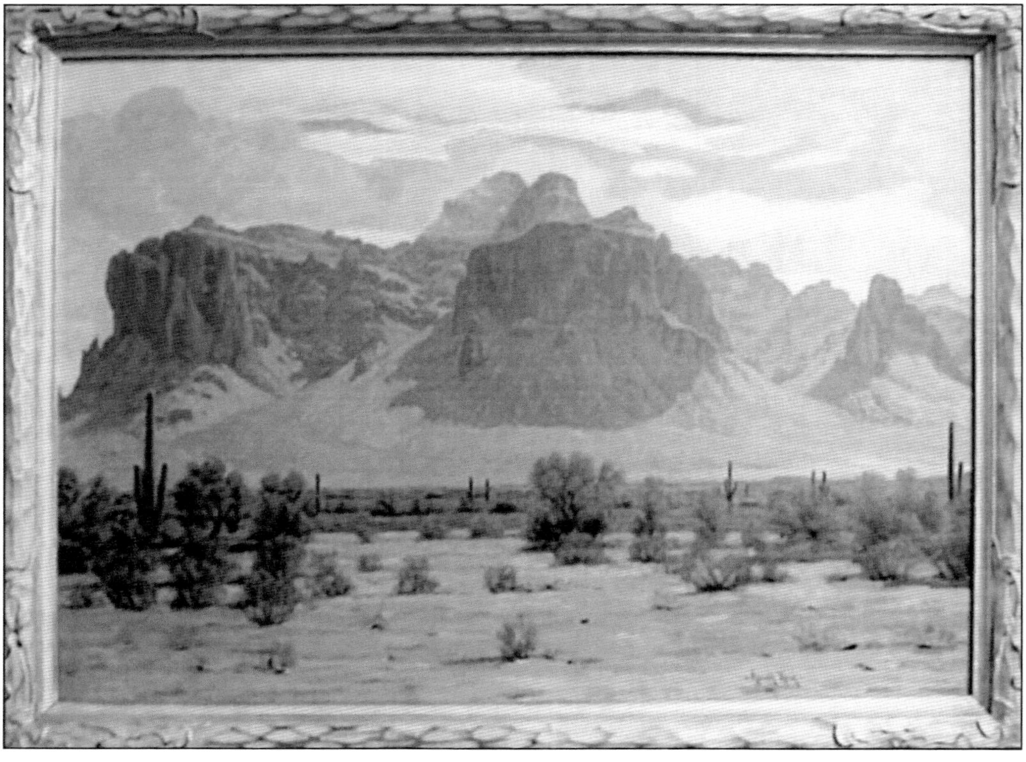

The Sligers' support of the arts followed many genres, from fine art to cartoons. It is uncertain how the couple first met Hal Empie (1909–2002), but once the connection was made, they soon employed his talents. A native Arizonan, Empie began his career in Duncan, Arizona, as the youngest licensed pharmacist in state history. In between formulating prescriptions, Empie was busy sketching—both as a self-taught fine artist and employing his penchant for cartooning. (Courtesy Hal Empie Gallery, Tubac, Arizona.)

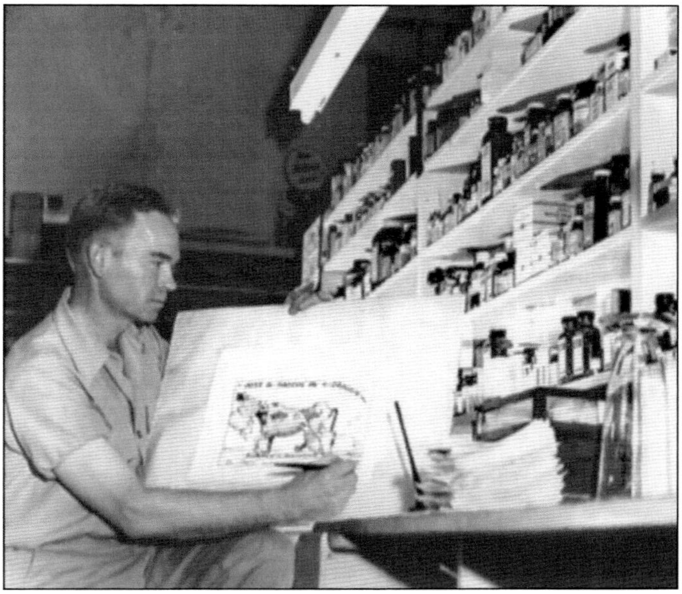

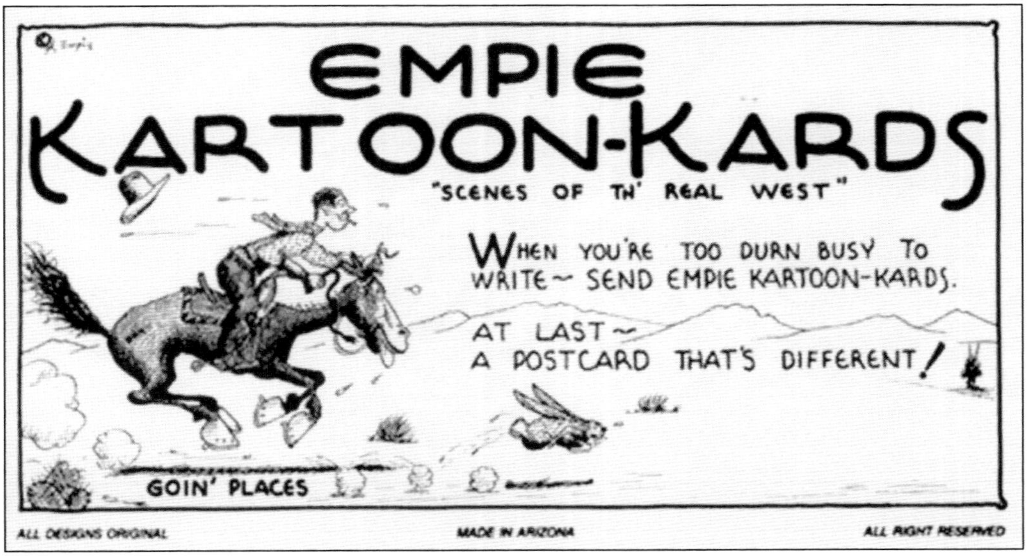

Gradually, art supplanted compounding medicines. By 1938, Hal Empie was creating his unique brand of Empie Kartoon Kards for a variety of businesses and publications like *Arizona Highways*. Before abandoning cartooning for fine art, Empie spent more than four decades creating cartoon postcards for customers in 38 states. (Courtesy Hal Empie Gallery, Tubac, Arizona.)

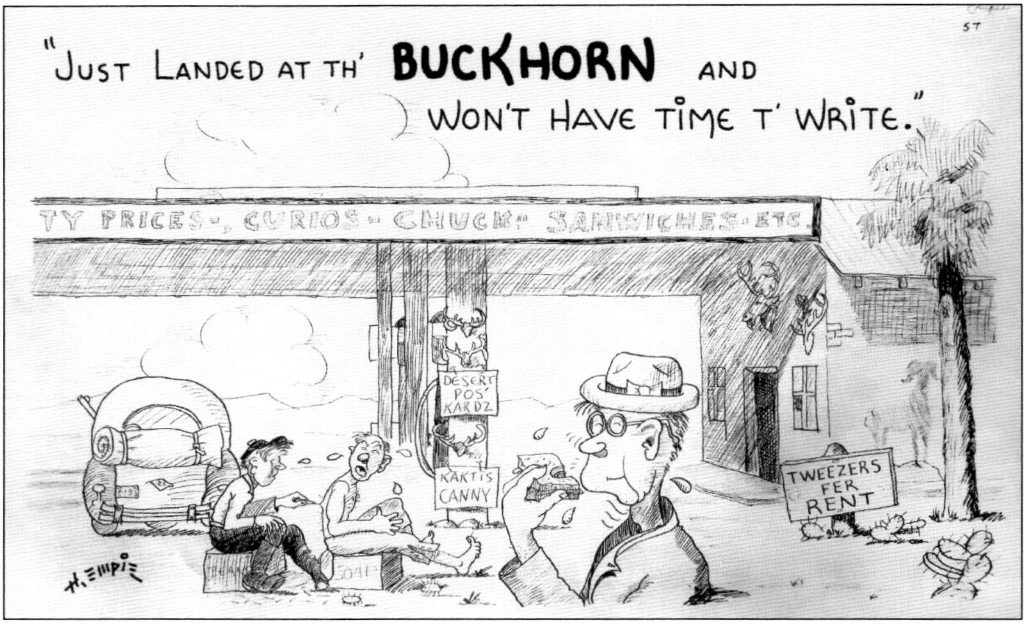

Only two Buckhorn Empie Kartoon Kards are known. In the absence of a date or inventory number, it is uncertain if this drawing was ever published. Empie's wry sense of humor soars, from the "Tweezers fer Rent" sign planted amongst prickly pear cacti to his not-so-subtle reference to "Desert Post Kards" for sale. The "Kaktis Canny" sign promoted one of the Buckhorn's more popular items—Cactus Candy. Hal Empie's cartoons delightfully captured an amusing spirit of the Old West. Unlike the previous illustration, this card is dated 1942 and features the Empie Kartoon Kard imprint. For unexplained reasons, the Sligers did not commission cartoon cards after that date, apparently preferring to produce more than 100 different cards photographically illustrating the Buckhorn campus and activities. (Both, courtesy Hal Empie Gallery, Tubac, Arizona.)

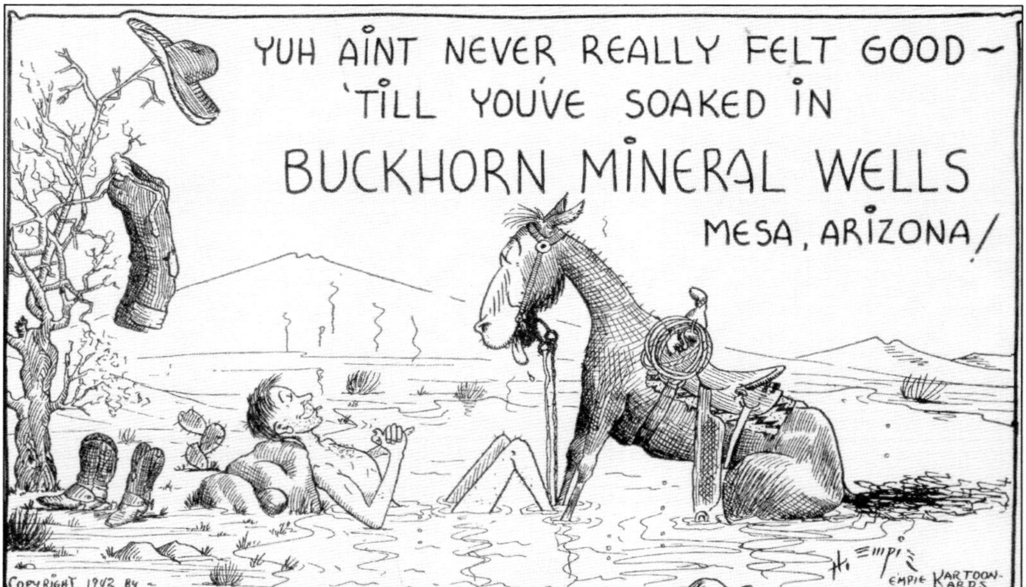

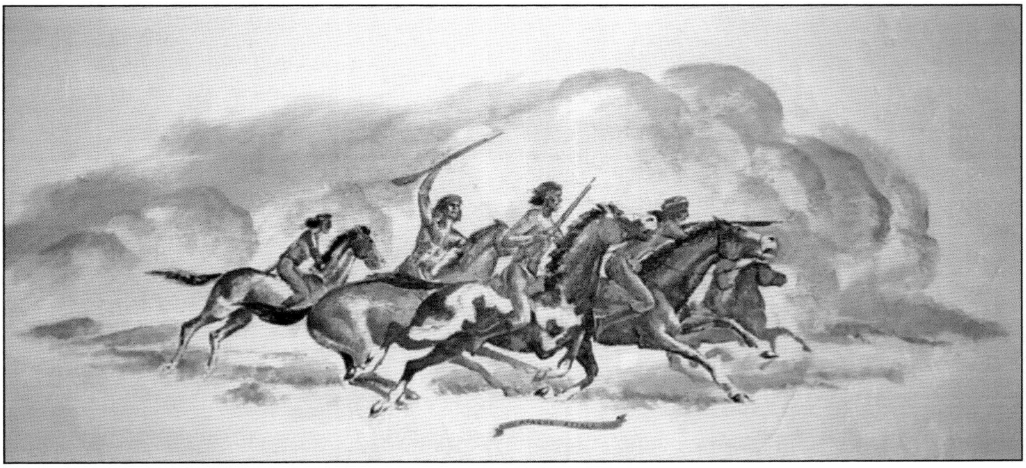

Nothing fascinated international and eastern American tourists more than Arizona's 19th-century Indian conflicts. Even in the 20th century, some mistakenly feared attacks. The Sligers were happy to provide guests with visions of the wars as they dined in the Buckhorn restaurant. A quartet of Indian-themed murals, created by an unidentified artist, presented chilling scenes of an "Apache Attack" and an Indian "Ambush." (Both, courtesy AZMNH.)

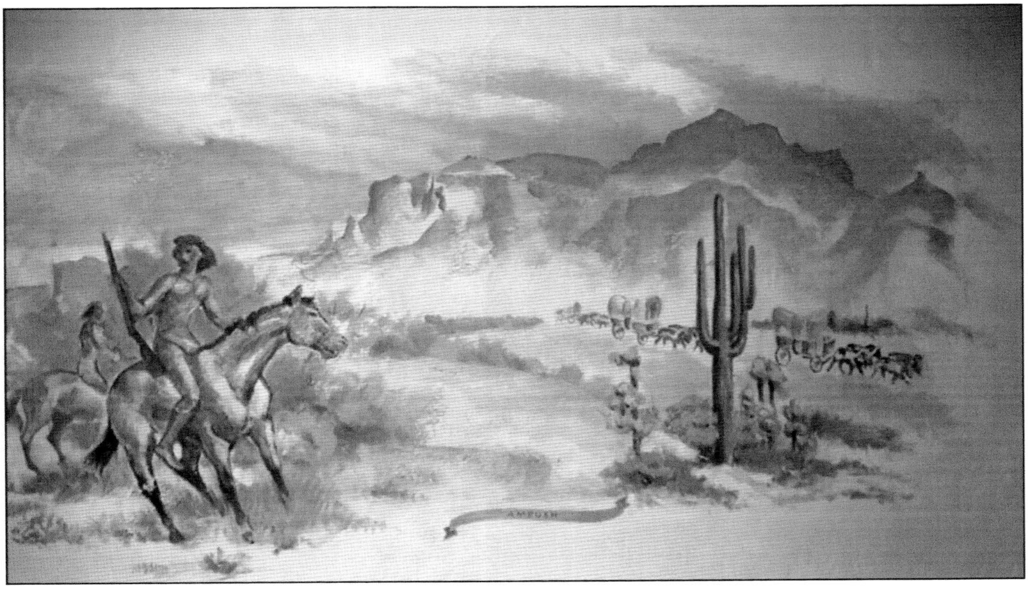

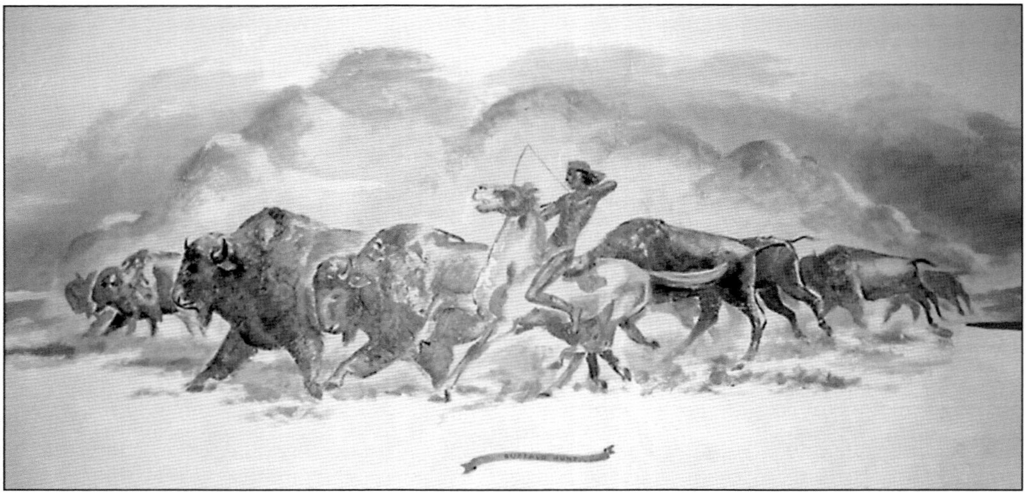

Two murals demonstrated the artist's complete lack of knowledge of Arizona history, Indians, and their cultures. But accuracy did not seem to bother the painter or the Sligers. This evocative but incorrect painting titled "Buffalo Hunt" portrays a Plains Indians activity never undertaken by the Apaches. (Courtesy AZMNH.)

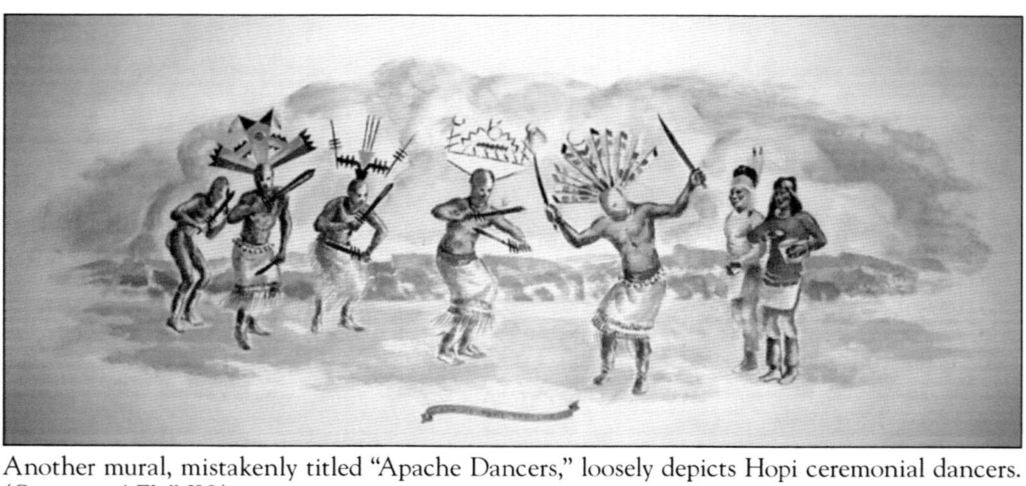

Another mural, mistakenly titled "Apache Dancers," loosely depicts Hopi ceremonial dancers. (Courtesy AZMNH.)

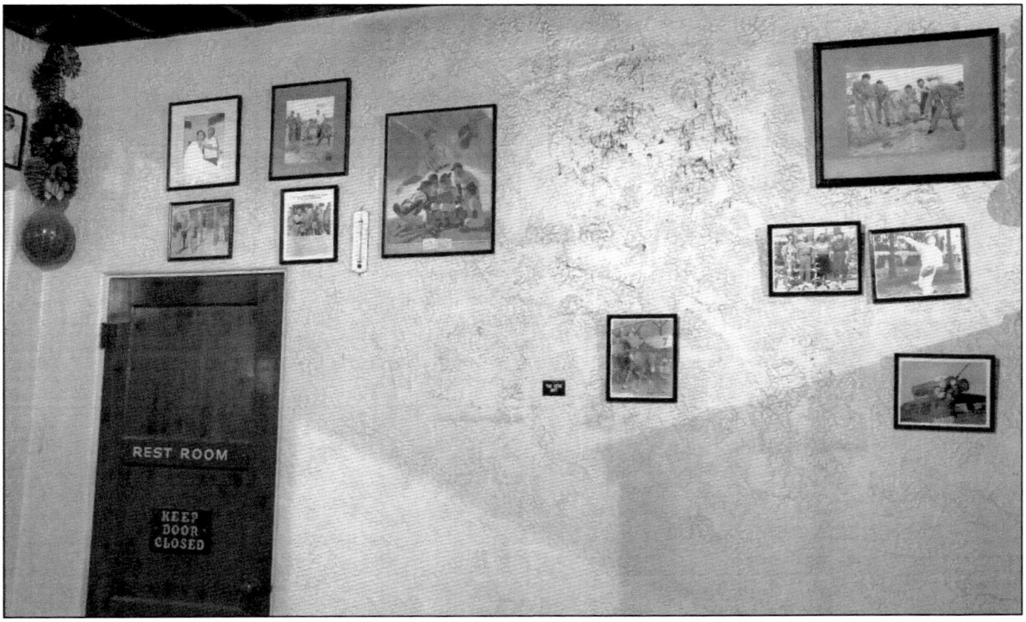

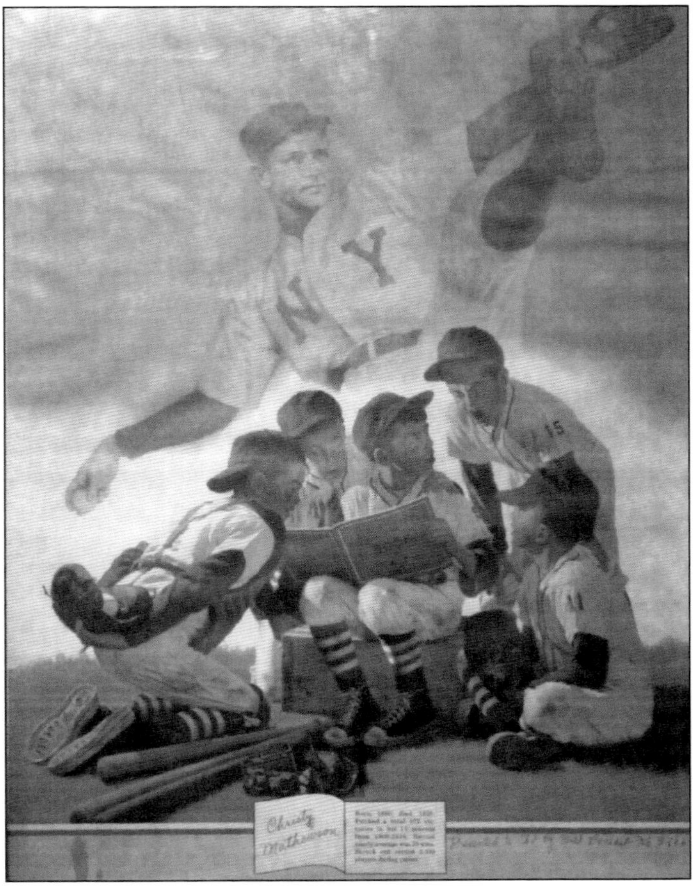

Although never billed as such, the Buckhorn was an art gallery of diverse subjects. Among original landscapes and portraits was an iconic print (above, fifth from left) featuring Christy Mathewson, one of early baseball's biggest stars. Hung in the player's bathhouse locker room, along with numerous baseball player photographs, the print was presented to Ted Sliger in 1966 by William "Barnacle Bill" Posedel, a right-handed pitcher who played in the big leagues between 1938 and 1946.

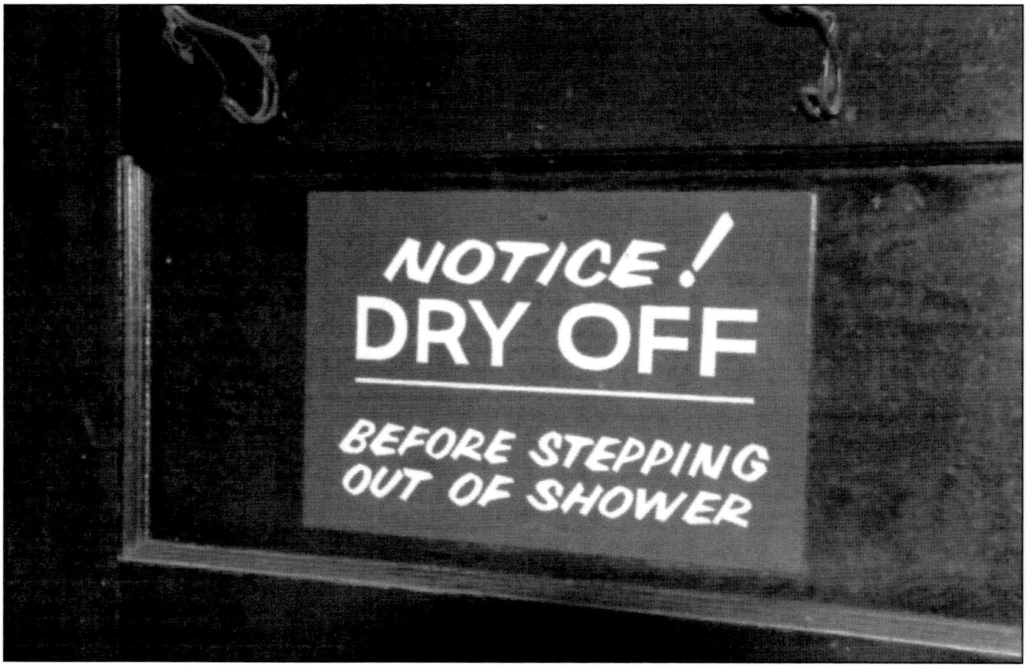

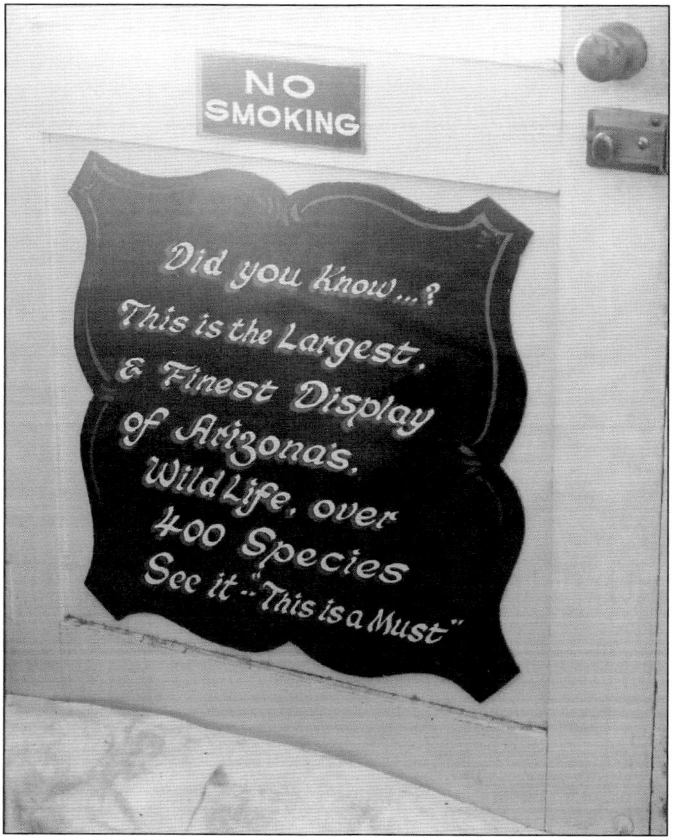

While fine artists like Frederick and Krug were painting portraits and landscapes, the Sligers were employing different artistic skills—sign painting. Rather than use commercially printed signs, they preferred more personal hand-painted plaques. Hundreds of these quaint signs were distributed throughout the campus, from dozens in the bathhouse, to the cactus garden, to the Wildlife Museum.

Six

LEADING THE WILDLIFE

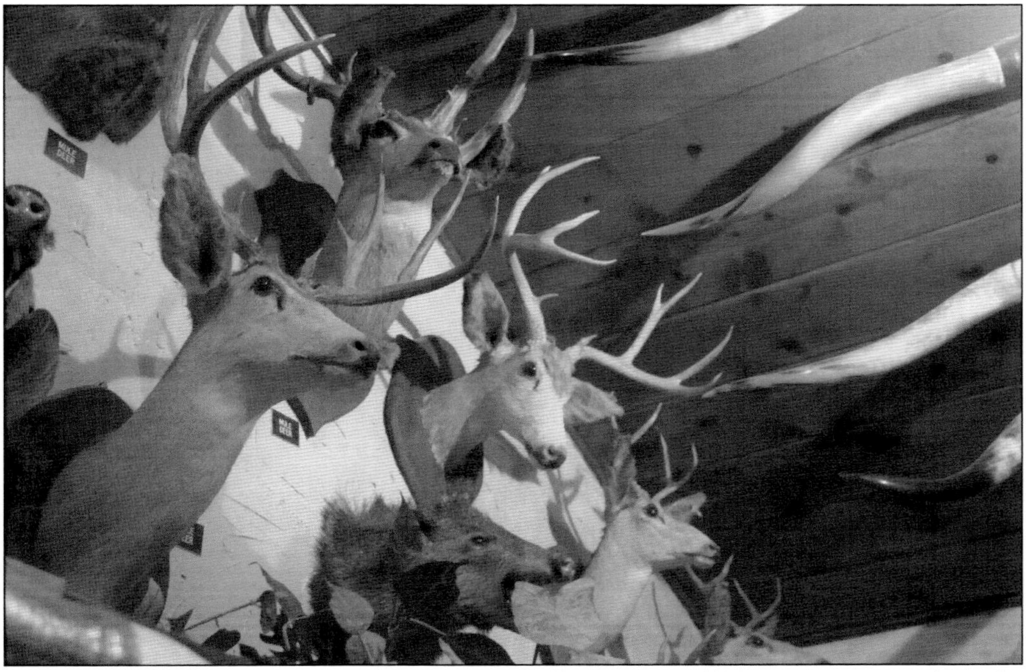

Of all the amenities and oddities the Buckhorn offered, the Wildlife Museum, touted as "the largest private museum in Arizona," was Ted Sliger's real pride and joy. Drawing thousands of people a year, the museum was the Buckhorn's biggest attraction. Ironically, Ted, a most capable and accomplished taxidermy artist, later in life confessed to his son, "I shouldn't have done it," referring to all the animals he had killed and mounted.

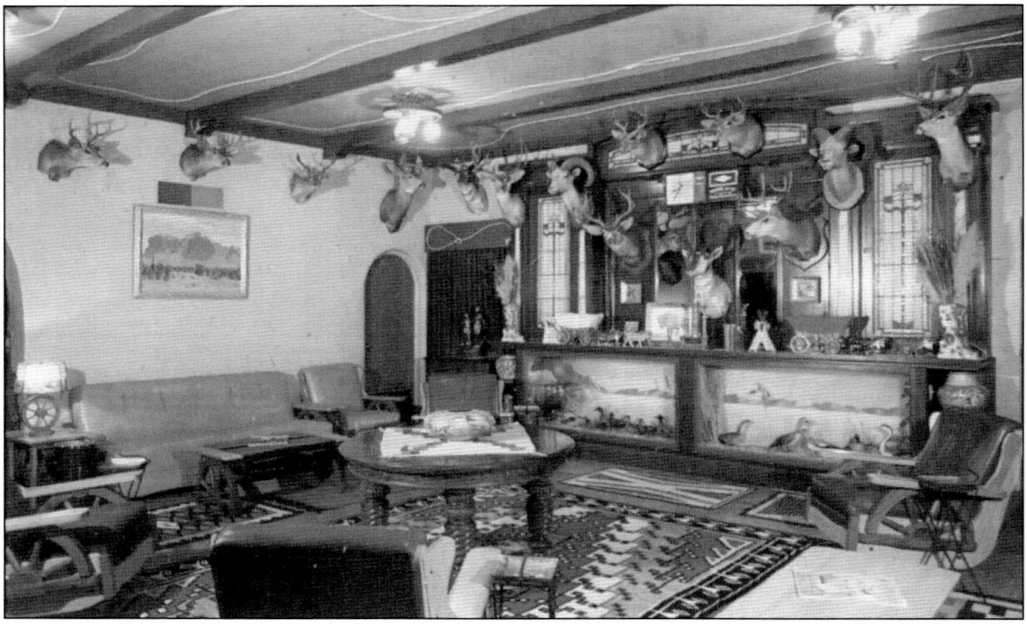

The Buckhorn's goal was to provide a welcoming and comfortable guest experience in a unique Western atmosphere. Just off the lobby was the living room, decorated with wildlife specimens and memorabilia from Ted's vast collection of guns and Native American artifacts. Here, visitors could meet in a homey setting and relax in leather-covered chairs. A pair of arches led to the Wildlife Museum, a room filled with more than 400 specimens, each prepared, stuffed, and mounted by Ted.

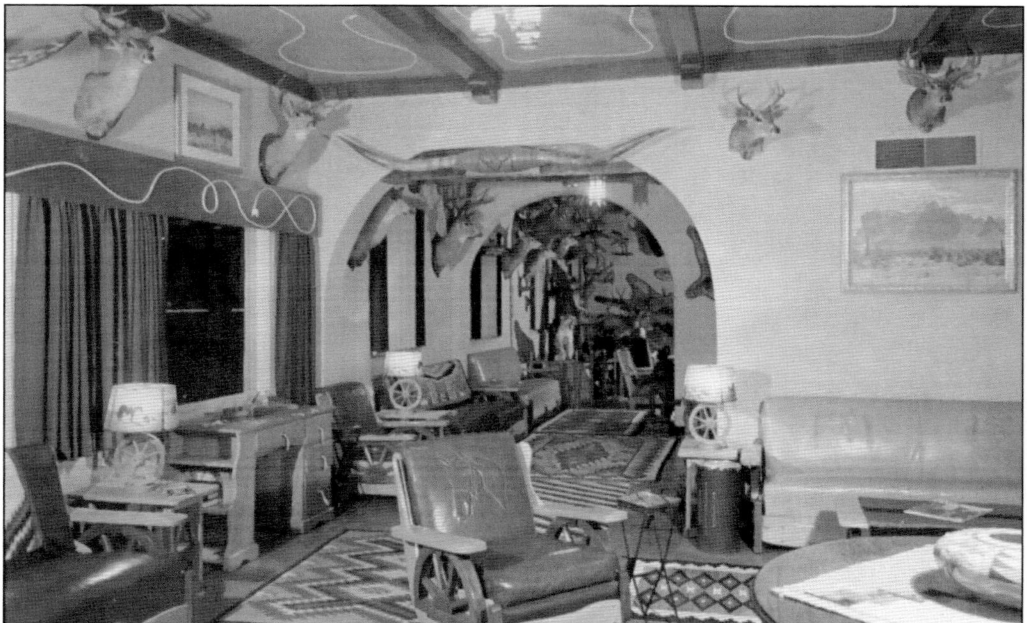

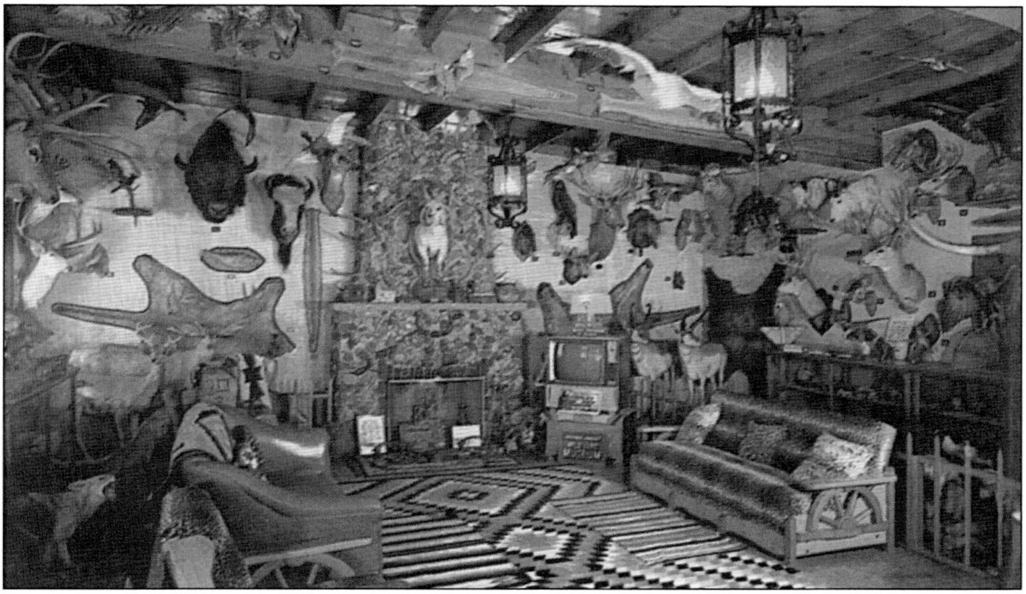

Ted Sliger was always an avid outdoorsman, especially after he and his father settled on the Arizona desert east of Mesa in 1923. Much of his free time was spent fishing and hunting. Those excursions led to a desire for preserving his best catches and kills. A self-taught taxidermist, Sliger's growing experience and talent for the art resulted in an avocation that allowed him to build an immense collection of wildlife, while earning extra money by performing this specialized service for others.

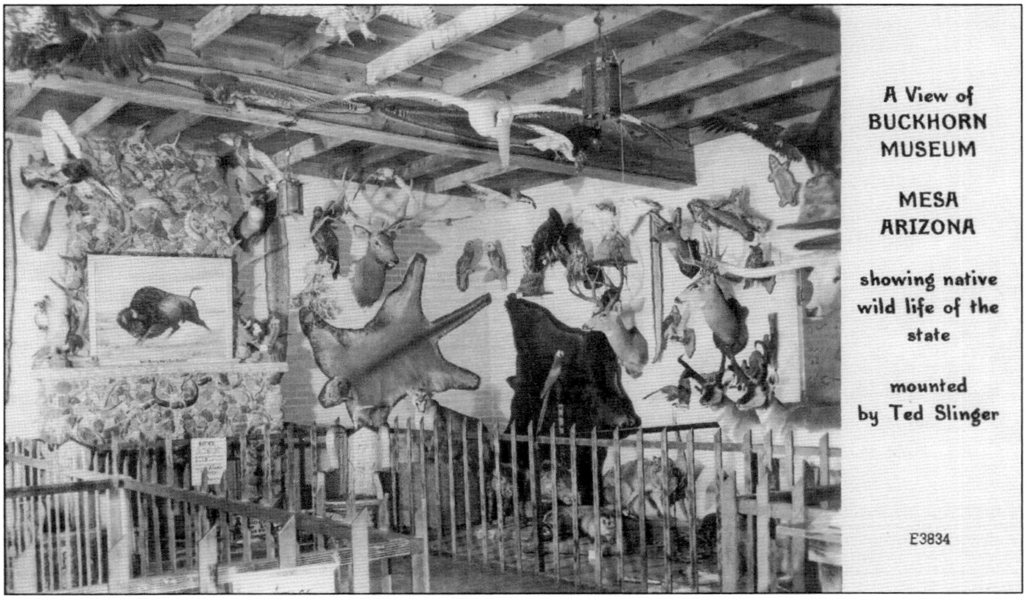

From the time the Sligers relocated to a new site after their 1935 Christmas Eve fire, Ted wanted to open a Wildlife Museum. After first setting up a gas station and curio shop, he constructed a building to house his growing wildlife collection. Even though some visitors never stayed long enough to enjoy the hot baths, thousands took time to tour the Wildlife Museum.

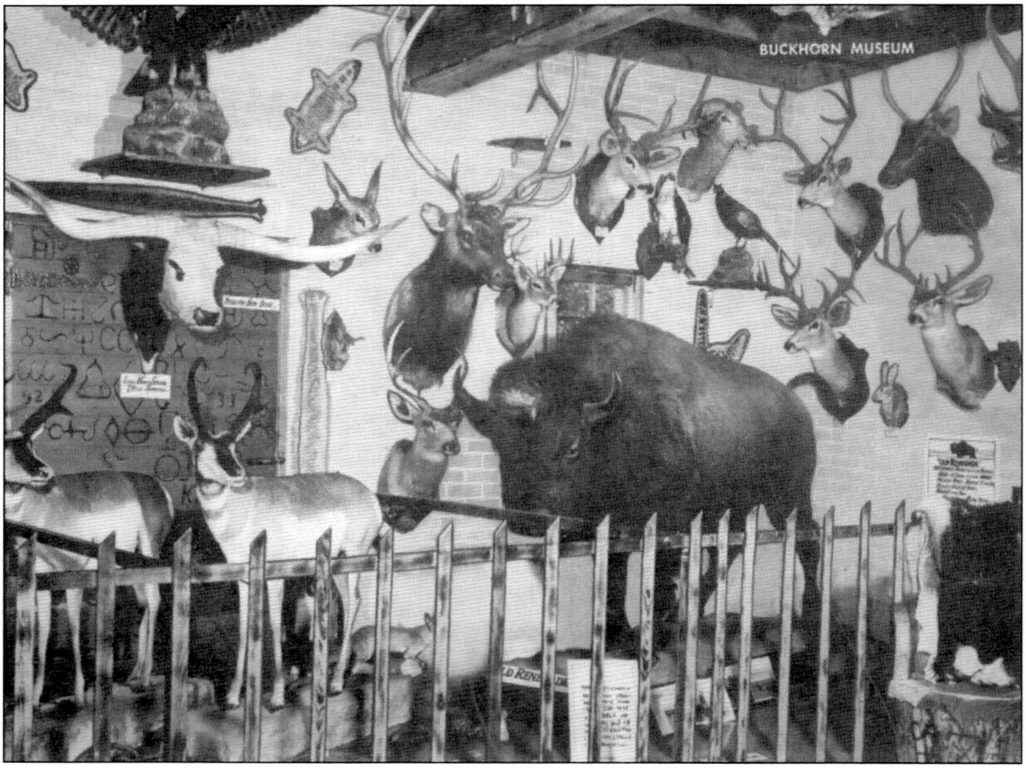

By far the grandest specimen in Ted Sliger's collection was Old Renegade, a quarter-century old "rogue" buffalo that had been creating havoc on ranches in the Buckskin Mountains near the Colorado River in western Arizona. In 1942, Arizona Game and Fish called upon Sliger to kill the old bull. It took two days of hunting with automobiles and horses to track down the elusive beast. The meat was served at a giant barbecue a month later.

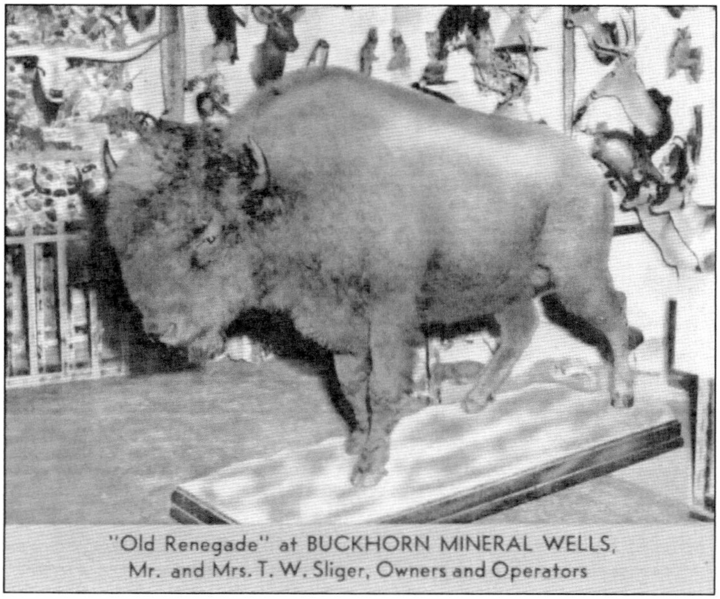

"Old Renegade" at BUCKHORN MINERAL WELLS,
Mr. and Mrs. T. W. Sliger, Owners and Operators

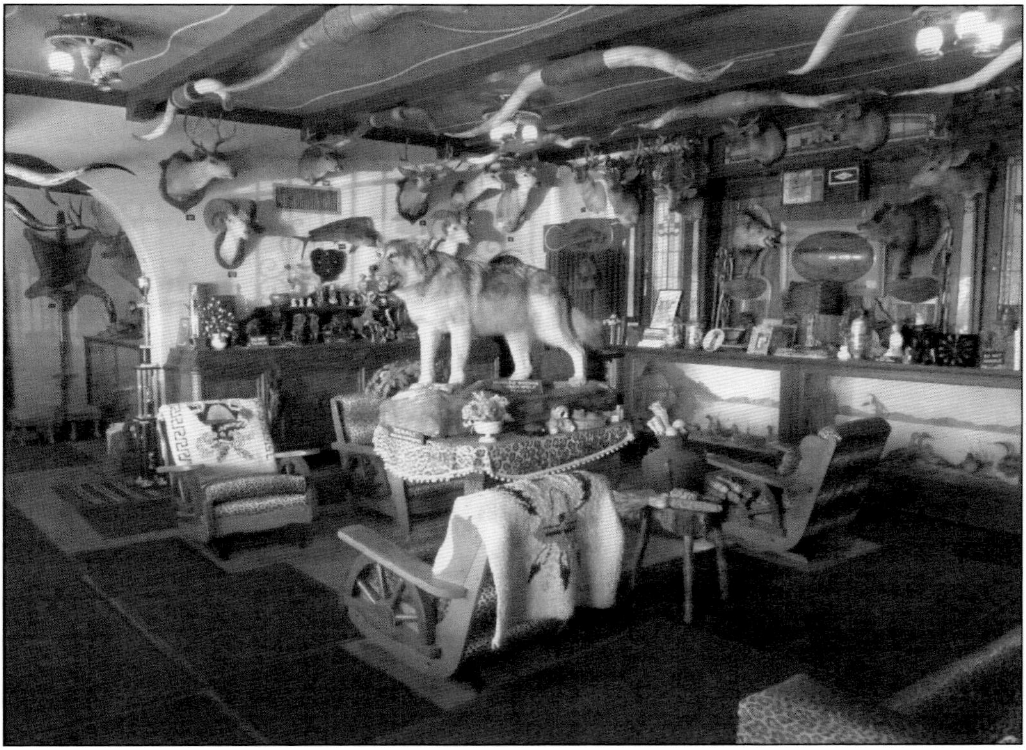

The Buckhorn's Wildlife Museum took two large rooms to house its vast collection; it almost exclusively featured Arizona specimens. One notable exception was the Alaskan Denali wolf that Ted prominently displayed on a front table in the living room area of the museum. Of the more than 450 pieces in the museum, many people found the Denali wolf, with its fangs bared, the most terrifying.

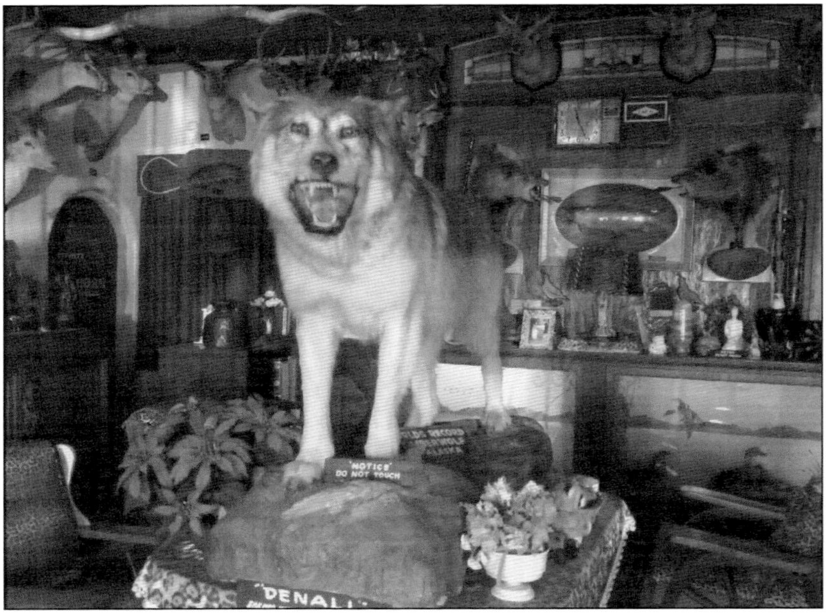

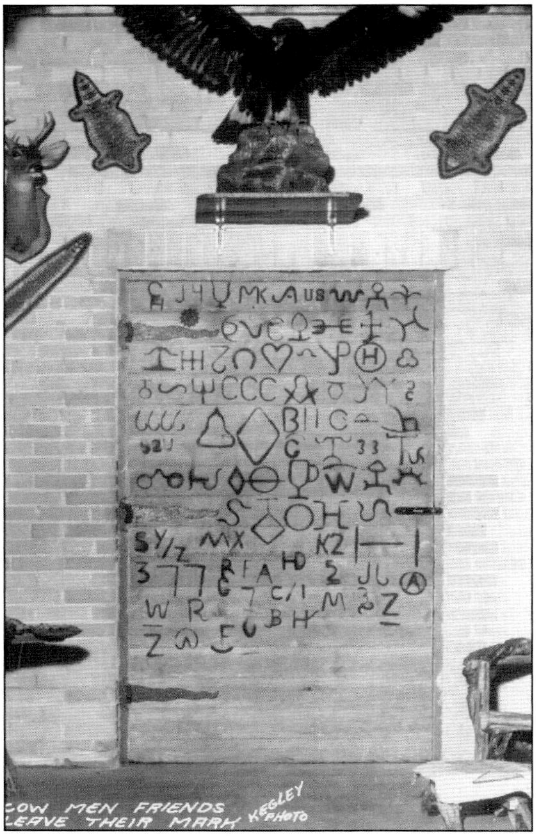

Every nook and cranny of the Buckhorn had a story, such as the Brand Door. By the 1940s, John Hale of Mesa had amassed what was considered the largest collection of branding irons in the United States. He was an often-consulted authority. A good friend of the Sligers, Hale decided one day that the Buckhorn should have a more Western theme. So he brought out a bunch of irons, heated them in a fire, and indelibly burned brands into the door.

A lack of space never deterred Ted Sliger from displaying his ever-growing collection of wildlife specimens. An enclosed breezeway ceiling became a perfect spot for his increasing assemblage of Texas longhorns. On the walls, Sliger thought nothing of displaying deer and javelinas together.

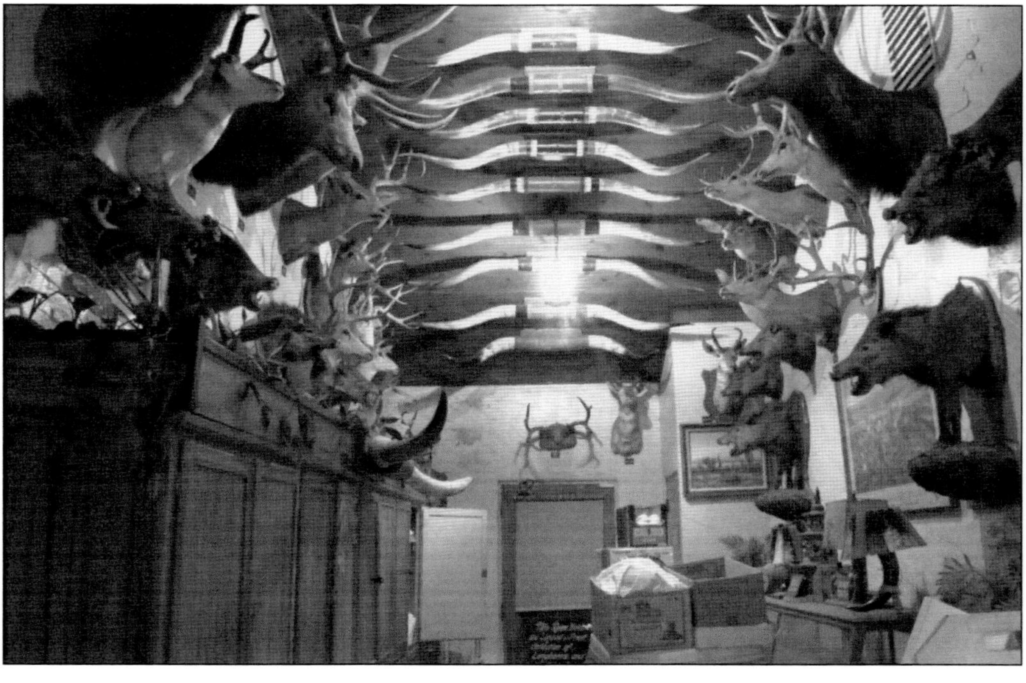

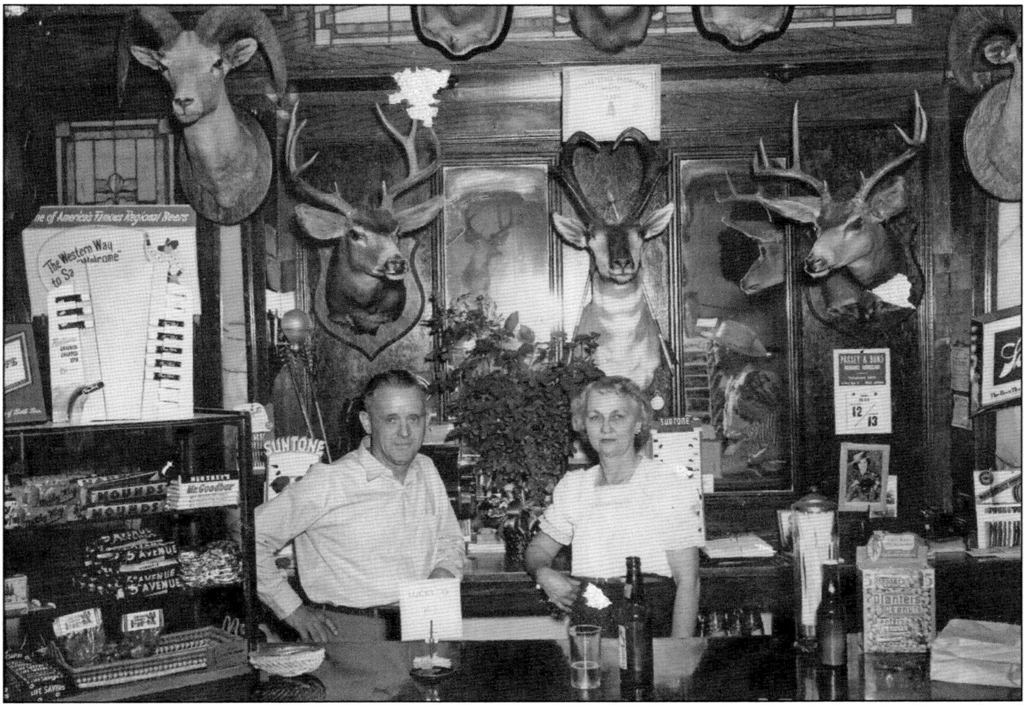

One of the more popular places for guests and motorists just gassing up was the bar and concession stand in the Wildlife Museum, seen in this 1951 photograph. Here, soft drinks, beer, candy, and sundries could be purchased while surrounded by deer. (Courtesy MHM.)

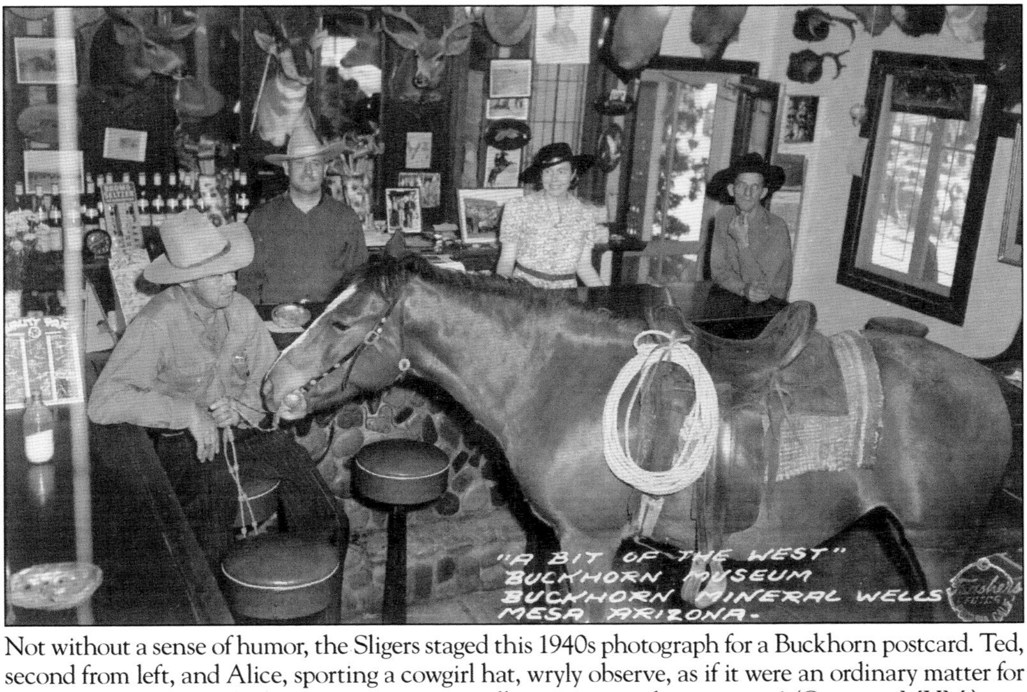

Not without a sense of humor, the Sligers staged this 1940s photograph for a Buckhorn postcard. Ted, second from left, and Alice, sporting a cowgirl hat, wryly observe, as if it were an ordinary matter for a horse to belly up to the bar. It was most assuredly not a normal occurrence! (Courtesy MHM.)

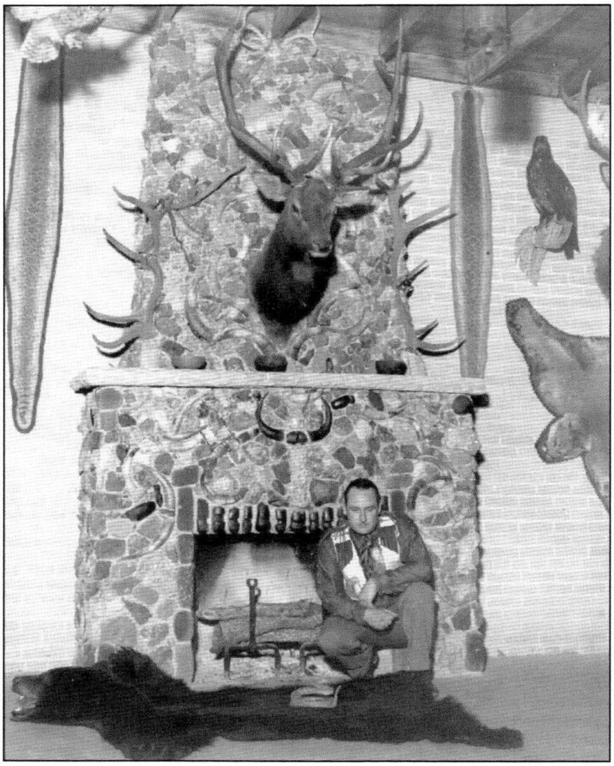

Along with an impressive array of Arizona wildlife, a custom fireplace was the centerpiece in the room that housed the collection. It too was a museum piece, incorporating native American artifacts along with minerals from throughout the state. Shortly after it was completed, Ted Sliger, dressed in a Western vest, posed in front of the fireplace with specimens from his collection. In the ensuing years, the somewhat sparse walls would be entirely filled with an assemblage of nearly 450 creatures. (Courtesy MHM.)

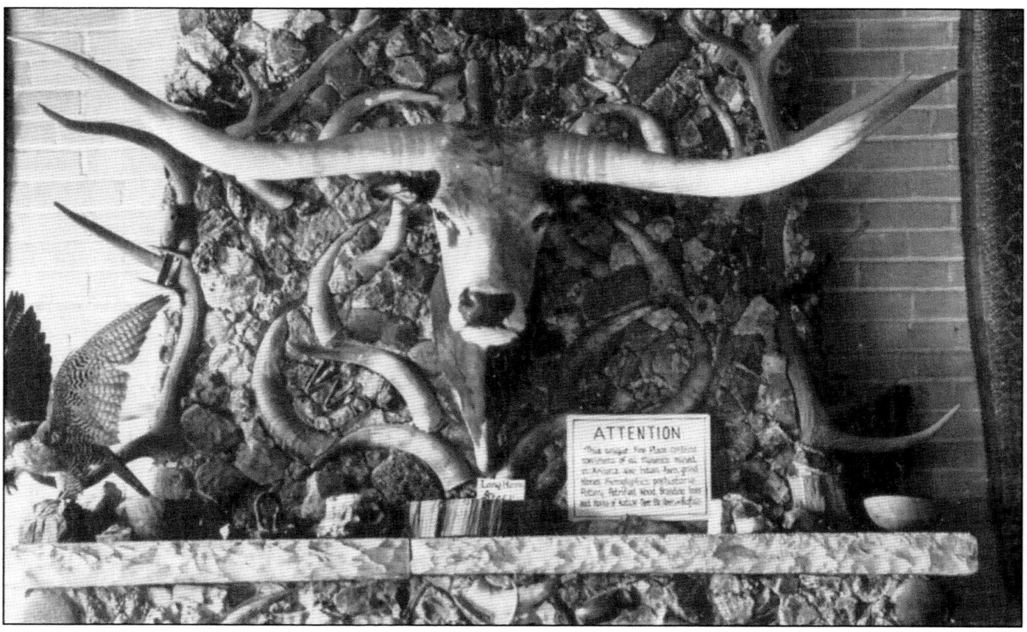

As the collection grew, Ted would replace specimens over the fireplace from time to time with bigger and better examples. A small, hand-painted placard boasted, "This unique Fire Place contains specimens of all minerals mined in Arizona, also Indian Axes, grind stones, Hieroglyphics, prehistoric Pottery, Petrified Wood, Branding Irons and Horns of Native Elk, Steer and Buffalo."

Seven

Sign of the Times

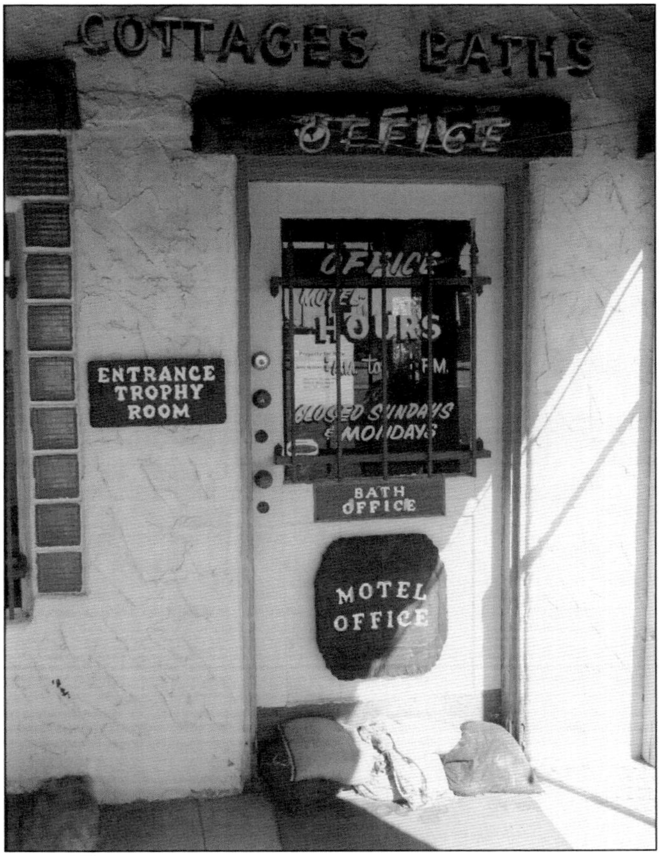

At the Buckhorn, neon and hand-painted signs abounded. They were one of the resort's most visible features—beginning with the guests' front door entrance to the lobby. Ted and Alice Sliger knew the marketing value of signage needed to attract travelers off the highway. They also valued the importance of signs to help navigate the large campus and understand all of the Buckhorn's amenities.

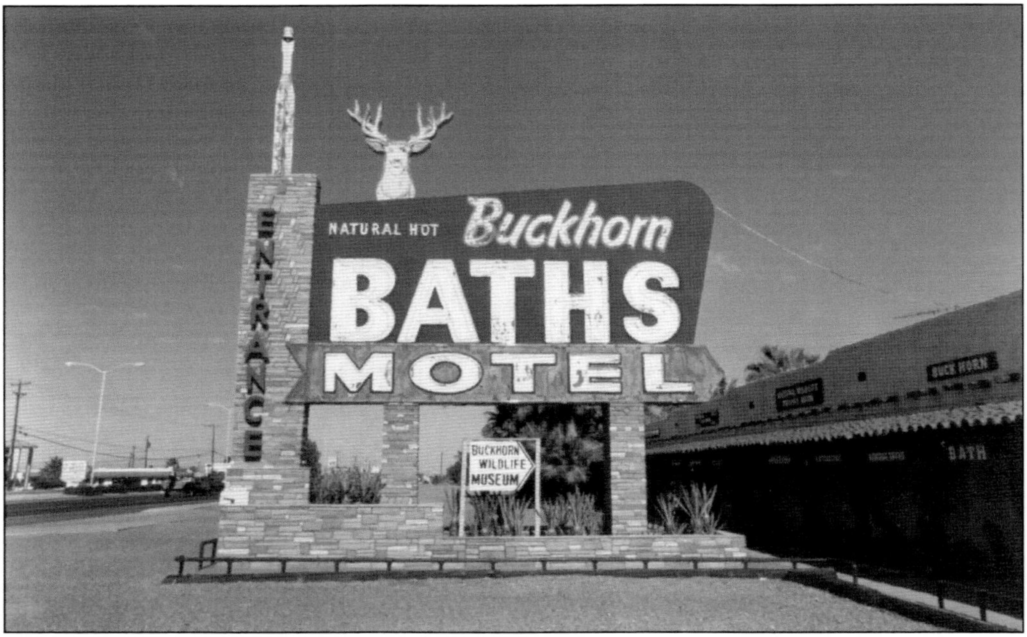

The monumental Buckhorn neon sign remains the resort's most recognized attribute. Conceived by noted sign designer Glen Guyette, it was manufactured about 1949 by legendary sign maker Paul Millet. Its brilliant glow could be seen from nearly a mile away, enticing travelers to pull out from the darkness into the inviting, warm embrace of the resort. This 1998 photograph, taken a year before the baths closed, shows paint beginning to peel.

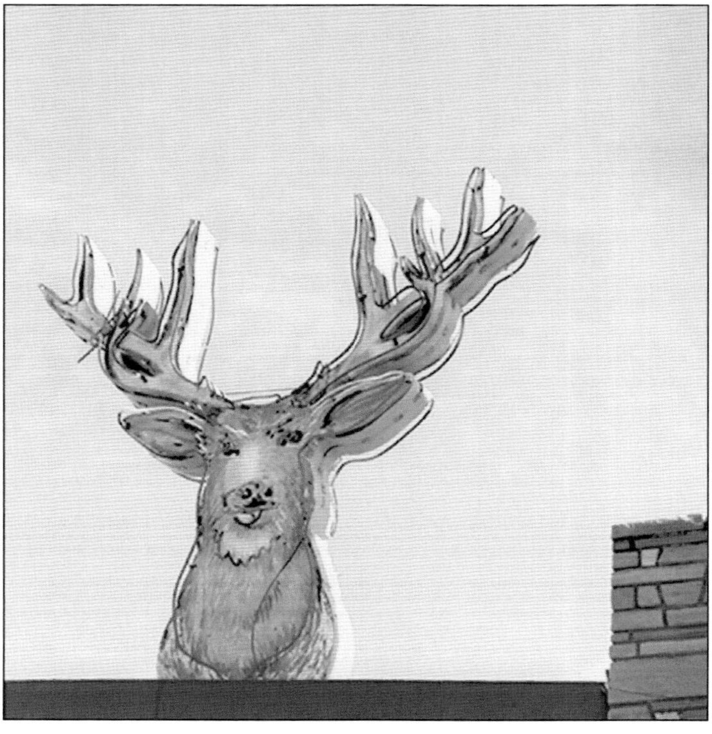

As word of Ted Sliger's taxidermy talents spread, he was inundated with requests from hunters and fishermen to preserve their treasures. The Buckhorn name derived from the catastrophic 1935 Christmas Eve fire that destroyed all of Ted's wildlife collection except for one specimen, a buck that he had earlier loaned to a local Mesa establishment. As the buck was the lucky sole survivor, Ted thought it appropriate to name the new business the "Buckhorn." The iconic antlered buck image became the business's brand. Even the post office opened in 1958 had mail stamped "Buckhorn Station."

The early years were not easy. Ted had to haul in water for the new business. When he dug wells in 1939, they gushed hot mineral water, opening up an additional opportunity for the Sligers. The baths helped the Buckhorn grow. It became a place for cattle and sheep men, hunters, and fishermen to gather and exchange stories of the big one that got away. Hand-painted signs were everywhere—even on benches that could be seen from the highway.

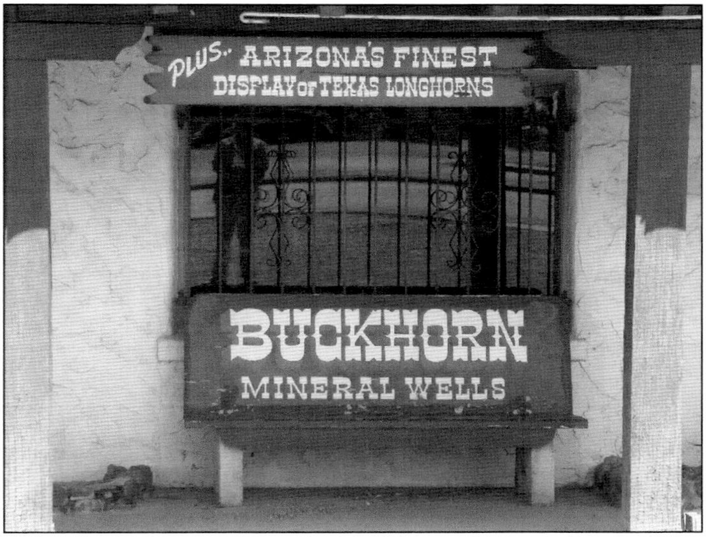

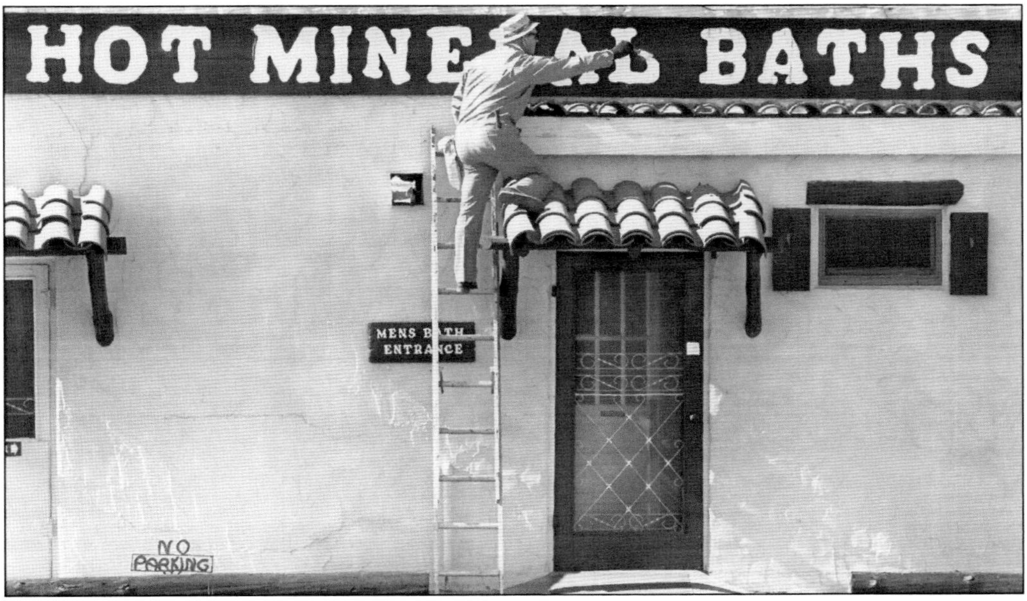

With an abundance of hand-painted signs around the Buckhorn, maintenance was a regular job. Edward M. Arbach (1918–1983) began painting and maintaining the myriad signs around 1973. Sign painting often required daredevil acrobatics. In this 1982 photograph, taken a year before his death, Arbach is seen precariously perched atop a ladder touching up the sign over the men's bathhouse entrance. Along with a "no parking" sign, a smaller Arbach sign is partially concealed by the ladder. (Courtesy MHM.)

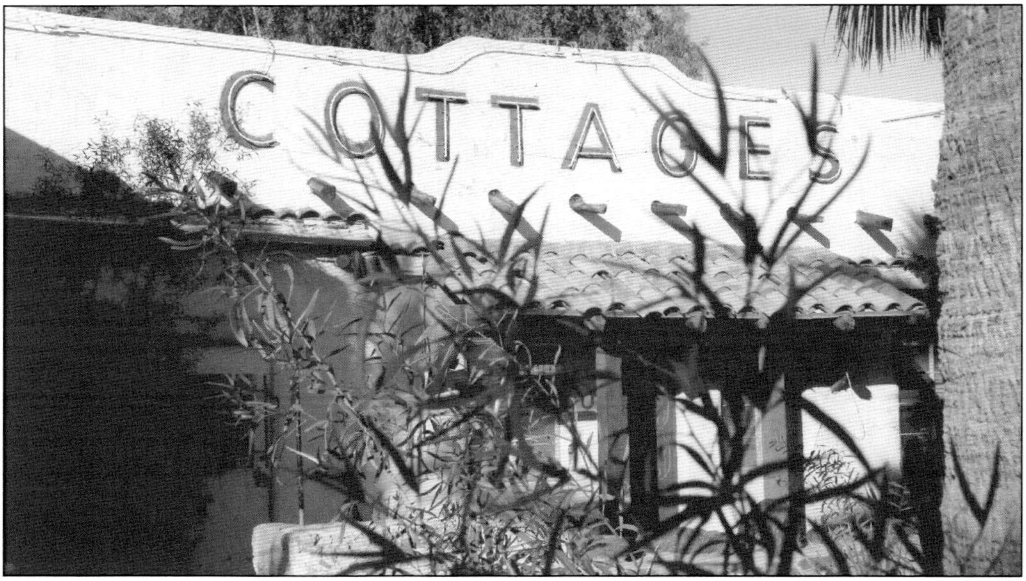

The use of the term "cottage" implied a homelike atmosphere that Ted and Alice sought to convey. The Sligers' use of Pueblo Indian–style architecture complemented the Western theme that drew in visitors. Beyond the lobby where they registered, women guests passed through the cactus garden to enter the bathhouse. Men used a separate door on the east side. After World War II, as more and more tourists were drawn to the Southwest, the "cottage" sign was updated to "motel," reflecting the more contemporary name for roadside lodging.

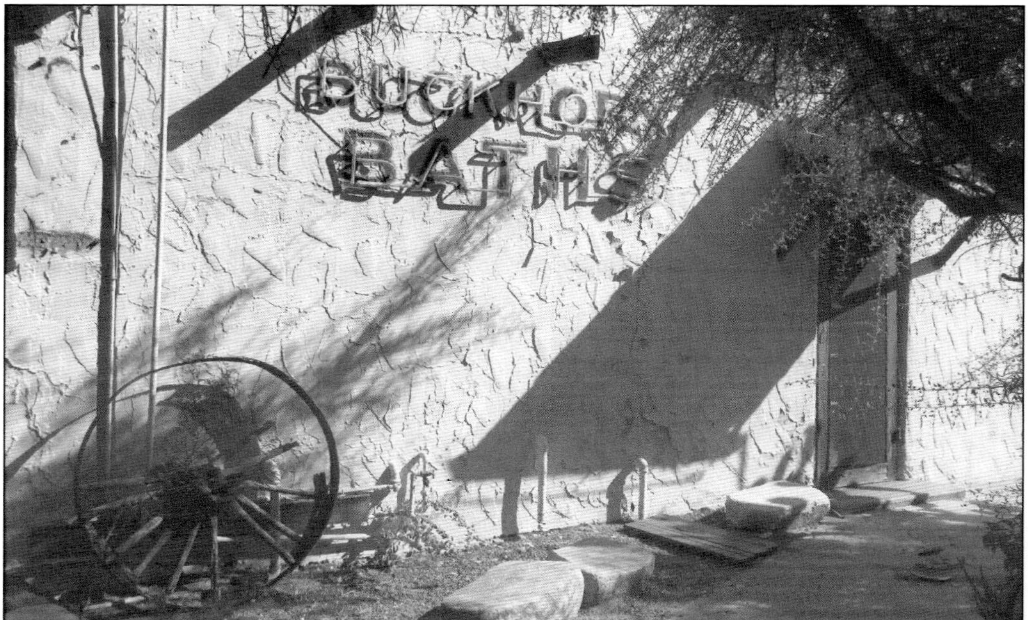

Without a doubt, Mesa sign maker Paul Millet was kept continually busy installing and maintaining a couple of dozen neon signs and the miles of decorative neon banding throughout the property. Surely, the Buckhorn at night was the most colorful, vibrant, and brightly lit business ever on Main Street.

No matter where a guest was on the campus, signs would remind them of their location. Distinctive Pueblo architecture provided a consistent theme throughout. *Pueblo* is a Spanish word for "town" or "village." When Coronado arrived around 1540, the inhabitants of the pueblos in Arizona and New Mexico were the apparent descendants of the Anasazi who had developed the unique building style. Throughout the west, restaurants, hotels, motels, railroad rest stops, and souvenir shops favored Pueblo architecture as the best for attracting tourists interested in exotic sights and local color.

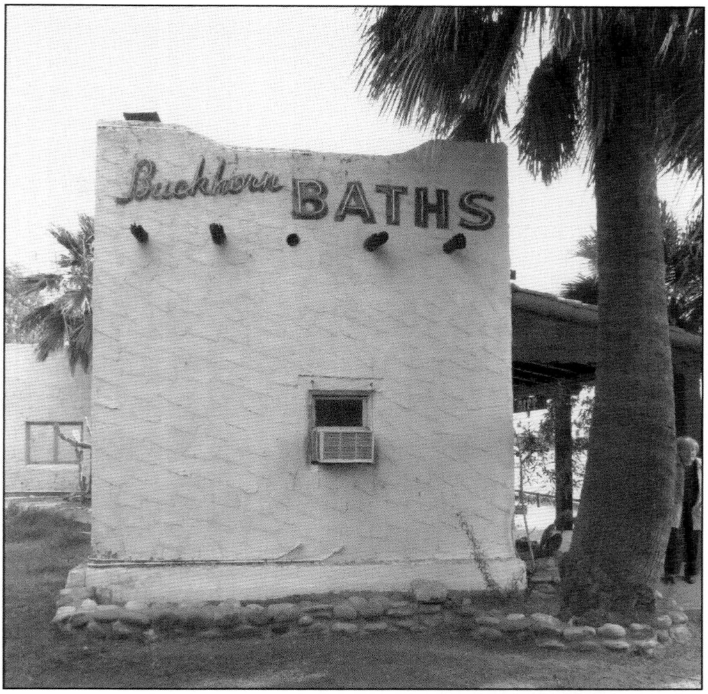

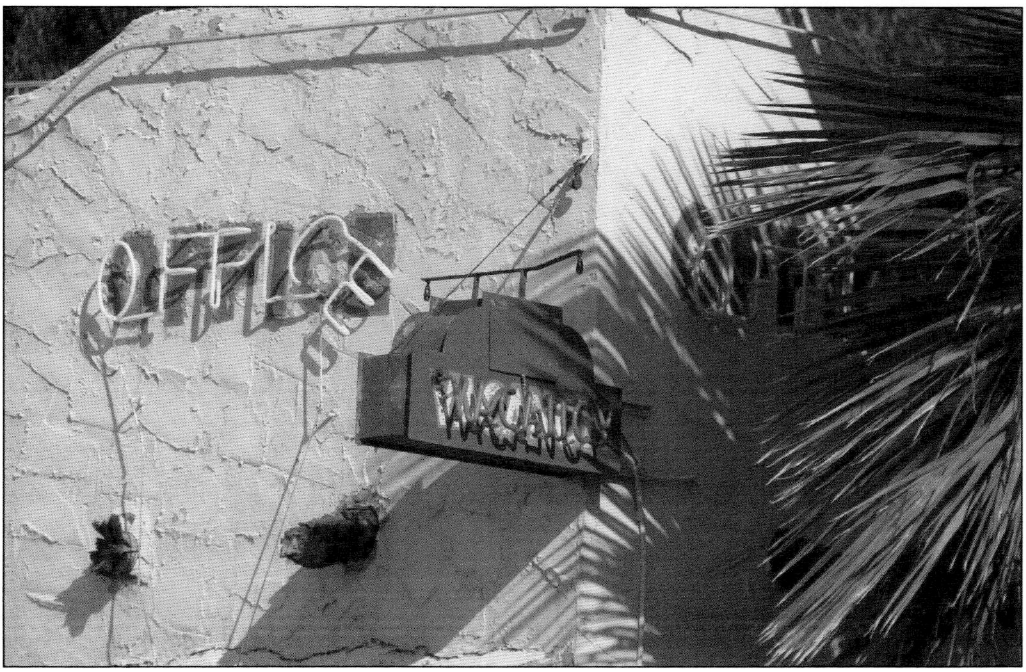

Over the years, the Buckhorn provided a variety of services and amenities—a post office, a Greyhound bus stop, a beauty shop, and a gift shop, along with cottages, the bathhouse, and the Wildlife Museum. A restaurant, opened around 1945, closed in 1975, but the building still stands. Other features included a metate collection, wishing well, and profuse signage, much of which still remains. Neon was a colorful addition to the eclectic nature of the Buckhorn.

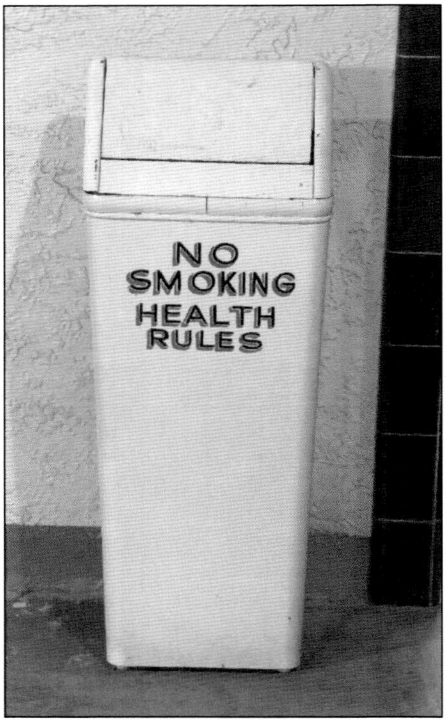

Numbering in the thousands, health-seekers throughout the world have basked in the Buckhorn's hot springs, hoping the mineral-rich waters would cure them of everything from rheumatism to fatigue. The Sligers reminded visitors it was not healthful to smoke in the bathhouse.

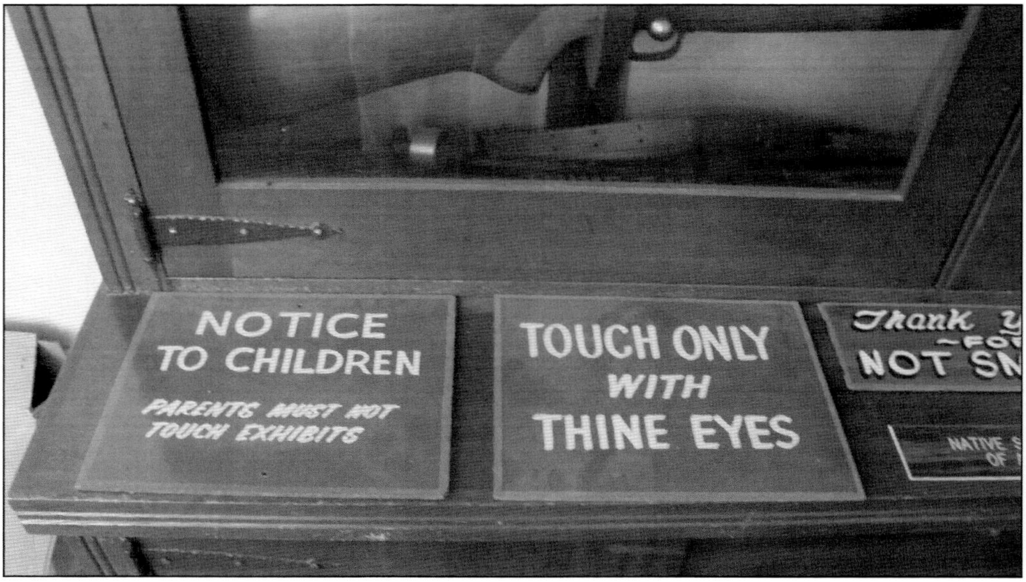

Given to superlatives, the Sligers proclaimed the Wildlife Museum contained "one of every native Arizona animal." Nearly 450 specimens—from a buffalo and Alaskan grey wolf to lizards and birds—hung from the ceilings and walls or were kept under glass. Giant Texas longhorns covered the ceilings, too. Included in the wildlife collection were rare and near extinct species like bald and golden eagles. All were preserved and mounted by Ted Sliger. Hand-painted signs provided details and admonished parents to keep their kids in tow. Most of all, "Touch Only with Thine Eyes."

Eight

The Buckhorn Hits a Home Run

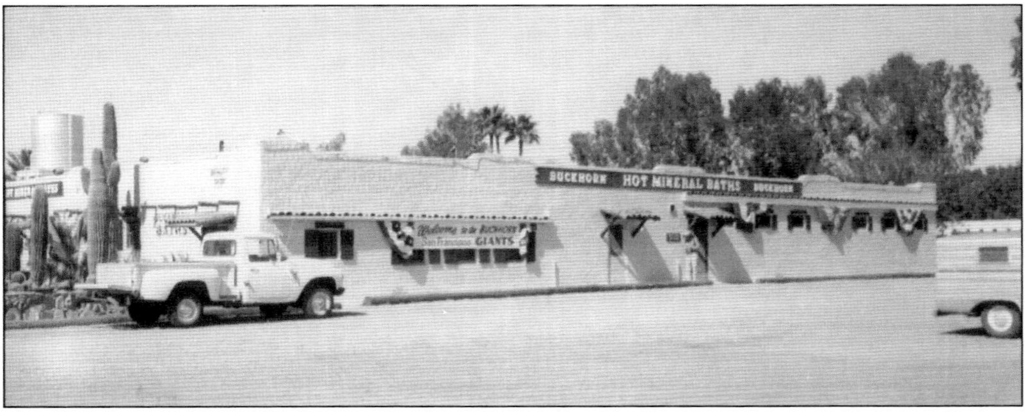

The Buckhorn and baseball were inextricably intertwined. New York Giants owner Horace Stoneham's chance discovery of the resort in 1947 is directly linked to what evolved into the Cactus League and its origins in Mesa. Returning every year for a quarter-century cemented a strong relationship and enduring friendship Stoneham had with Ted and Alice Sliger. Even in the face of competition, no other health spa ever enjoyed the annual spring ritual of hosting ballplayers like the Buckhorn. (Courtesy Larry Ward.)

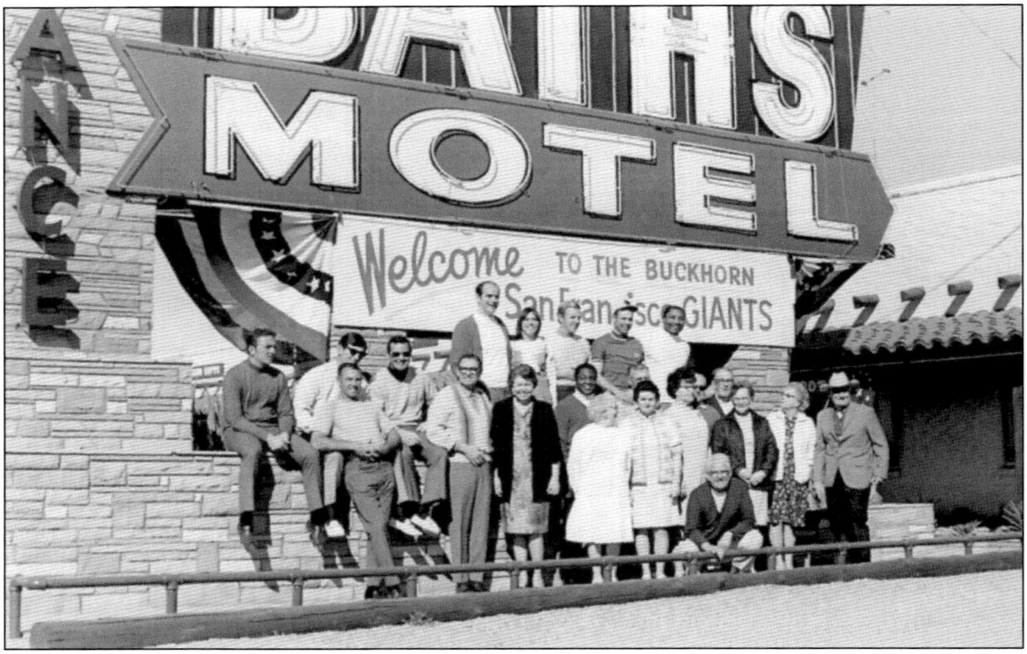

It is difficult to say with any measure of certainty how the Buckhorn might have fared without the support of major-league baseball. Would it have been a comet that shone brightly for a brief moment before quickly fading away like the other nearby competing mineral baths? One can reasonably conclude that without the Cactus League, the Buckhorn would never have attained the status, notoriety, and longevity it enjoyed. (Courtesy MHM.)

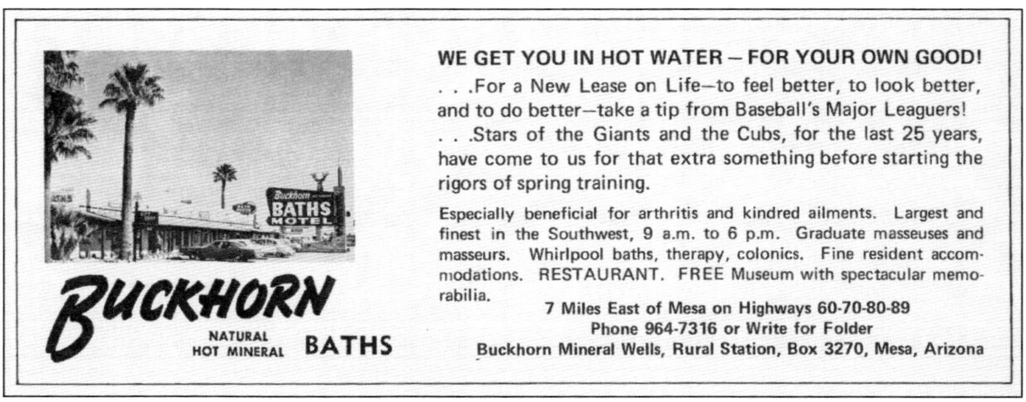

Ever the consummate promoters, the Sligers would never pass up an opportunity to brag about baseball's attraction to the Buckhorn. A delightful 1971 advertisement asked potential guests to "take a tip from Baseball's Major Leaguers [who] have come to us for that extra something." If the baths were good enough for baseball stars, they were certainly good for the average patron. (Courtesy MHM.)

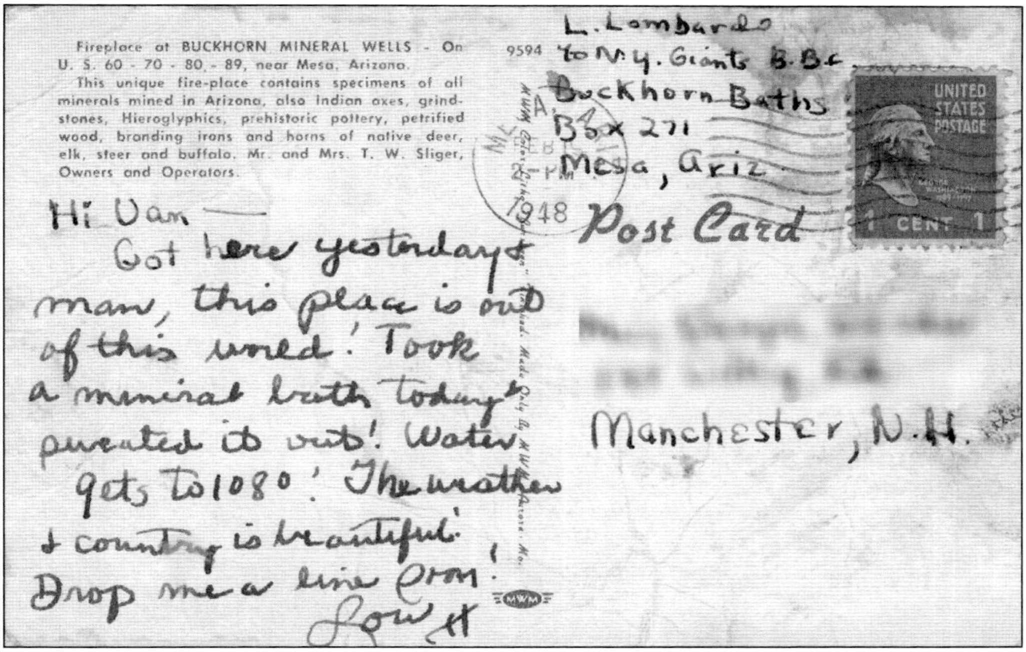
Fireplace at BUCKHORN MINERAL WELLS - On U. S. 60 - 70 - 80 - 89, near Mesa, Arizona. This unique fire-place contains specimens of all minerals mined in Arizona, also Indian axes, grindstones, Hieroglyphics, prehistoric pottery, petrified wood, branding irons and horns of native deer, elk, steer and buffalo. Mr. and Mrs. T. W. Sliger, Owners and Operators.

9594

L. Lombardo
to N.Y. Giants B.B.C.
Buckhorn Baths
Box 271
Mesa, Ariz.

1948

Post Card

Hi Van —
Got here yesterday & man, this place is out of this world! Took a mineral bath today & sweated it out! Water gets to 108°! The weather & country is beautiful! Drop me a line [illegible]!
Lou

Manchester, N.H.

There could not be a better testimonial than that of New York Giants pitcher Lou Lombardo, who penned this postcard and mailed it back east in February 1948, the second year the Giants came to the Buckhorn. It is easy to understand why Horace Stoneham was so delighted to send his best players to the resort for pampering. (Courtesy MHM.)

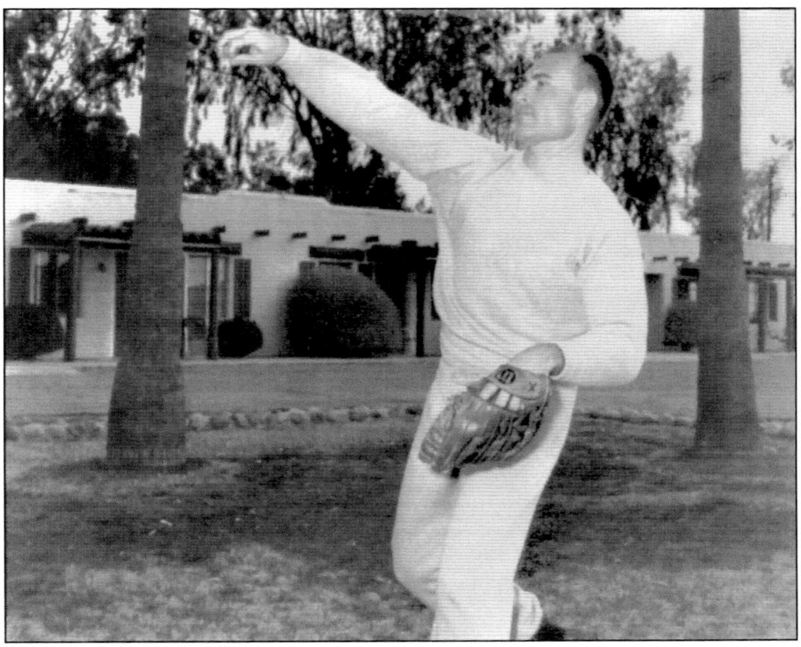

Out of uniform, big-league baseball players looked just like everyone else. But even relaxing before the start of the Cactus League season, they were never far from a bat or ball. Here, San Francisco Giants pitcher Ron Herbel plays catch just for fun on the Buckhorn's expansive center lawn in 1966. (Courtesy MHM.)

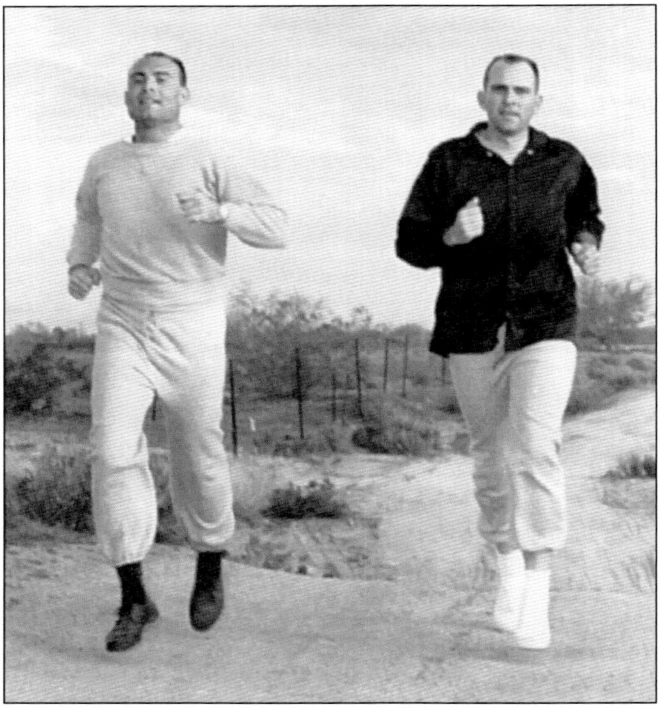

With mostly sagebrush and sand—and the occasional rattlesnake—the unpopulated desert around the Buckhorn provided a perfect place for jogging, as San Francisco Giants pitchers Ron Herbel (left) and Joe Gibbon (right) are doing in 1966. (Courtesy MHM.)

After a hot soak and massage, the bathhouse locker room was where ballplayers could relax or talk shop away from the general public, who might be seeking autographs. From left to right in this 1958 photograph are Marv Grissom, Dusty Rhodes, Hank Sauer, and Curt Barclay. What they are discussing one can only speculate. (Courtesy MHM.)

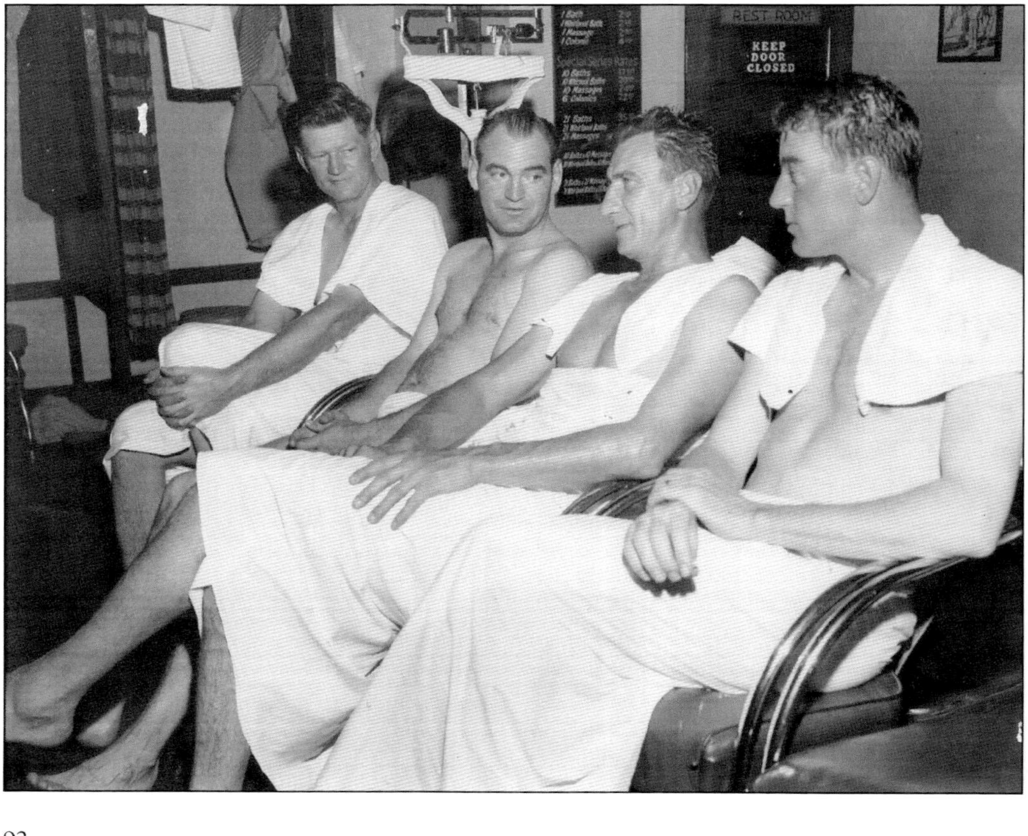

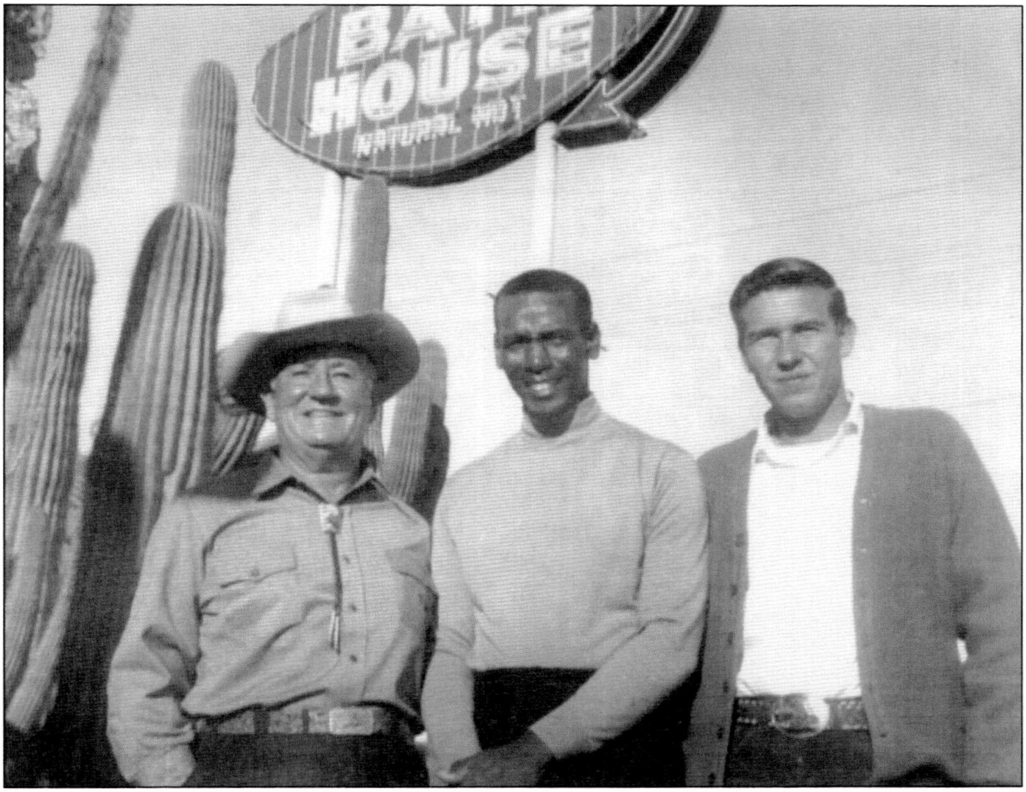

Over many spring training seasons, the Sligers built up a remarkable album of photographs taken with some of the nation's best mid-century baseball players. Here, beneath the early bathhouse sign, Ted Sr. and Jr. pose with Ernie Banks, considered by many one of the greatest players of all time. (Courtesy MHM.)

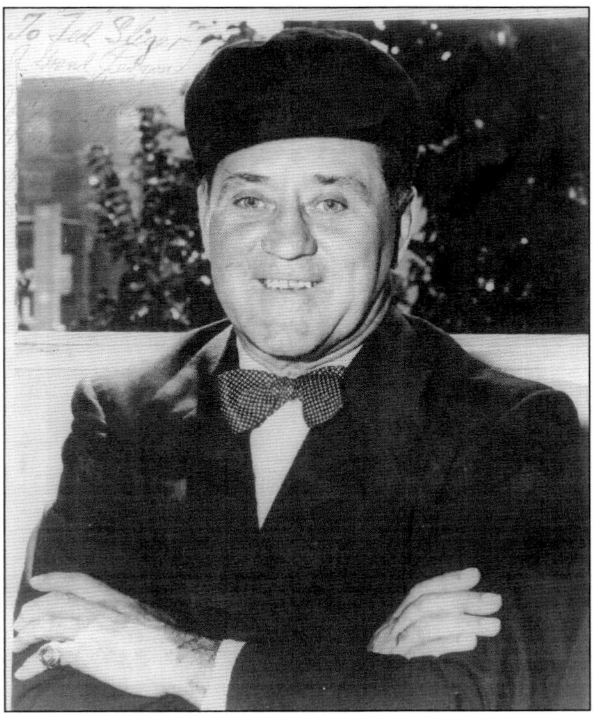

The Sligers' baseball friendships extended far beyond the players themselves. They included owners, managers, and coaches, as well as Jocko Conlan, lesser known for his brief time as a Chicago White Sox outfielder in the 1930s than for his 25-year career as a National League umpire, which included five World Series and six all-star games. Conlan inscribed this 1959 photograph, "To Ted Sliger—A Grand Person." (Courtesy MHM.)

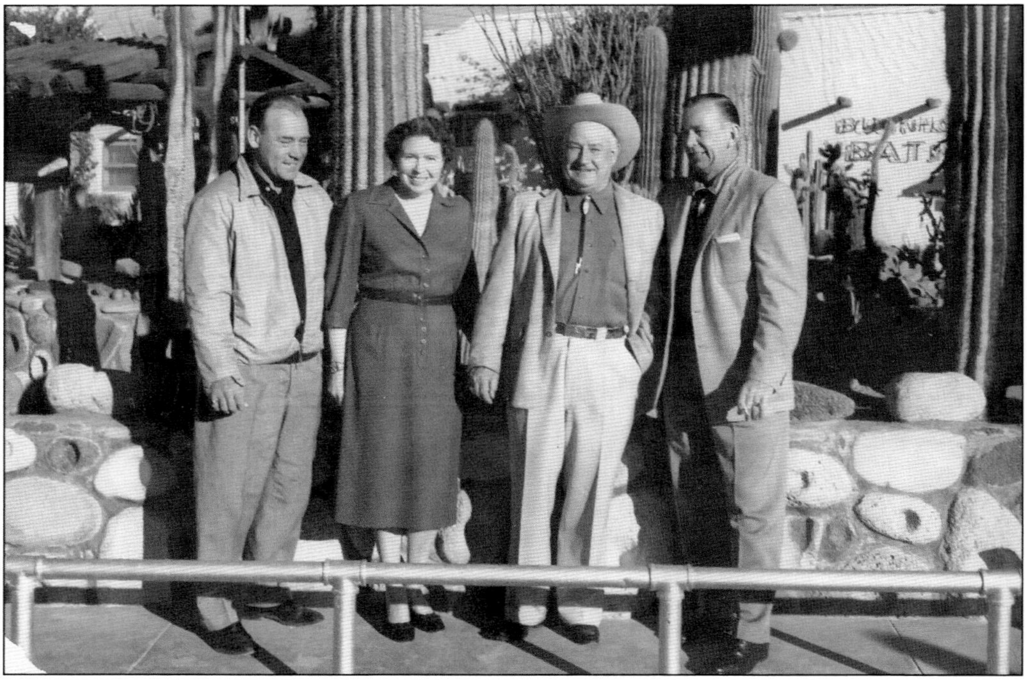

A camera was always handy at the Buckhorn to capture special moments when the Sligers were with celebrities, like in the cactus garden with National League umpire Jocko Conlan (left) and an unidentified New York Giants executive (right). (Courtesy MHM.)

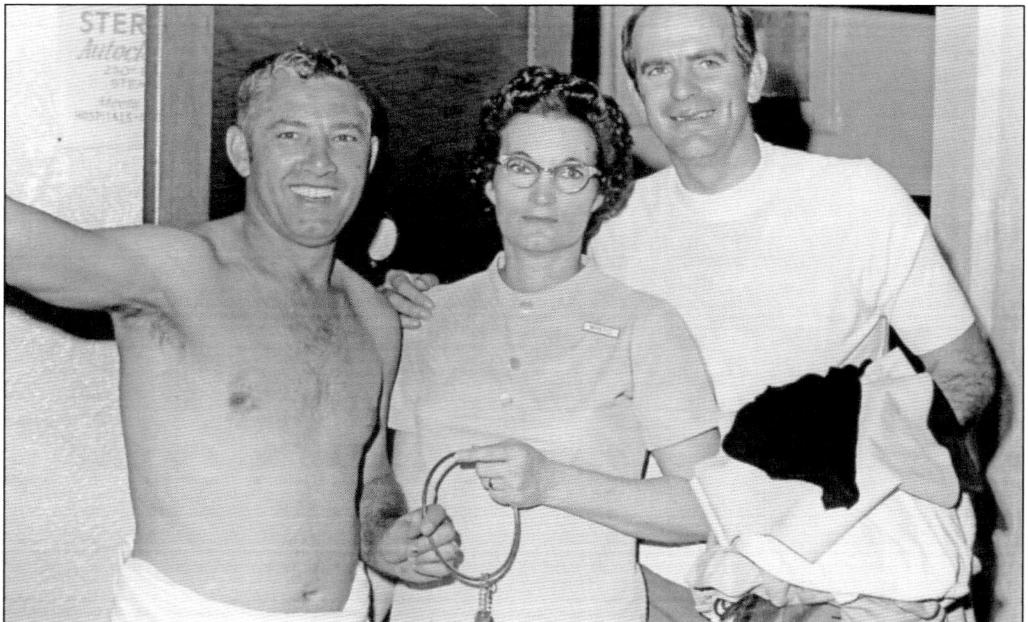

Baseball players spent considerable time in the bathhouse being pampered. Myrtis Gann, who managed the baths for more than 40 years, stands between an unidentified player (left) and Gaylord Perry (right). (Courtesy Larry Ward.)

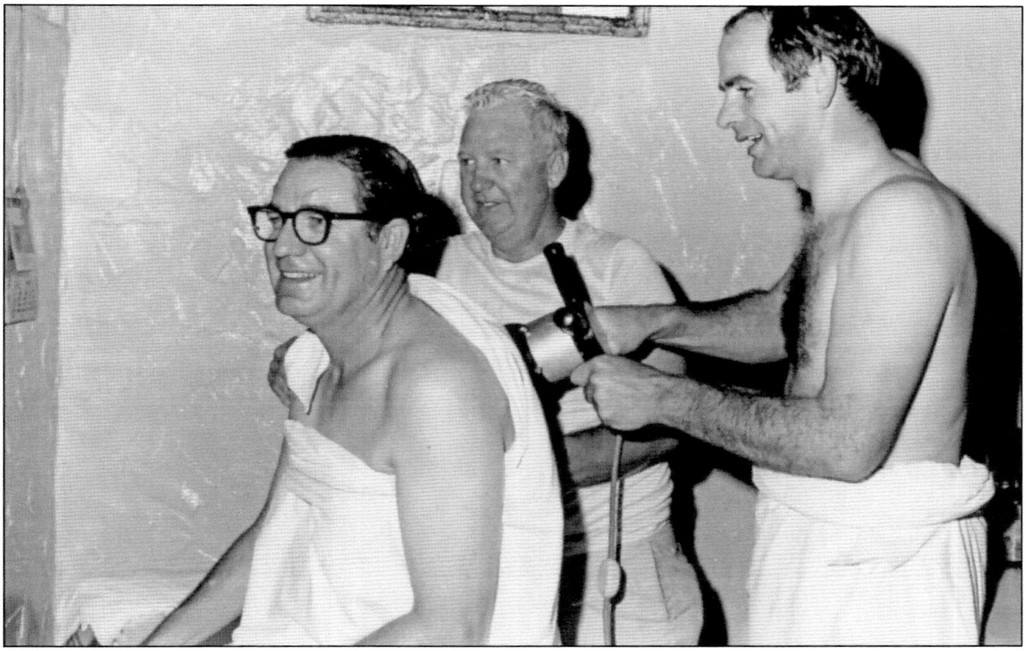

Everybody got in on the act in the bathhouse. With head masseur Ed Nordquist providing "expert" advice, San Francisco star pitcher Gaylord Perry gives a vibrating back massage to pitching coach Larry Jensen in the 1960s. Jensen was a star pitcher himself a decade earlier. (Courtesy Larry Ward.)

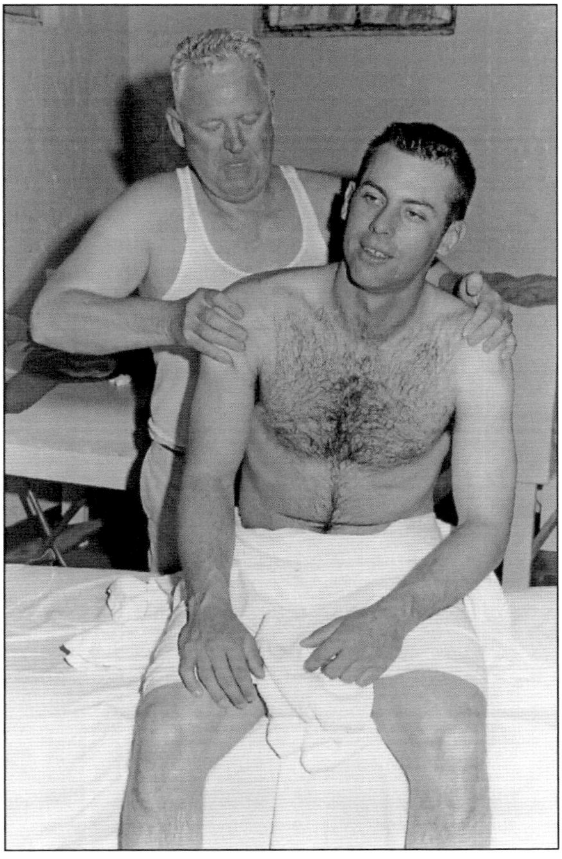

In preparation for the start of the Cactus League spring training season, San Francisco Giants pitcher Ron Hunt gets a shoulder massage from muscular bathhouse masseur Ed Nordquist. Hunt pitched for the Giants for three seasons starting in 1968. (Courtesy Larry Ward.)

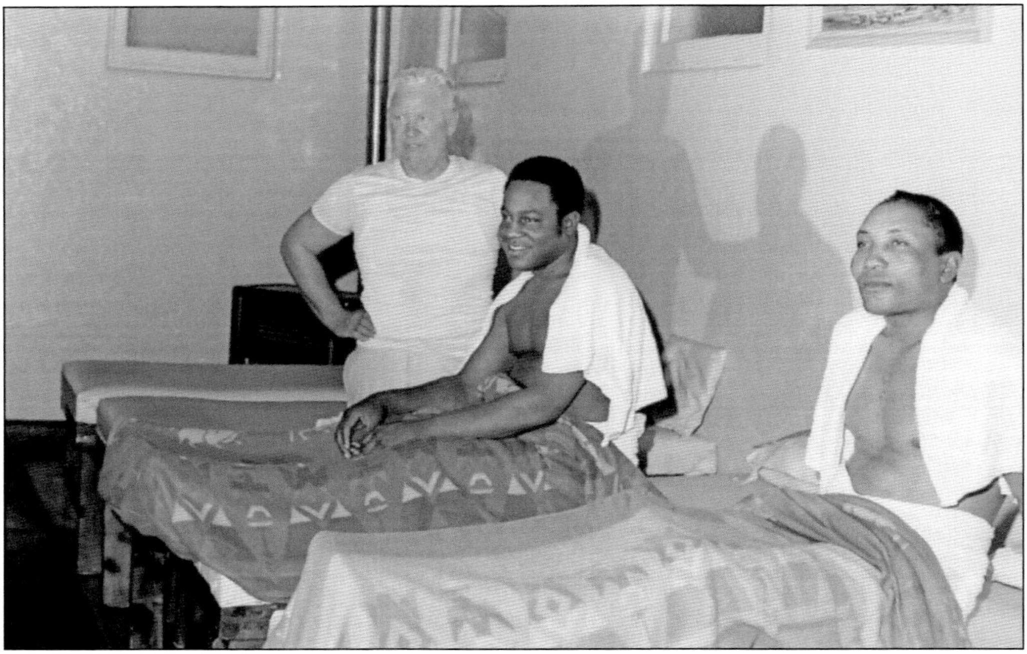

Back in 1947, when the New York Giants began sending players to the Buckhorn and Jackie Robinson became the first modern African American ballplayer in the major leagues, segregation was the norm. Black players could not stay at the same hotels or eat in the same restaurants as their white counterparts. But that was never the case at the Buckhorn. The Sligers always warmly welcomed all races and ethnicities, like Monte Irvin (right). (Courtesy Larry Ward.)

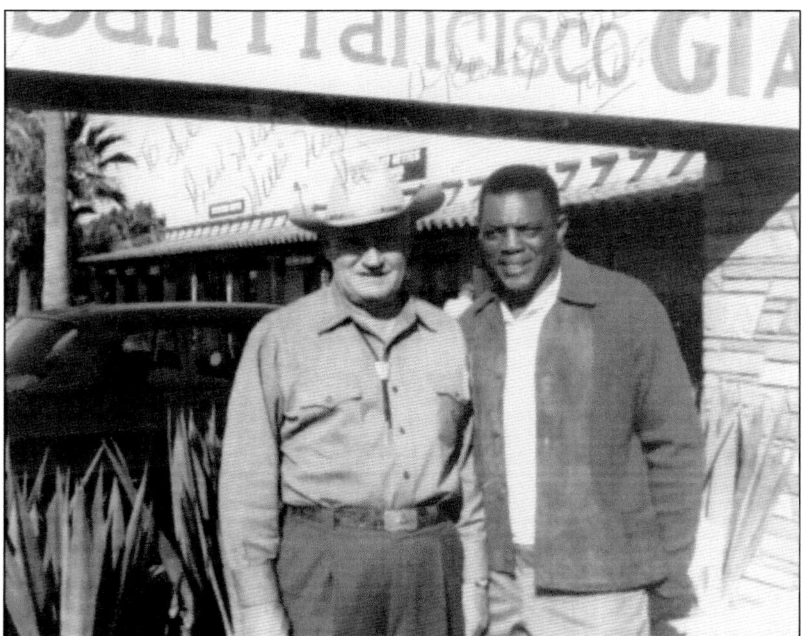

Willie Mays was certainly one of Ted and Alice's favorites at the Buckhorn. Mays inscribed this 1965 photograph to Ted, calling him "A really good friend." (Courtesy MHM.)

Nine

Be Our Guest

Phone 34 Friday, March 27, 1942

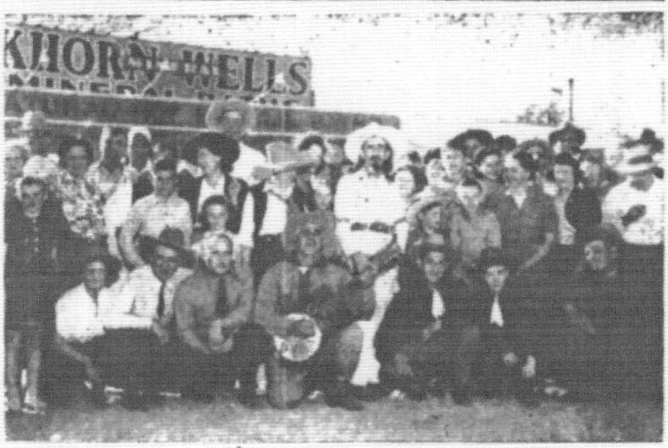

When Sligers Fed 4,000

Recipe for a crowd of 4000: Mix well together 3000 pounds of meat (one buffalo, one steer, three muttons, two wild hogs) 100 pounds of beans, 100 pounds of potatoes, 100 onions and 300 loaves of bread. And you have the meal Mr. and Mrs. Ted Sliger dished out to their friends at Buckhorn Mineral Wells last Sunday afternoon. Ted supplied the buffalo, Old Renegade, Roy Hancock brought the mutton and supervised the barbecuing, Arthur Price delivered the steer and Harry Connolly contributed the javelina hogs. Mrs. John Verney, and Mrs. Luther McAllister, Don LeBaron, Mrs. Thelma Brown and Mrs. May Sliger assisted in the serving. Entertainment was furnished by Porter's orchestra, Wild Horse Pete, expert rifleman and Powder River Jack and Kitty Lee. A small portion of the crowd is shown, above, with Powder River and his guitar, center. Genial Host Ted Sliger is on Jack's right. Everyone agreed that it was some blow-out.

● The Stitch and Chat club met Thursday at the First Ward chapel for an afternoon of quilting. Hostesses were Mrs. Lily Webb, Mrs. Edwin Miller, Mrs. M. L. Griner, and Mrs. Van B. Brinton.

Imagine hosting a barbecue that had to feed 4,000 people with 3,000 pounds of meat—steer, buffalo, sheep, and wild hogs—not to mention 100 pounds of potatoes and 300 loaves of bread. But that is just what Ted and Alice Sliger did in March 1942. No war rationing here. The buffalo meat came from Old Renegade, a rogue beast Ted had shot the month before. On its expansive barbecue patio, hundreds and sometimes thousands could be served, making the Buckhorn's cookouts wildly popular. Providing the best guest experience was always foremost in the minds of Ted and Alice Sliger. (Courtesy Ted and Jerri Sliger.)

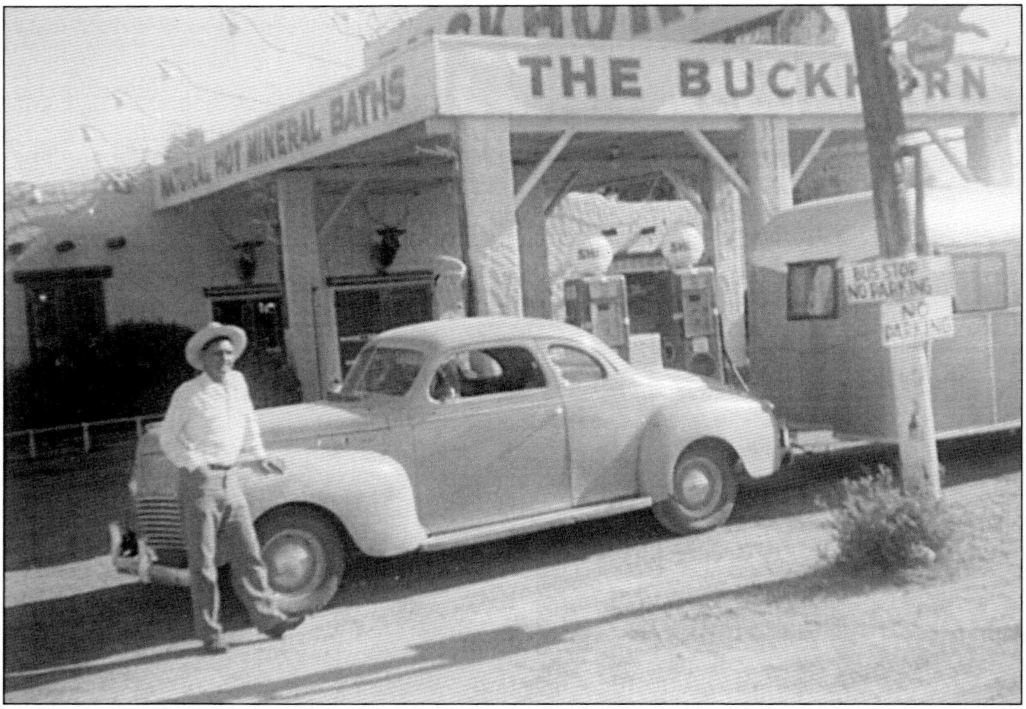

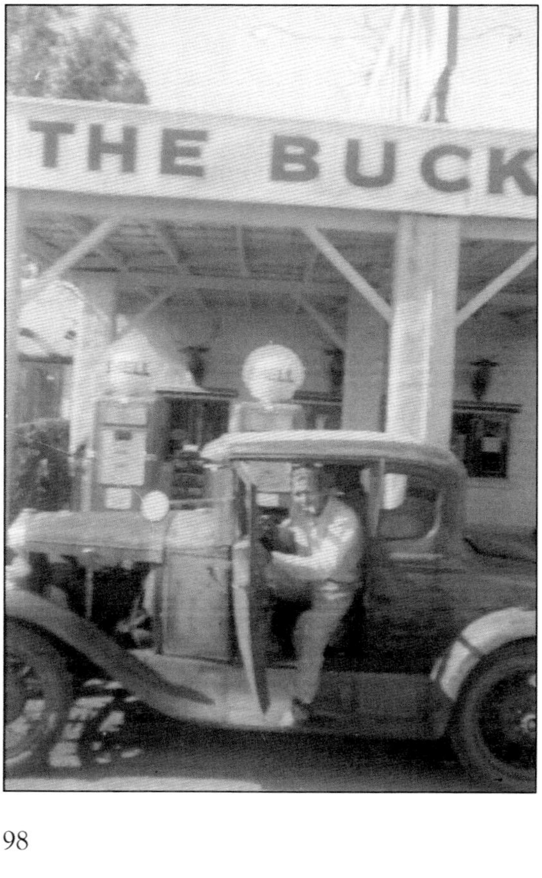

Following the 1935 fire that destroyed their gas station and business, the Sligers relocated to 10 acres on the northwest corner of Main Street and Recker Road. There they built a new gas station, souvenir shop, and taxidermy business. The Buckhorn Shell station was a busy place. In this 1940s photograph, a motorist pulling a travel trailer behind his coupe stops for a fill-up and refreshments. (Courtesy Janette Carr.)

The first auto tourists were often upper- or middle-class families who could afford both cars and leisure time. In the early years, hotel service was generally designed for traveling businessmen. When families took to the road, they frequently found hotels to be too expensive. The auto-camping industry sprung up in response. It became popular in the 1920s as an inexpensive, alternative return to a simpler lifestyle. Campers got a closer look at nature, and trailers provided a sense of freedom. It was casual and sociable. But gas and places to refresh were always needed. The Buckhorn graciously provided both. (Courtesy of Jeanette Carr.)

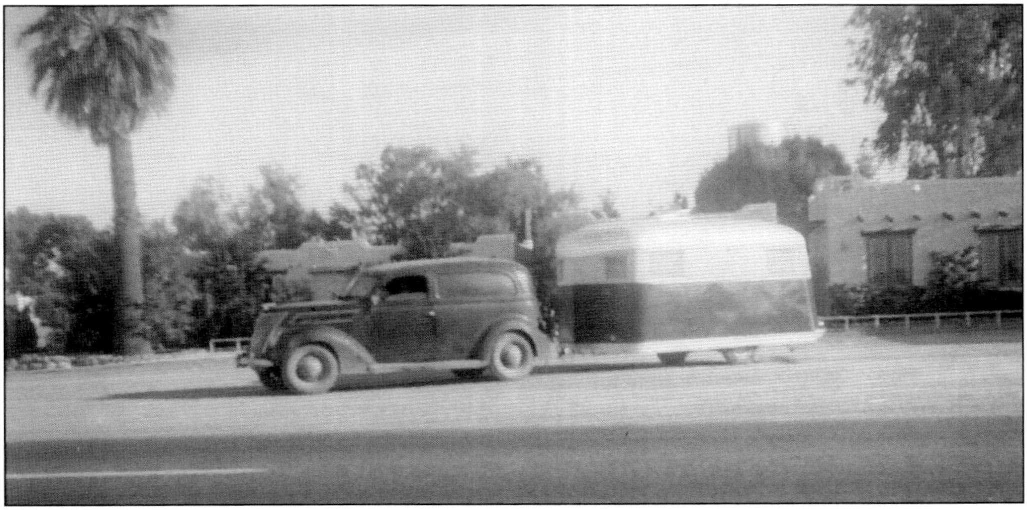

The automobile gave rise to the roadside lodging industry. By 1950, there were about 155 motels and tourist courts in the valley. While health resorts were a lure for thousands of health-seekers and tourists, there still had to be an easy way to get to them. Although the railroad was important to the growth of the West, it was the rise of personal transportation that changed the landscape. The 1916 Federal Aid Road Act became the nation's first federal highway funding legislation. The Federal Highway Act of 1921 allowed the government to offer financial assistance for general road construction. By 1929, these two acts, as well as the use of a gasoline tax to fund highway improvement, resulted in an interconnected system that made most of the United States accessible. (Courtesy of Janette Carr.)

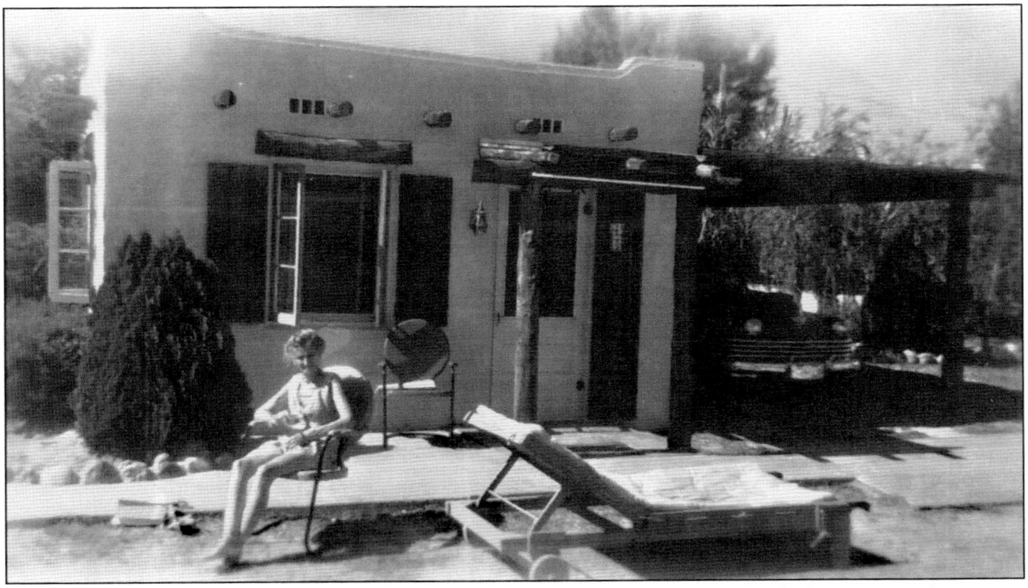

A guest basks in the warm winter sun in front of her cottage. In the 1940s, before air-conditioning, cross ventilation cooled the rooms with dry Arizona air. Cars were parked in the shade under attached carports. The 225-square-foot cottages had minimal bath and kitchen facilities because guests were encouraged to shower in the mineral baths and dine and socialize in the restaurant. (Courtesy of Janette Carr.)

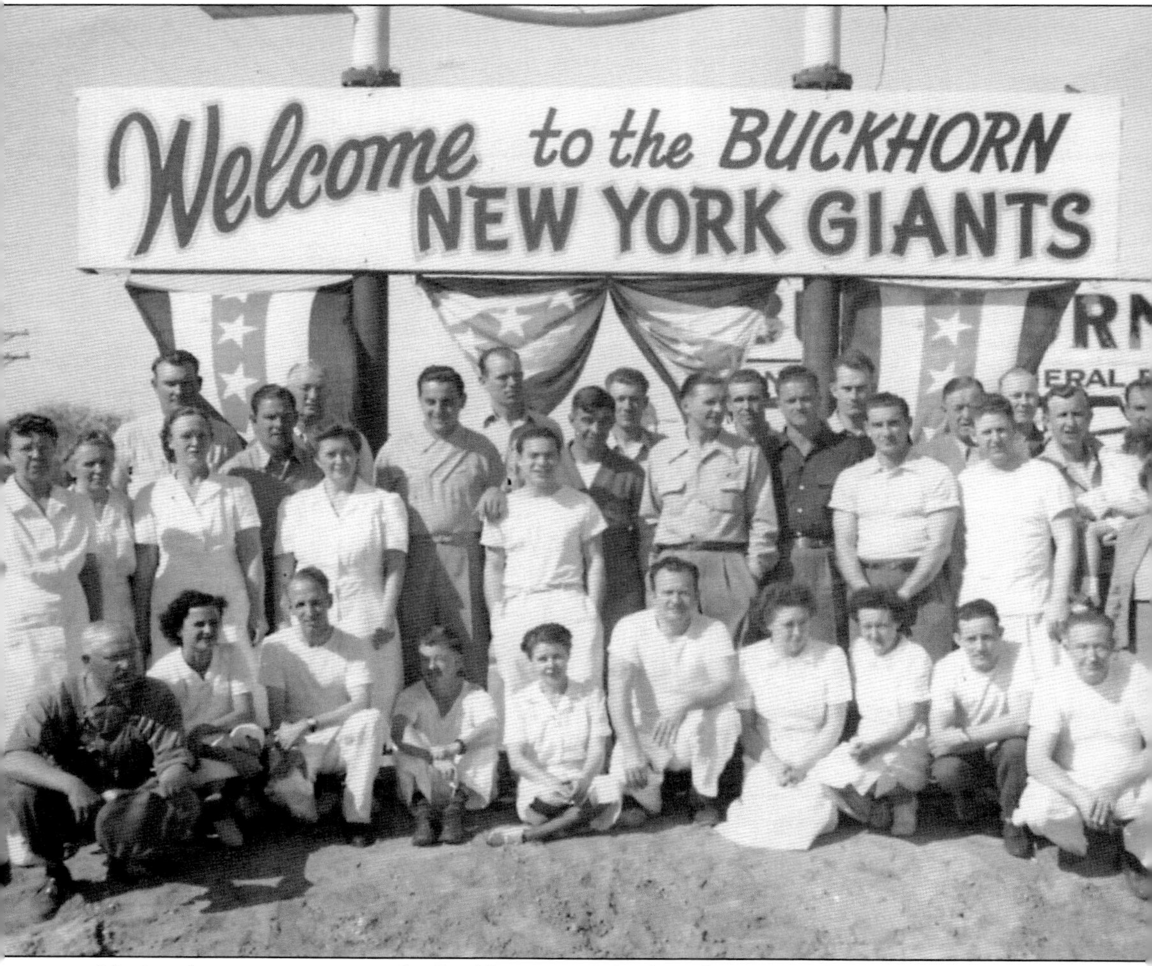

National attention came to the Buckhorn in 1947 when the New York Giants arrived in Phoenix looking for winter quarters. The healthful benefits of the mineral baths clearly cinched the deal. For 25 years, the Buckhorn was the base of operations for the Giants, and later the Chicago Cubs, as a prelude to spring training. An annual tradition was a group photograph in front of the Buckhorn. This 1948 image shows the large Buckhorn staff, ready to serve their celebrity guests, posing in front of a welcome banner. (Courtesy MHM.)

The Sligers often ran full-page advertisements like this 1974 piece promoting the Buckhorn Mineral Wells and Wildlife Museum. A physical street address is added to the PO box/route number, reflecting the encroaching growth between the resort and Mesa. Beneath portraits of Ted and Alice Sliger, the advertisement unabashedly asserts, "You haven't seen Arizona until you have seen Arizona's largest Wildlife Museum—the famous museum featuring 400 mounted specimens." The building boasts a new portal and gift shop.

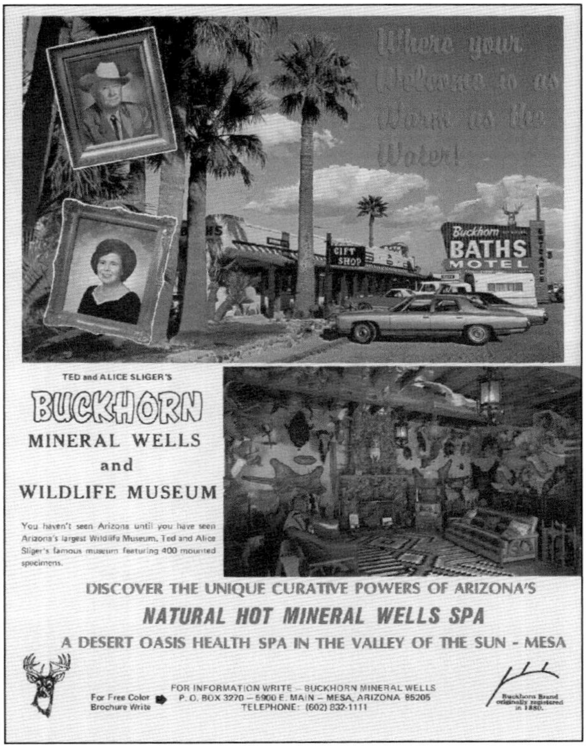

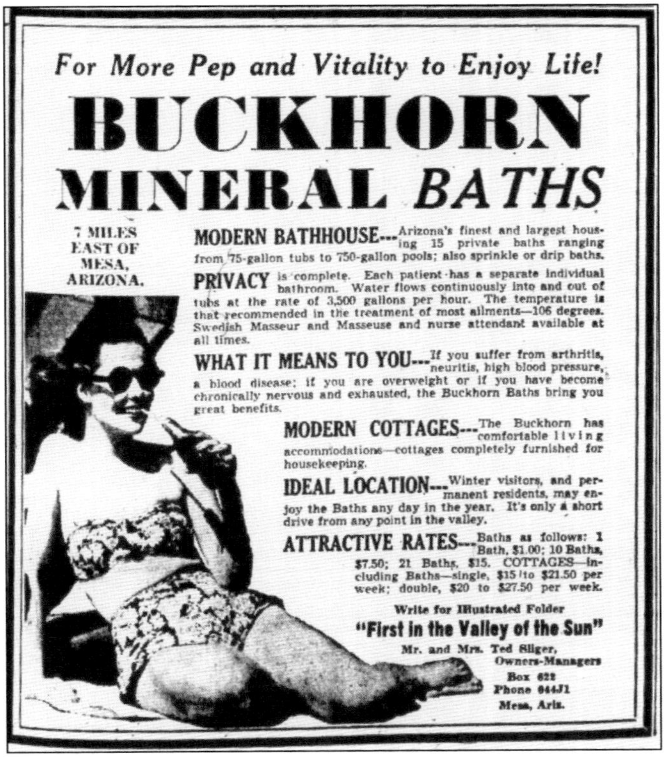

The Sligers shamelessly promoted the Buckhorn. A 1942 newspaper advertisement promised "More Pep and Vitality to Enjoy Life. If you suffer from arthritis, neuritis, high blood pressure or a blood disease . . . the Buckhorn Baths brings you great benefits." The modern bathhouse featured "15 private baths ranging from 75-gallon tubs to 750-gallon pools." The 106-degree water was recirculated at a rate of 3,500 gallons per hour. An individual bath was just a dollar.

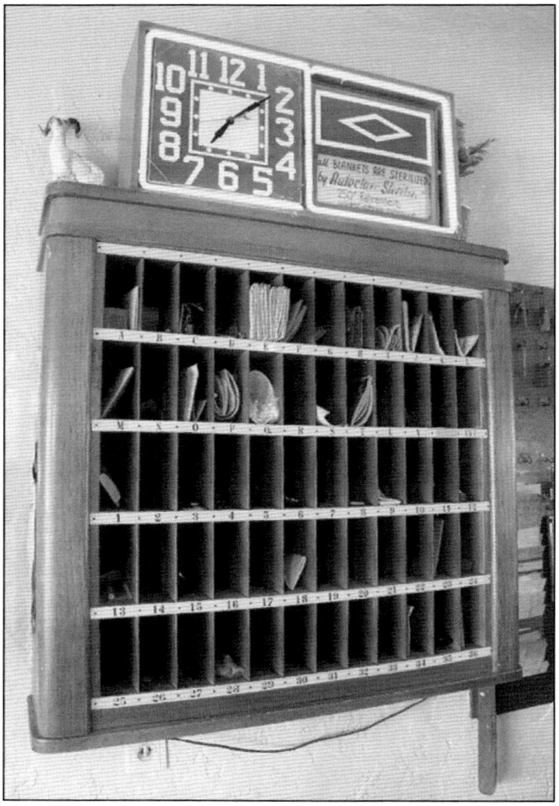

The Buckhorn office and lobby, where guests checked in and received their room key, remains a well-preserved time capsule. The mailboxes still contain letters and other ephemera. Portraits of Ted and Alice Sliger welcoming guests hang on an opposite wall. Behind the lobby is an informal sitting room where celebrities and regular folk gathered. Beyond that is Ted's Wildlife Museum.

Being seven miles from downtown Mesa meant that without a nearby post office, guests would need to travel into town to mail and receive letters. In 1956, the Sligers solved that problem by opening a post office station, operated under contract with the Mesa postmaster. It remained in service for 28 years—15 by the Sligers, the remainder with another contractor. (Courtesy Greg Marek.)

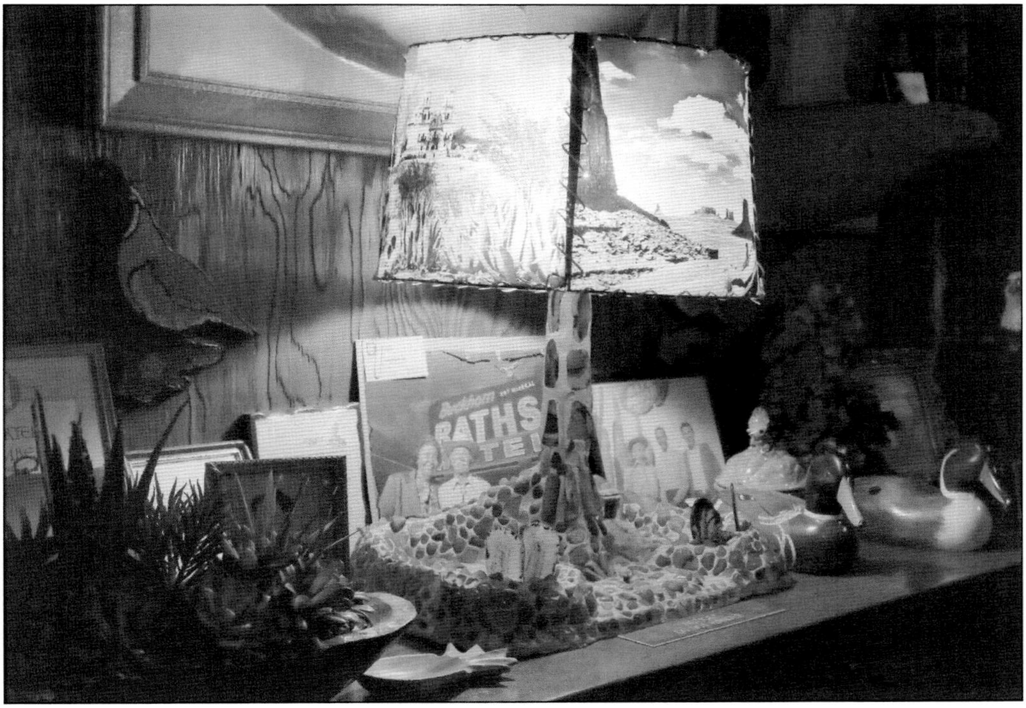

The Buckhorn consistently focused on offering its guests a unique and memorable experience, even including table lamps. In a photograph behind this lamp, Alice and Ted Sliger are seen posed in front of their iconic neon sign.

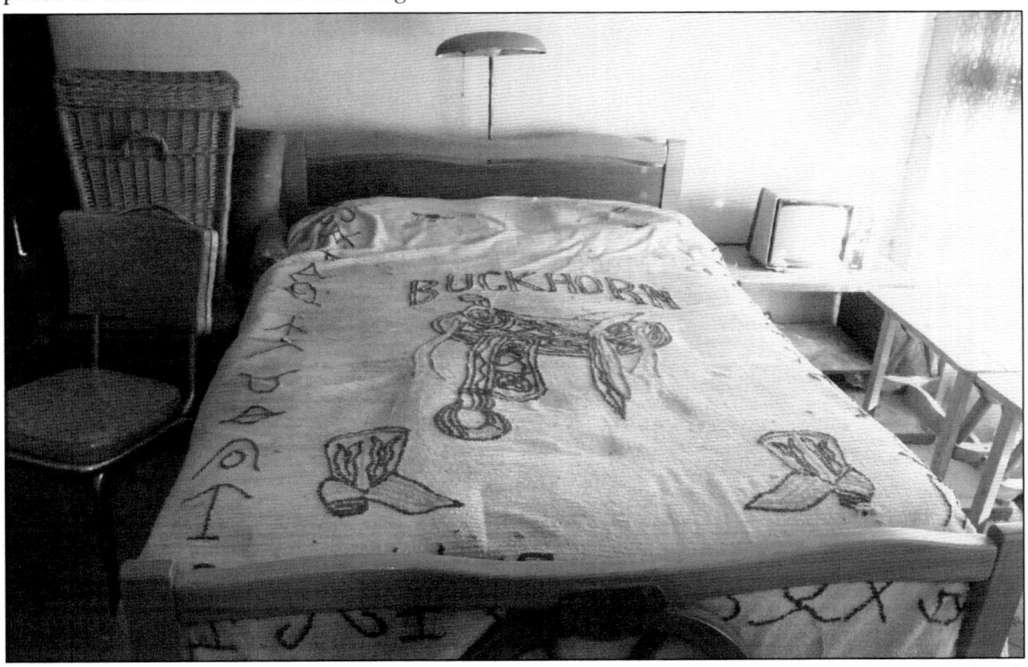

Keeping Buckhorn iconography in front of guests was important, right down to custom-embroidered, Western-themed Buckhorn bedspreads.

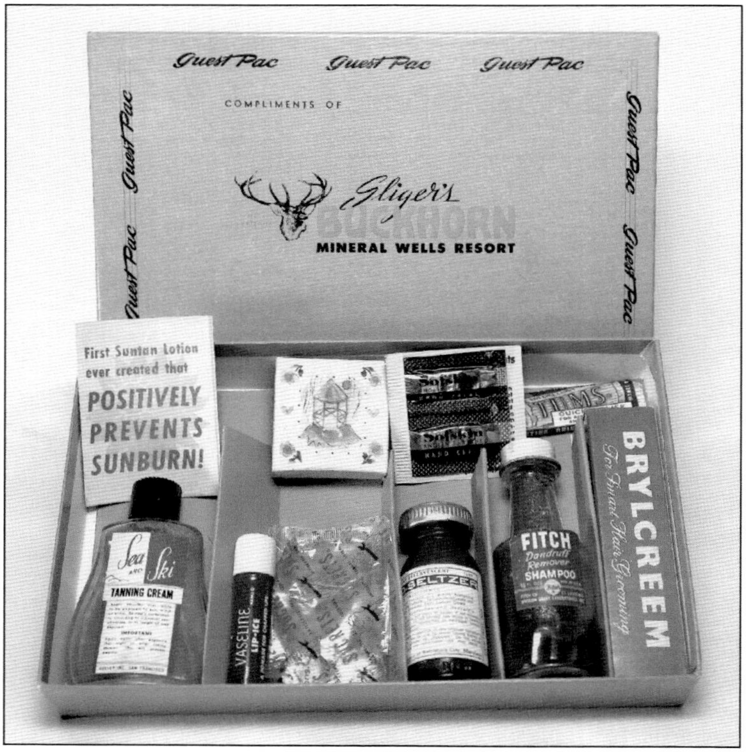

Pampering was paramount at the Buckhorn. In each guest room was a complimentary Guest Pac with, of course, the Buckhorn logo prominently displayed. The gift box was filled with items a guest might need to make a stay more enjoyable. Everything from breath fresheners to suntan lotion was provided. (Courtesy Ted and Jerri Sliger.)

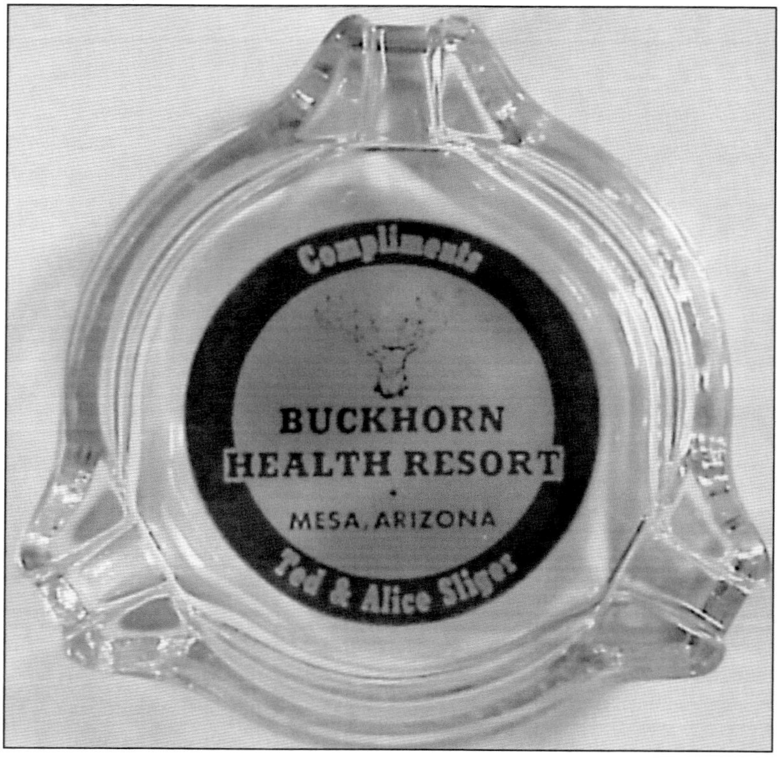

Seldom seen today, ashtrays were common in the Buckhorn era. Along with the free Guest Pac, visitors were encouraged to take home a souvenir ashtray—anything to help spread the word of this unique resort and spa. (Courtesy Ted and Jerri Sliger.)

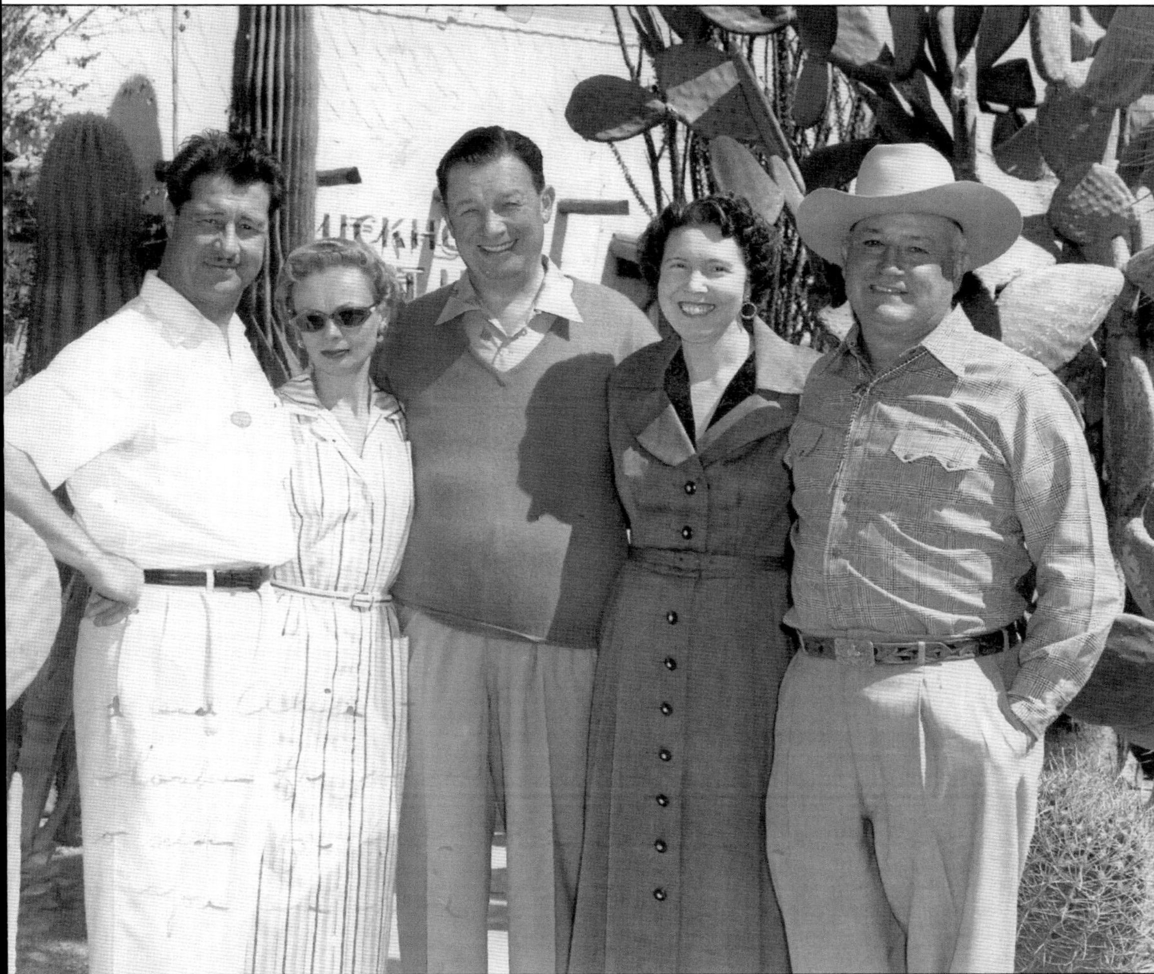

Coming from humble beginnings, the Sligers particularly loved entertaining the rich and famous. The list of big names was long and varied. The year 1956 was a busy one at the Buckhorn. Movie star Don Ameche (left) is standing next to Marion "Baby" Shor and her husband, Toots Shor (1903–1977), the celebrated New York restaurateur. One wonders how much restaurant advice the outspoken Toots Shor may have imparted to Ted and Alice. Shor's long connection to baseball was revealed when granddaughter Kristi Jacobson profiled his life in *Toots*, a 2006 documentary. It was voted best picture at the National Baseball Hall of Fame's first annual film festival that same year. Don Ameche (1908–1993), along with Bob Hope and Bing Crosby, once owned the Los Angeles Dons football team in the All-America Football Conference the trio helped create. (Courtesy MHM.)

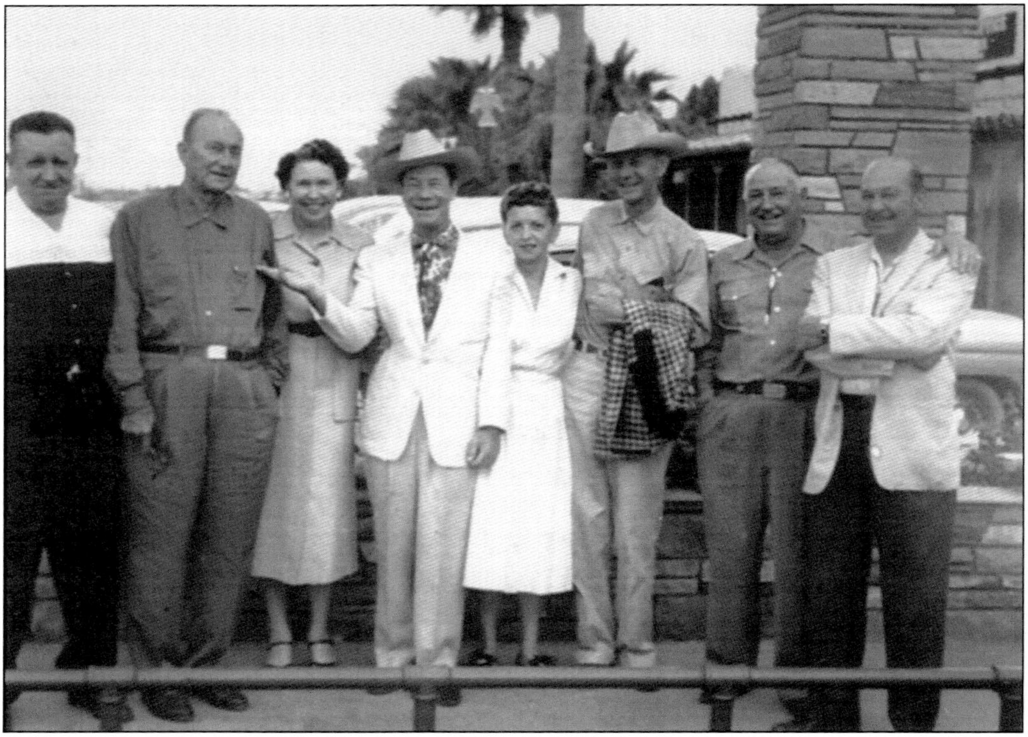

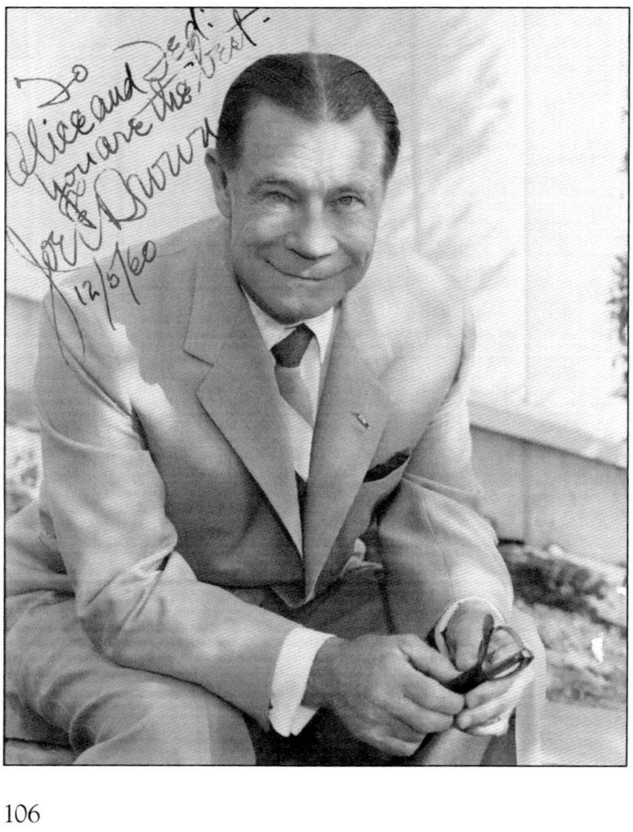

Celebrities were regular guests at the Buckhorn. Joe E. Brown (1891–1973), in white jacket and hat, was an avid sports enthusiast. Early in his career, Brown toured nationally with vaudeville and circus groups but later became a semiprofessional baseball player. When offered a big-league opportunity, he turned it down in favor of a show business career. In 1953, Brown was a New York Yankees pregame and postgame announcer. A close friend of Ty Cobb (second from left), Brown was with Cobb in the days before he died in 1961. Alice Sliger stands between the two stars, and Ted Sliger is pictured second from right. (Both, courtesy MHM.)

Selfies might just have originated at the Buckhorn—particularly in front of the "Worlds largest collection of Metates" sign, where this man is posed. Beyond the garden wall was the bathhouse where guests were invited to not only luxuriate in the healing waters but also have their "innards irrigated." Antiquated equipment and stricter health regulations, however, did away with that practice in the late 1970s. (Courtesy of Jeanette Carr.)

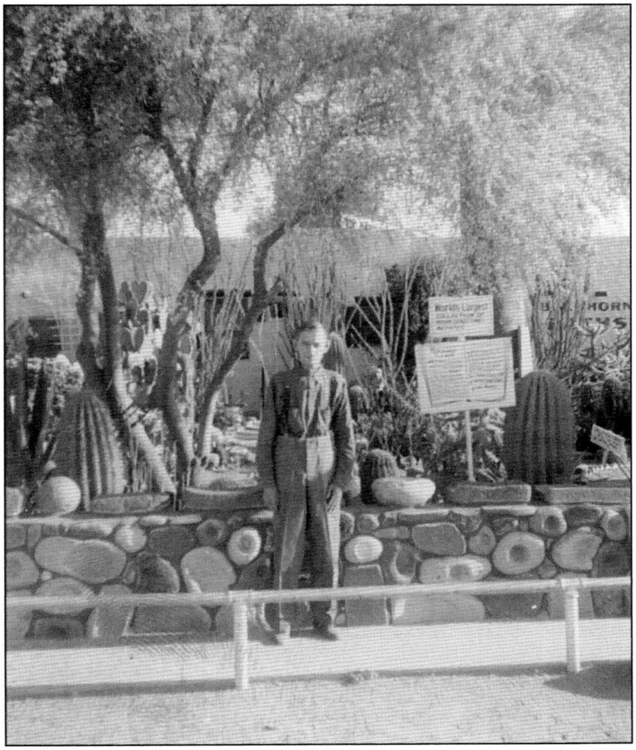

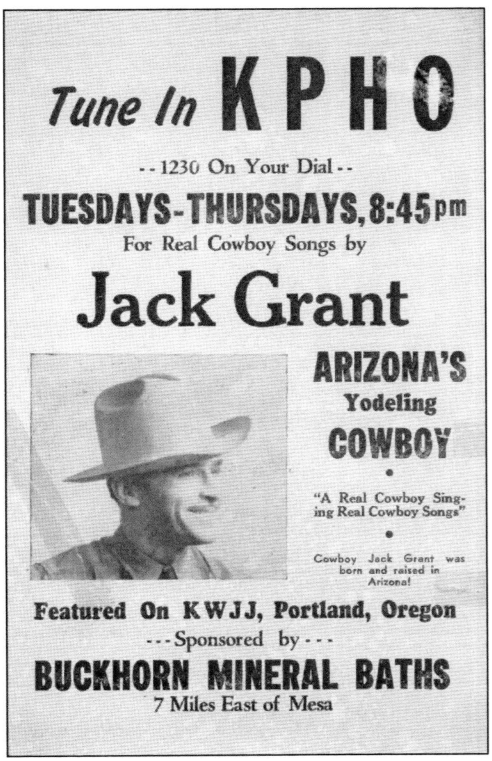

After the sun set on the desert, keeping guests entertained was an important part of Buckhorn activities. Jack Grant, "Arizona's Yodeling Cowboy," appeared regularly in the late 1940s. A big-ranch operator "born and raised in Arizona," the singer was touted as "A Real Cowboy Singing Real Cowboy Songs." In this advertisement, the Buckhorn promotes its sponsorship of Grant on local radio station KPHO. (Courtesy MHM.)

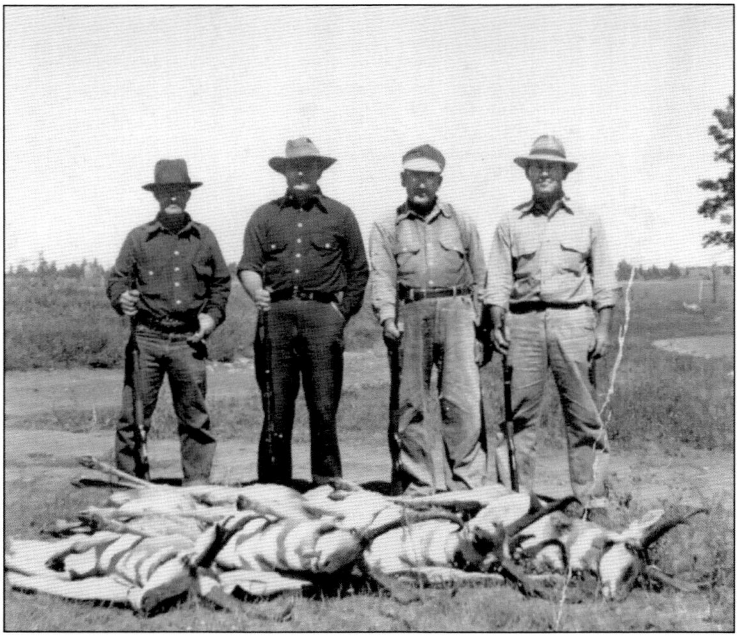

Hunting and fishing were two of Ted Sliger's favorite pastimes, especially when accompanied on excursions by local cronies and guests. Sliger is pictured second from left in 1941 with a day's kill—four antelope. At far left is Ronald Ellsworth, local Shell distributor, who loaned the Sligers money to reopen their gas station and get back on their feet after the disastrous 1935 fire. (Courtesy Ted and Jerri Sliger.)

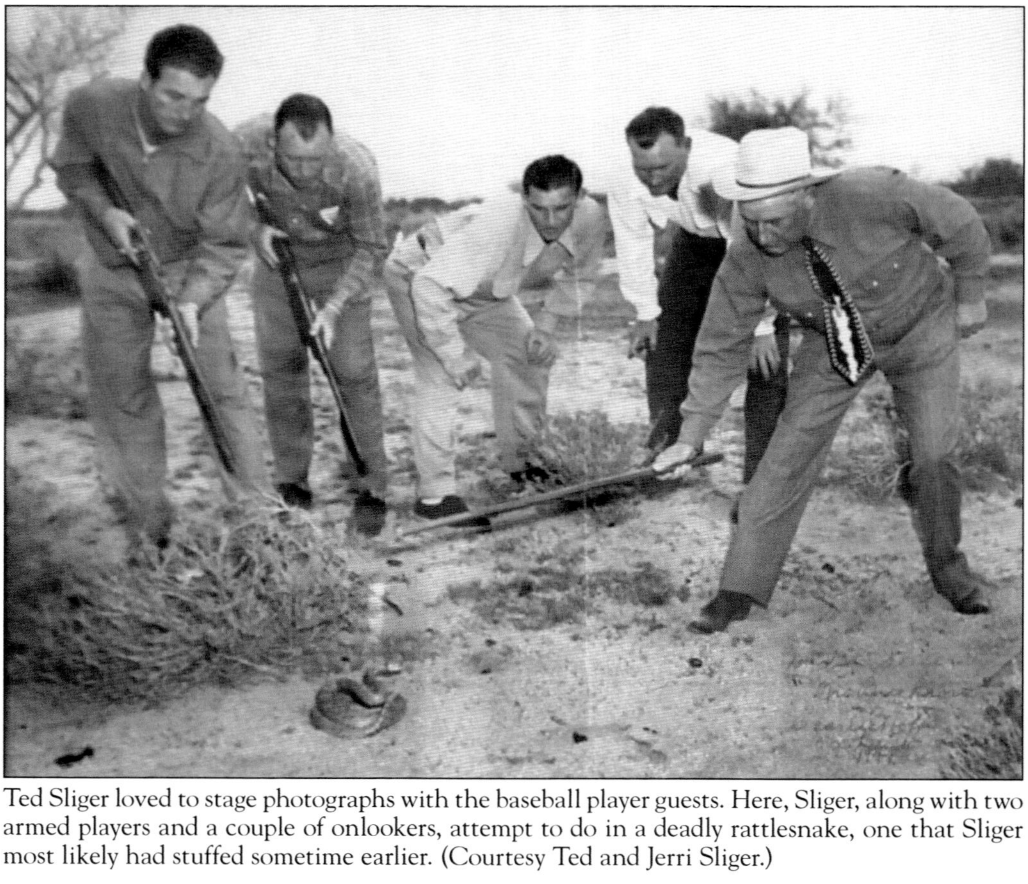

Ted Sliger loved to stage photographs with the baseball player guests. Here, Sliger, along with two armed players and a couple of onlookers, attempt to do in a deadly rattlesnake, one that Sliger most likely had stuffed sometime earlier. (Courtesy Ted and Jerri Sliger.)

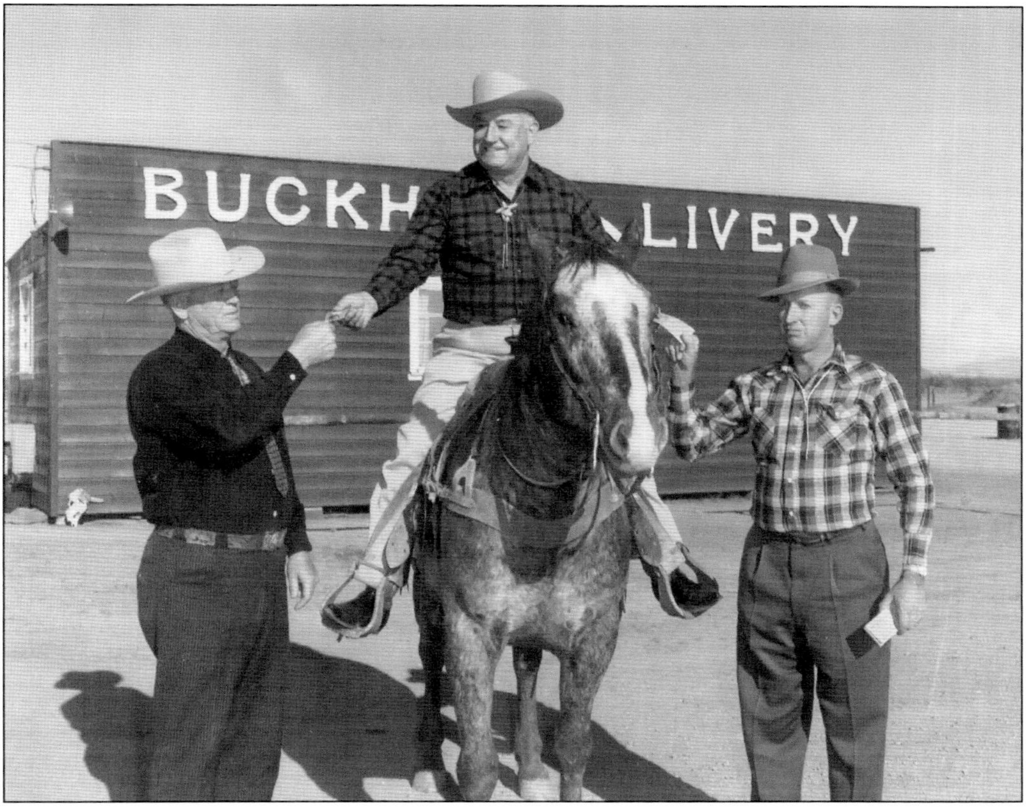

No visit to a Western resort was complete without a horseback ride. The Buckhorn continually strived to offer guests and visitors the broadest experience possible. One short-lived amenity was the Buckhorn Livery, located on the northwest corner of the property. "Four ranch horses, four gentle parade horses and two kid horses" were available for guest use. An avid community supporter, Ted Sliger is seen in the c. 1960 posed photograph above purchasing a ticket for a Mesa charity event. (Both, courtesy MHM.)

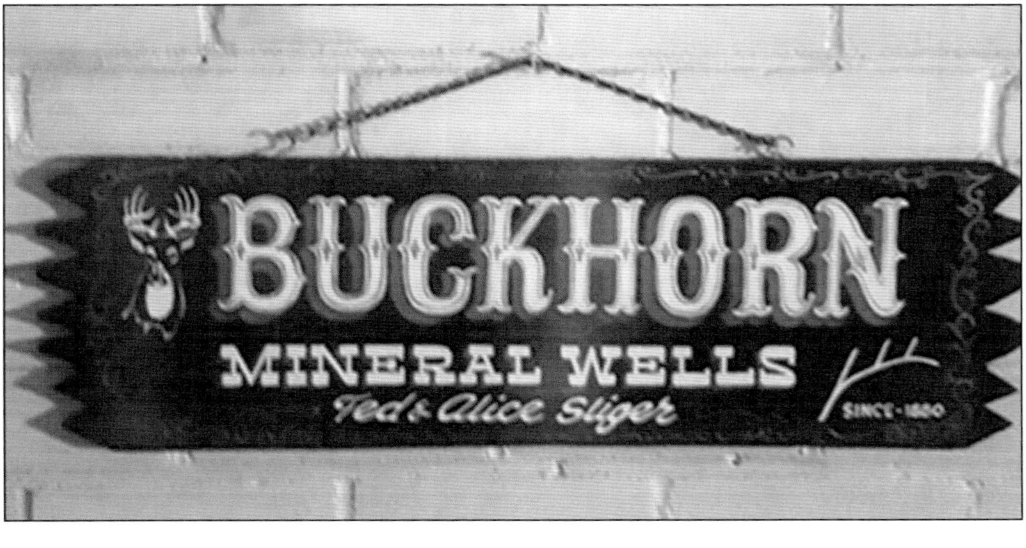

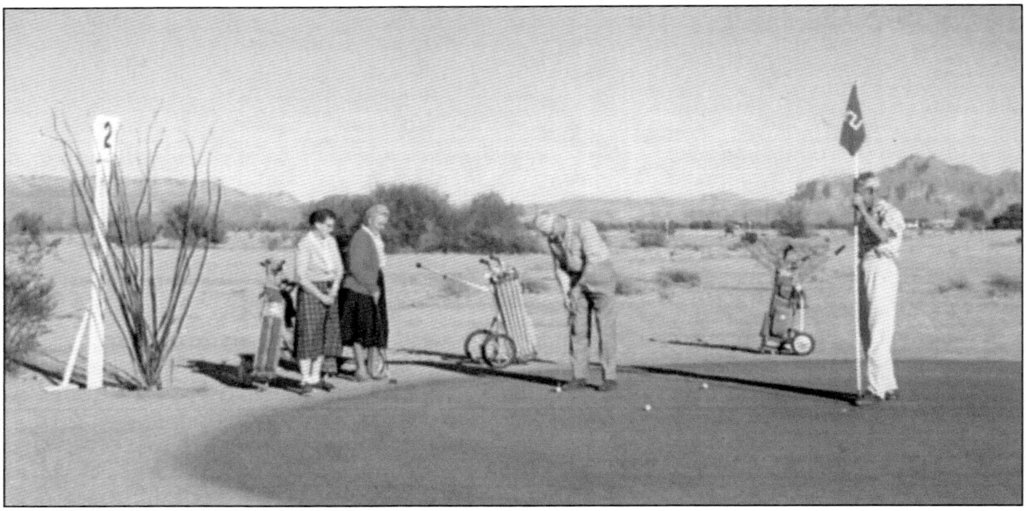

Golf in the desert? Why not? The Sligers cleared some brush and rock, put in some holes, and created a sand golf course, one of the Buckhorn's several recreational amenities. No caddies or electric carts were found here, just acres of sand. This undated postcard view represents the only known photograph of the short-lived course. Ted Sliger Jr. placed its location at the northeast corner of the property, now the site of a strip shopping center. The majestic Superstition Mountains form a backdrop for this image of the second hole.

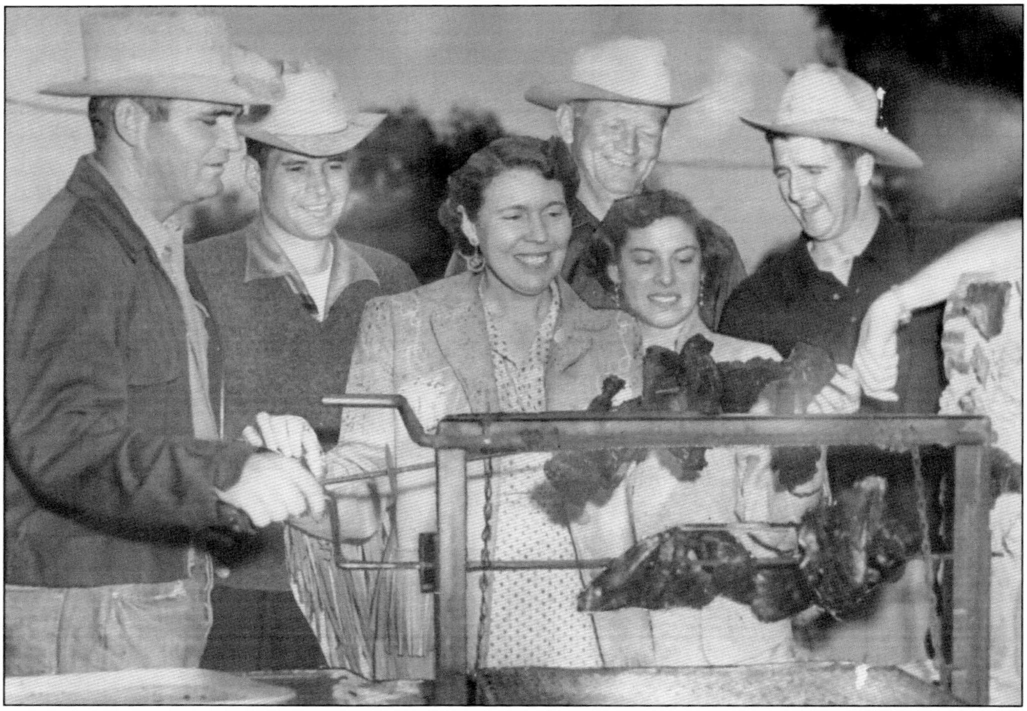

On the broad patio with a large grill, hundreds of guests would gather to enjoy a delicious Buckhorn barbecue. Here, with a crew of hungry onlookers, Alice Sliger (center, in a polka-dot dress) checks to see if the meat is ready. Seen with her are, from left to right, Dusty Rhodes, Bill Sarni, Shirley Worthington, Marc Grissom, and Don Mueller. (Courtesy MHM.)

Ten

Age and Decline

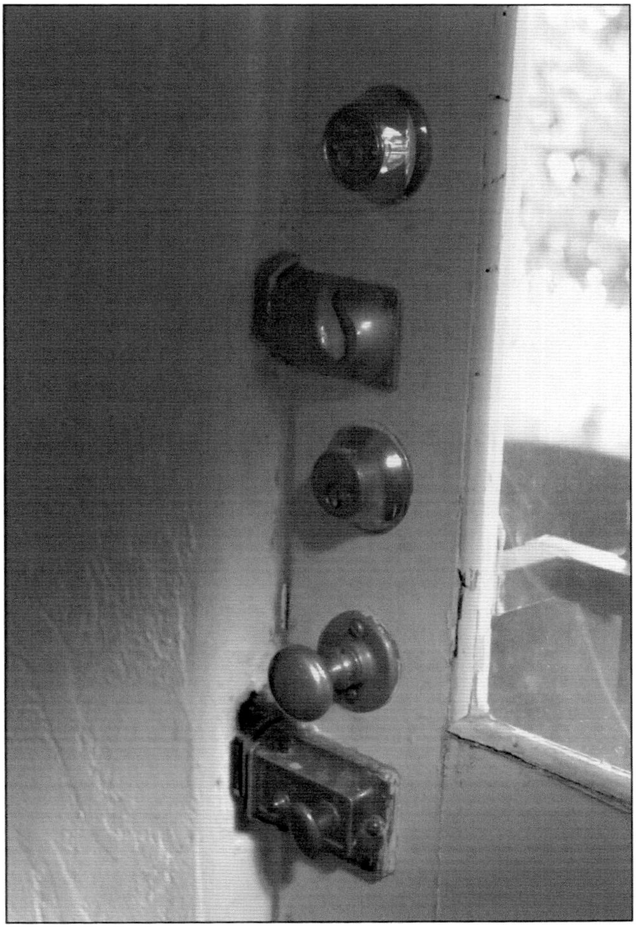

A visit to the Buckhorn in its heyday was very much like entering an oasis. Its grounds were meticulously kept. Water flowed in abundance. Trimmed trees offered comforting shade. Even after Ted Sliger's death in 1984, Alice continued running the Buckhorn for another 15 years, until advancing age made the challenge of maintaining such a large site and complex business more difficult. In 1999, when most would have retired years before, 92-year-old Alice reluctantly turned off the tap in the baths for the last time. Finally, in 2007, as she neared 100, Alice closed the motel and locked the doors for good, starting a long period of decline that has continued to this day.

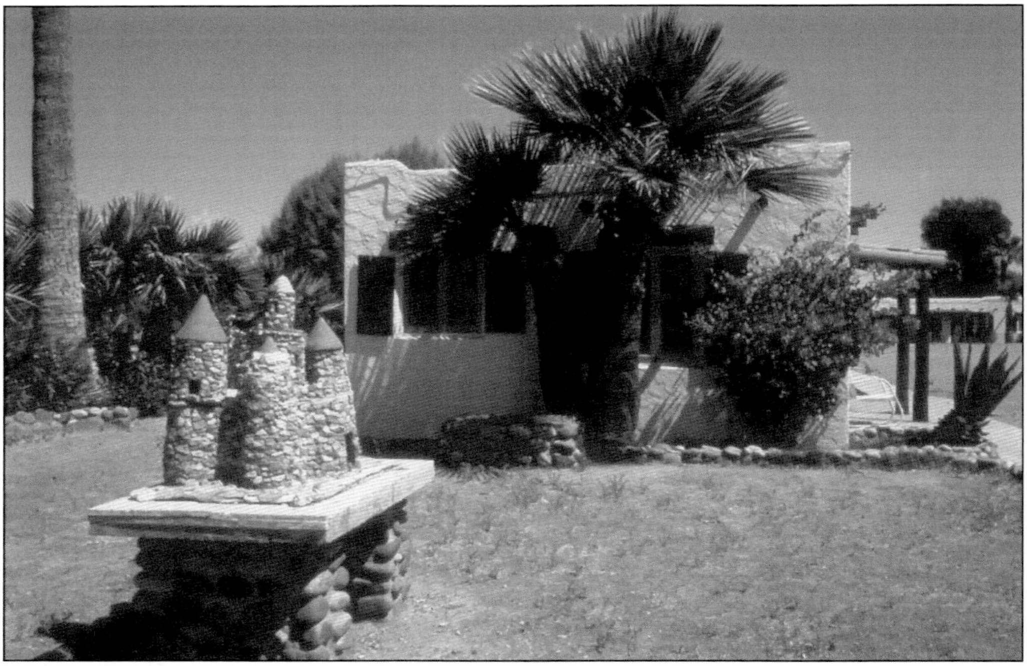

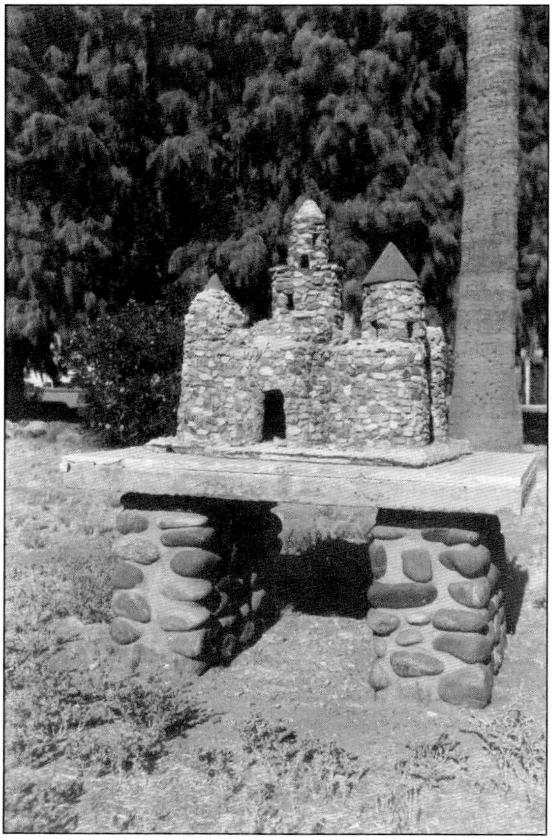

Several distinctive small stone castles, crafted from locally harvested rock, were constructed near the cottages. Alice Sliger said artistic guests were always encouraged to contribute something unique to the Buckhorn. In a 2000 interview, she could not recall who crafted the miniature castles or why, stating it was "just someone who stayed here and wanted to add something to our collection." No matter who created them, they added an unusual bit of European flavor to the Western setting. Of the several that once dotted the site, only one survives intact.

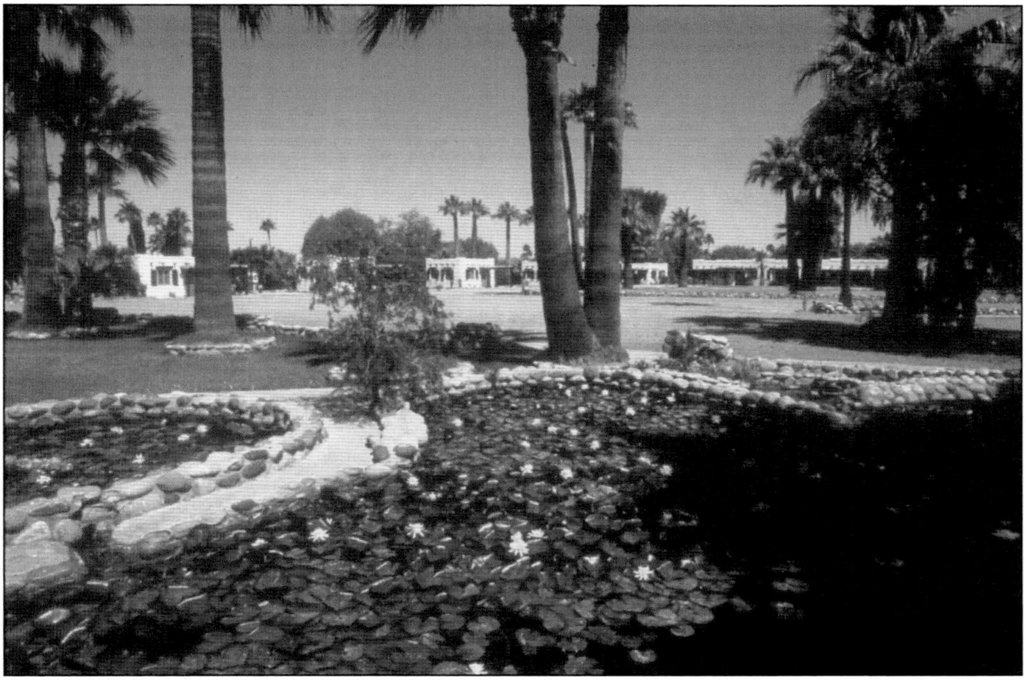

Local rock surrounds, embedded with metates and other artifacts, were used in the site's numerous water features and were filled with fish, frogs, and other critters. In the desert, where water brings life, the Buckhorn was indeed an oasis, providing guests with a cool, inviting environment filled with the sounds of rushing water and filtered sunlight through numerous palm trees. Wading was discouraged, but probably more than a few guests could not resist the temptation to dip their toes into the cool waters. A few water features had bubbling fountains that regrettably no longer work. Some ponds are now dry. Vegetation choked the life out of others.

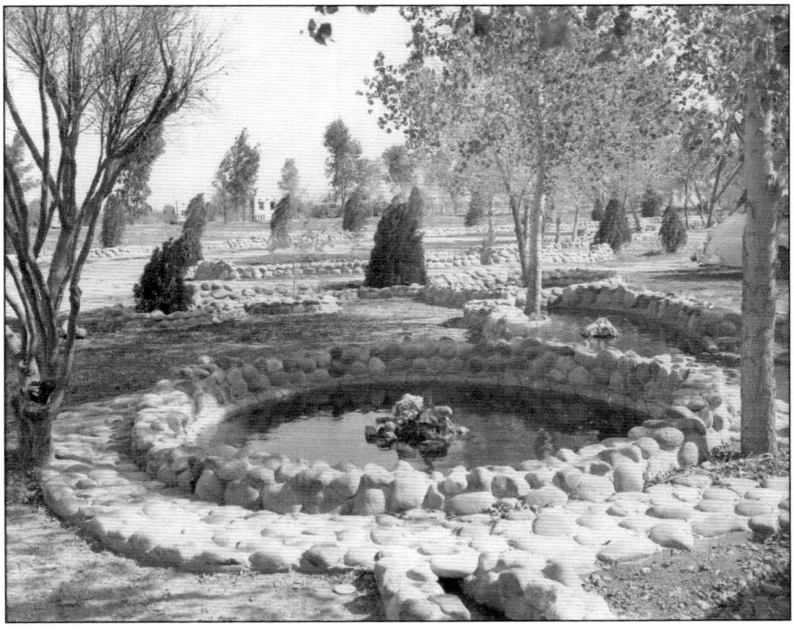

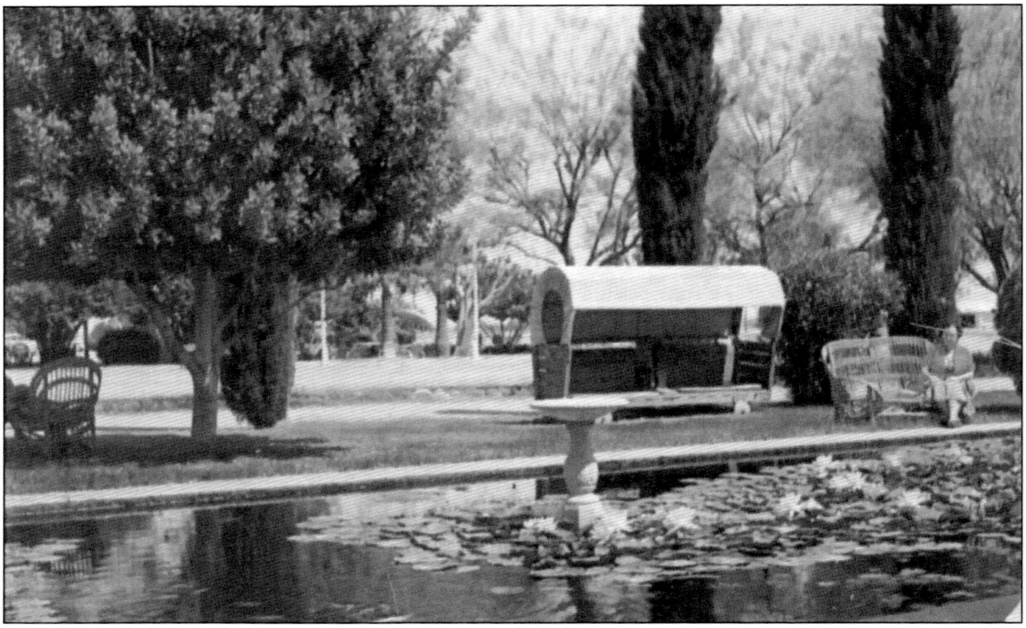

A large reflecting pool once dominated El Maro, the short-lived competitor just west of the Buckhorn. Too shallow for swimming, the "fishpond," as it was called, was constructed of local rock, surrounded by trees and covered wagon structures used by guests as refreshment areas. Today, the pond is filled in with soil.

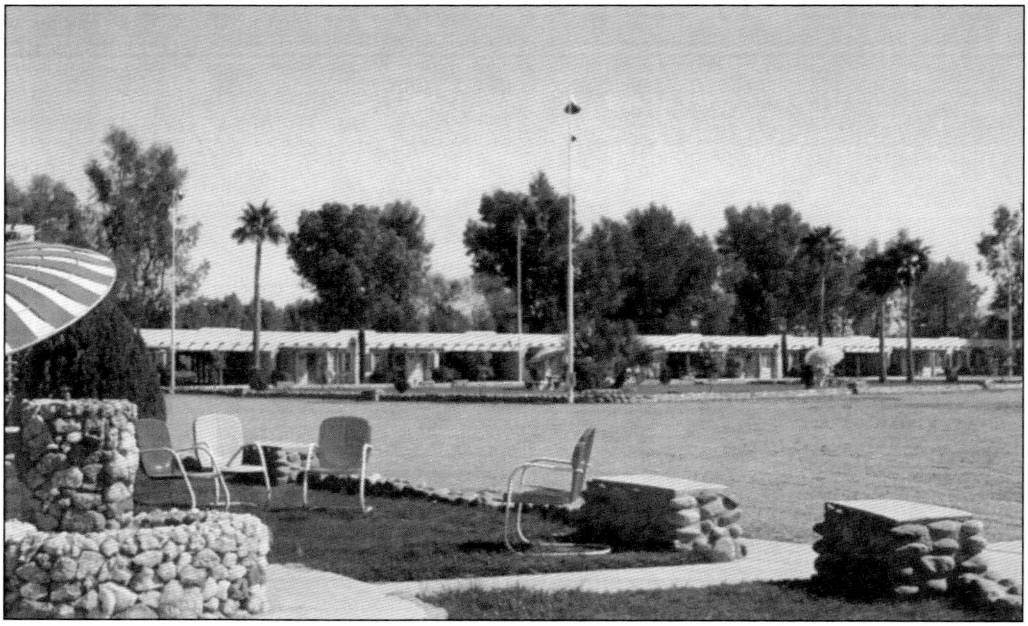

If the Sligers ever had plans for the centrally positioned, expansive greensward, they never materialized. It remained as a large open green space where ballplayers once used to toss a ball around and stay loose before the start of the spring training season. Also a sunbathing and play area for children, it was never transformed into anything more than a "central green." Flood irrigation once kept it lush, but now desert heat has left it a dry space.

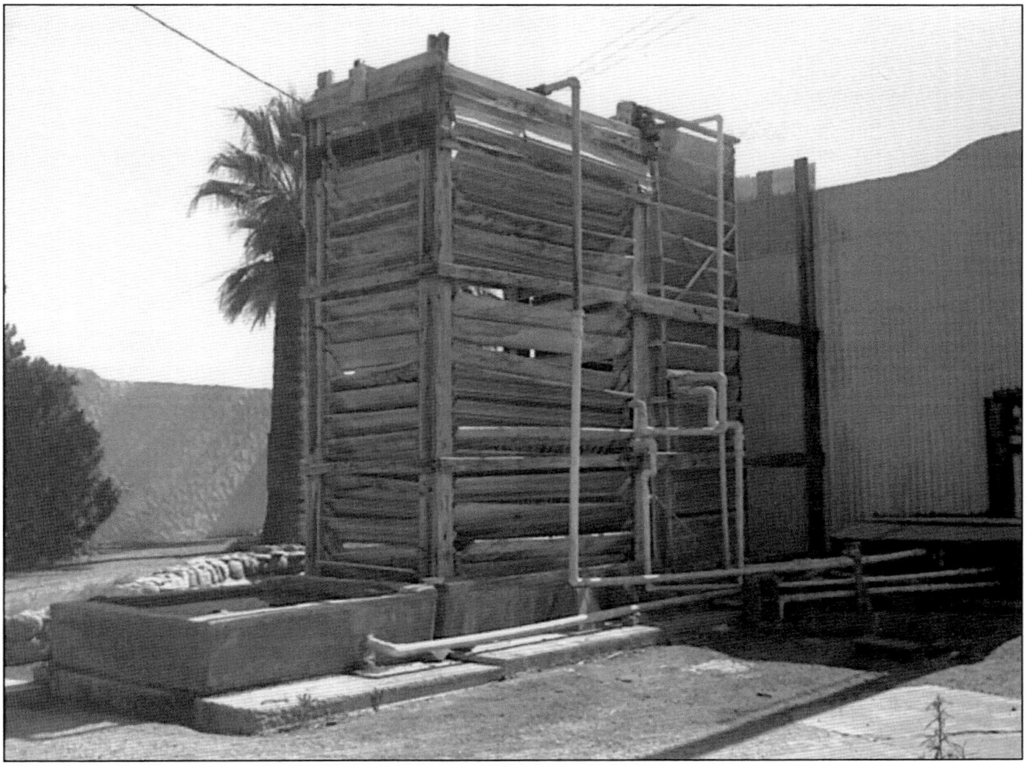

Water for the bathhouse emerged from the ground at temperatures ranging from 130 degrees in the deepest well (1,000 feet) to 112 degrees in the shallower wells. By using large wooden cooling towers to reduce the temperature, the water was then conveyed to the bathhouse at around 106 degrees. Water was pumped to the top of the tower and filtered down over the fins. Air passing through lowered the water temperature as it fell into the pool at the bottom. Minerals took their toll on the wood. One surviving tower stands as an eerie specter from the past.

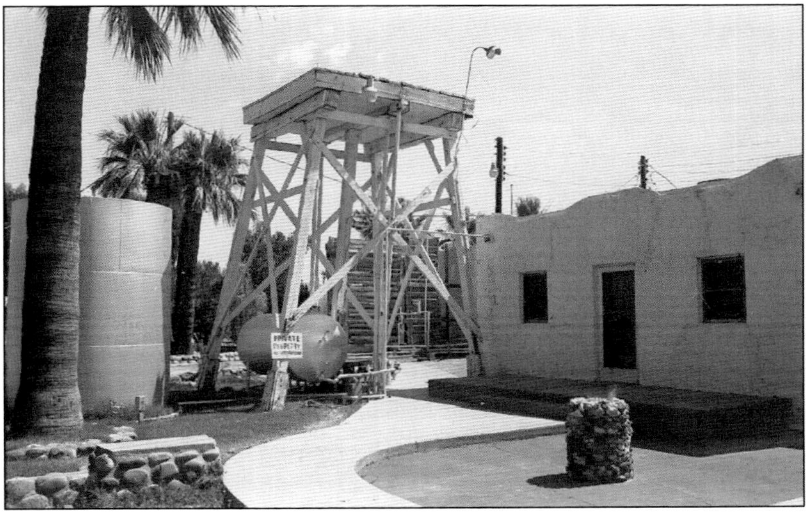

An elevated water tank was replaced by modern ground-level storage, leaving an abandoned wooden tower. A now dry reflecting pool (lower right) once featured a bubbling fountain.

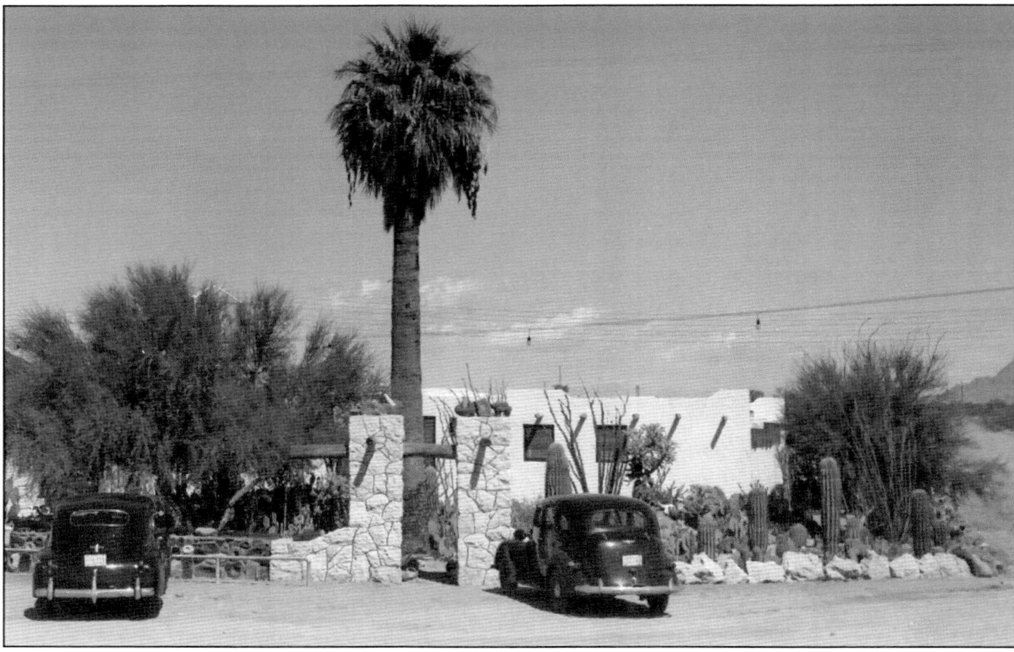

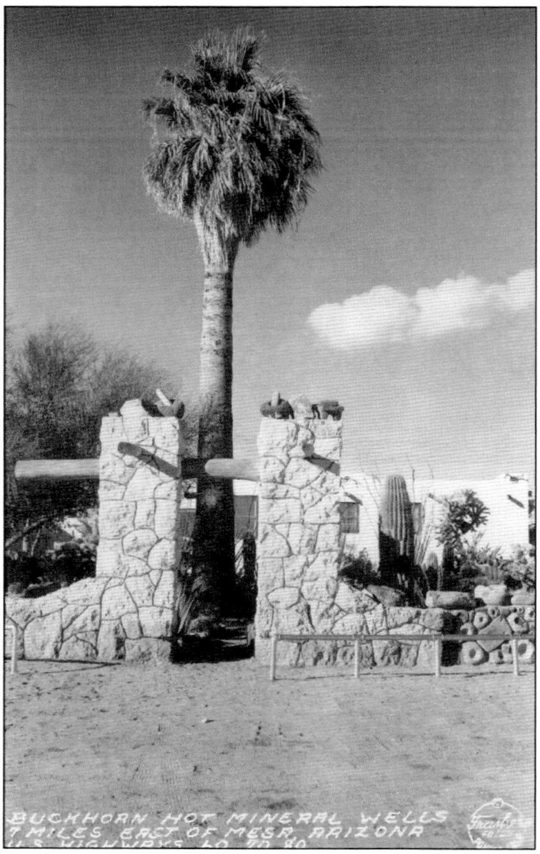

Most roadside restaurants, hotels, motels, railroad rest stops, and souvenir shops adopted indigenous architectural styles to pull in travelers from the road. The distinctive rock-walled cactus garden signaled "oasis," offering visitors a cool contemplative space. Saving ancient metates was the Sligers' goal when they began building the cactus garden. Walls embedded with metates and other Indian artifacts became a curiosity. Not long after Ted Sliger completed the cactus garden, he began building another attraction, the wishing well.

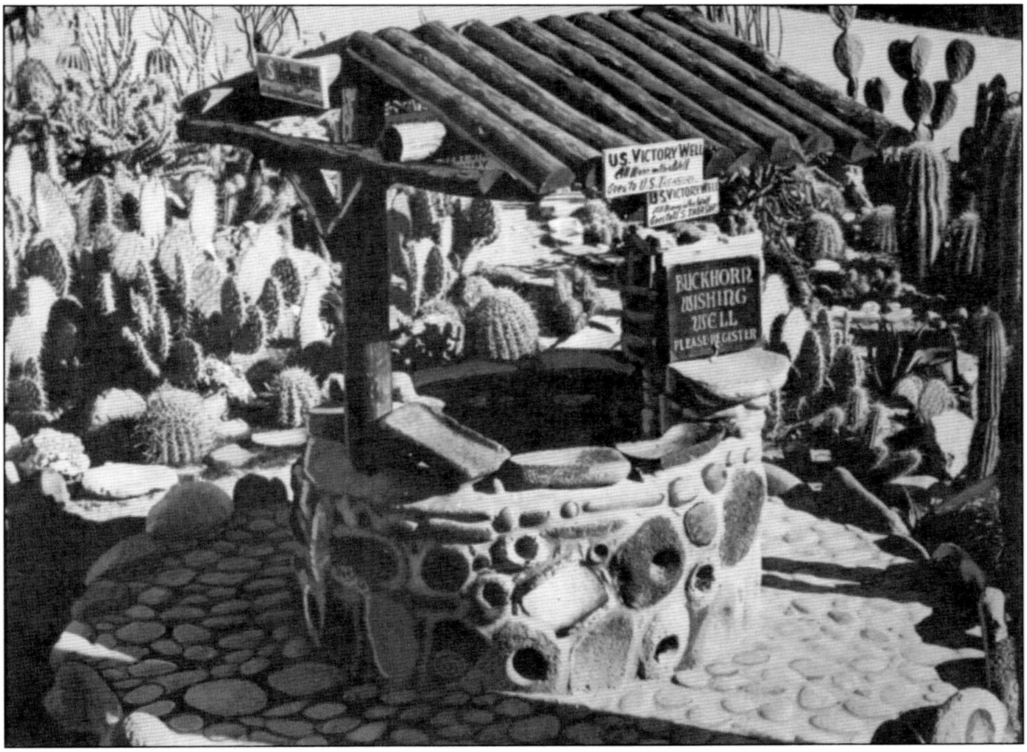

Alice Sliger wrote in 2007: "The well was dug to [a depth] of about fourteen feet. Large metates make up the body of the well, the circular top, and sides leading to a log roof. Connections were made so some water could be kept in the 'well.' When it was built, our nation was at war with Japan, so one of the signs . . . read 'Coins on which you make a wish will go to the war efforts.' Many people visited and made wishes and coins piled up. Periodically volunteers would come and help us. They would use ladders to go down into the well with large containers [and] bring up the coins. These made an interesting contribution to the government," for which the Sligers received a certificate of appreciation for the donations. She continued, "When the war was over, the sign was changed to 'Coins on which you make a wish will go to the March of Dimes to fight polio.' Coins continued to pour in, and for many years the yearly contribution from this well made headlines in the *Mesa Tribune* and served a great cause."

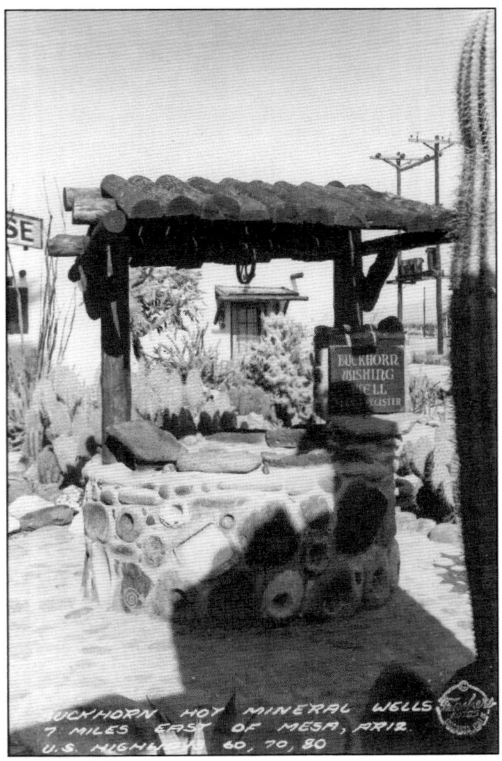

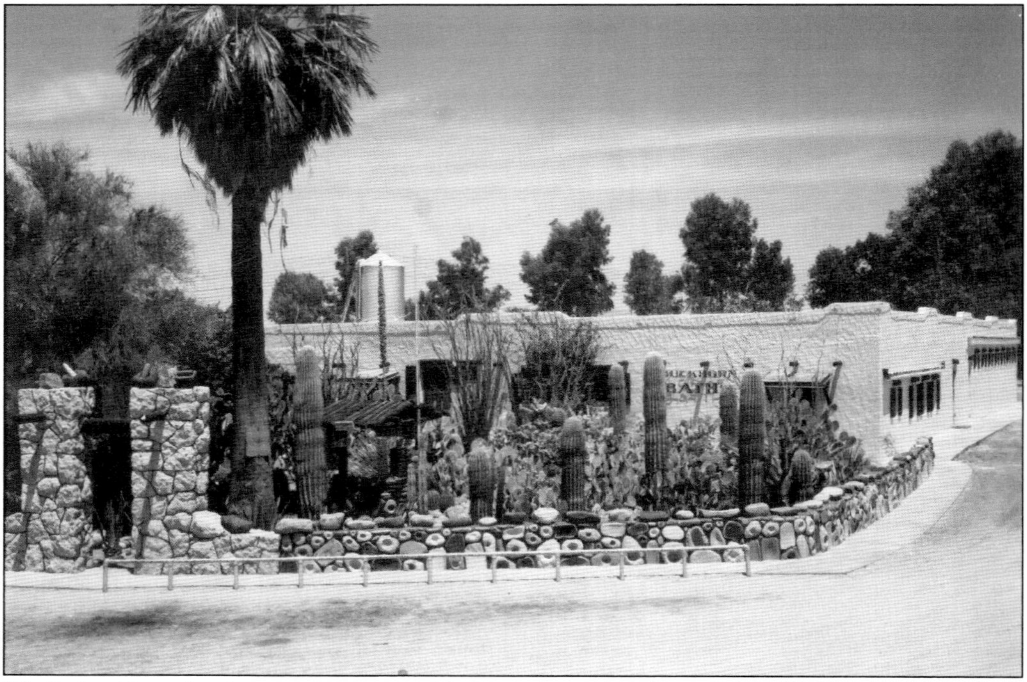

While building the distinctive stone-walled cactus garden fronting the bathhouse, Ted Sliger was often asked, "What are you going to do with all those odd rocks?" "Well, they aren't just rocks but Indian grindstones called metates," he replied. The Buckhorn boasted that it displayed the largest collection of metates in the world. Sliger's ingenuity led to embedding them, along with manos (pestle-like stones used with metates) and stone ax heads, into landscape walls and elsewhere on the Buckhorn campus. Easily visible but well conserved, these decorative elements have stood the test of time.

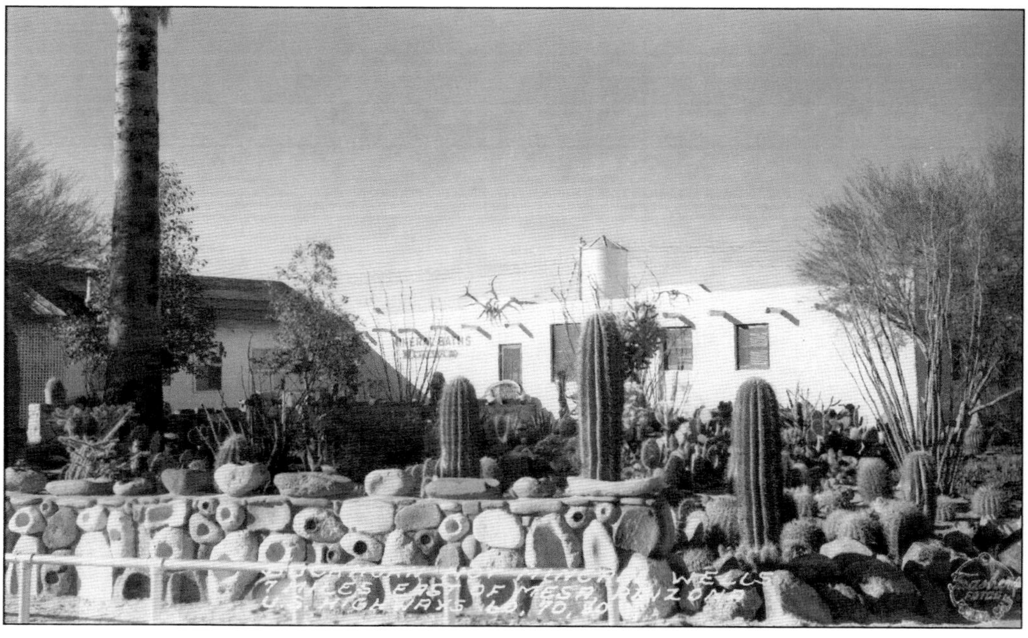

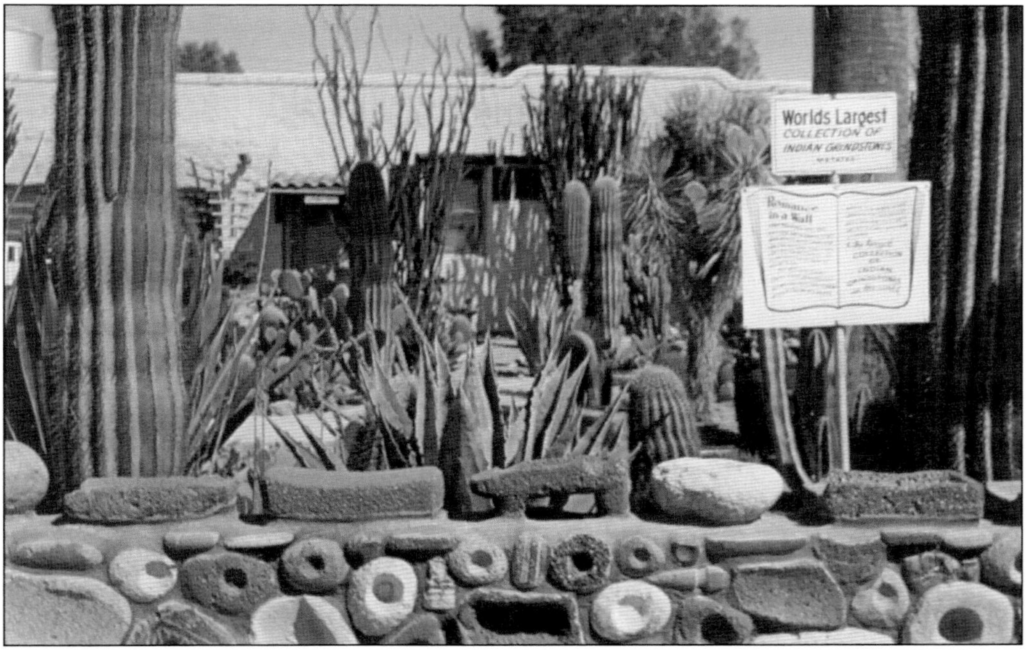

Photographic postcards detailed the hundreds of metates ingeniously incorporated into landscape walls. Evidence of metate use by native Arizona cultures for crushing and grinding grain and seeds dates back thousands of years. Coined by the Spanish from the Náhuatl word *metlatl*, a metate is a stone with a carved depression to hold corn and other grains. A smaller stone called a mano did the crushing through a horizontal grinding motion. In the Buckhorn's early years, metates were abundant, often found just lying on the ground.

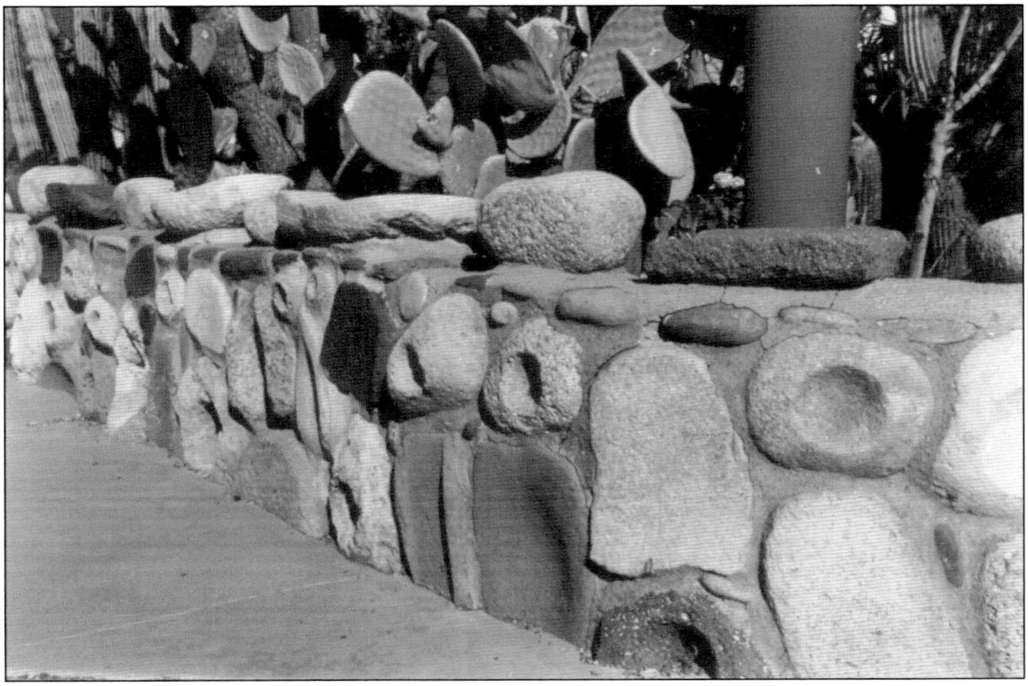

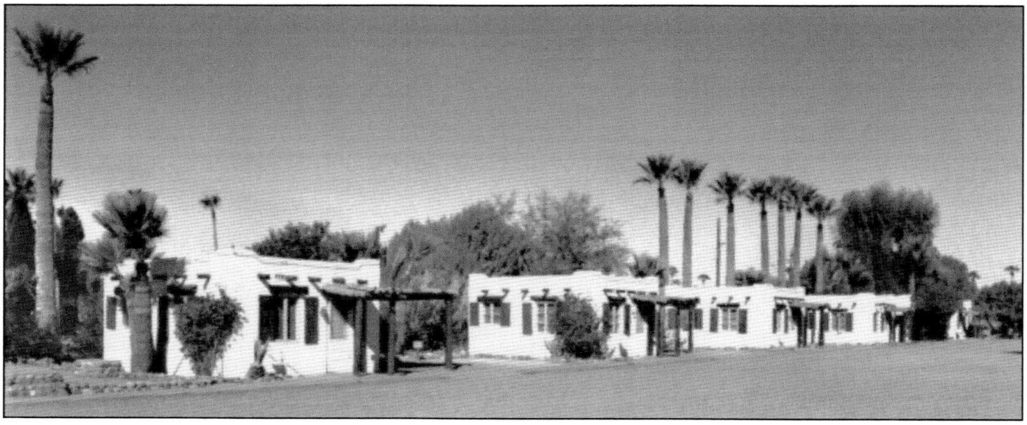

With the opening of the baths in 1939, providing guest lodging was next. A government loan helped build the first cottages in a vernacular Pueblo style. Without an architect, Ted Sliger created the characteristic designs. The Buckhorn cottages, constructed of concrete block with a skip trowel stucco finish, were detached units (approximately 225 square feet). Wood shutter trimming offered a Craftsman touch to the Pueblo style. A small front porch highlighted the entry, with round columns supporting a sloping clay tile roof. Eight-inch circular columns held up an attached carport. Accenting the petite structures, Sliger trimmed their outline with neon lighting. Could one of these cottages be where Willy Mays or Don Ameche or Joe Brown slept?

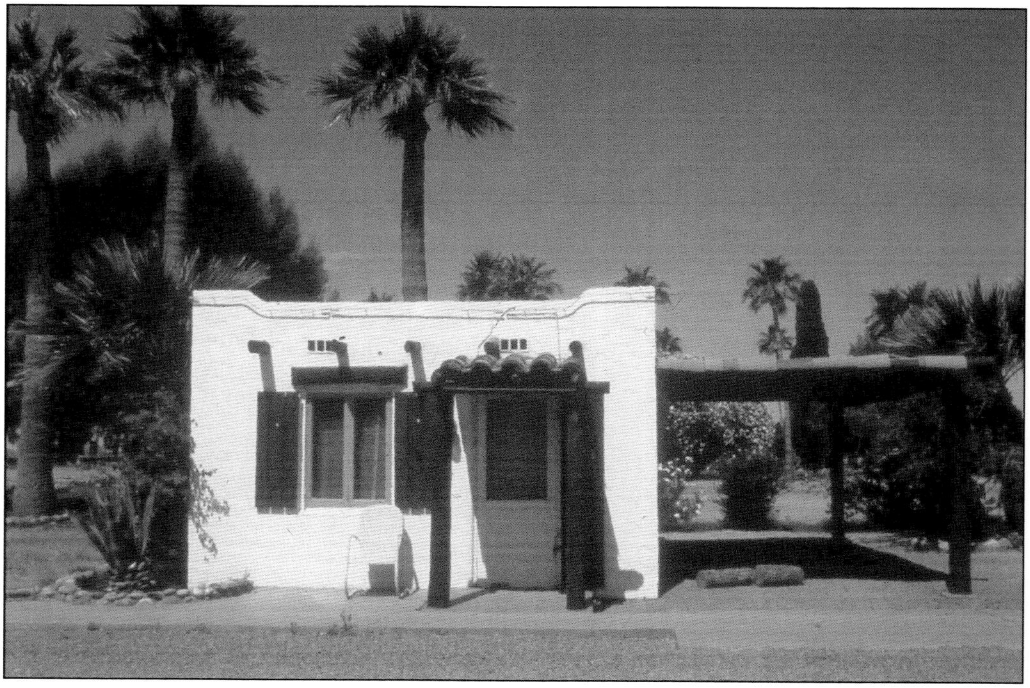

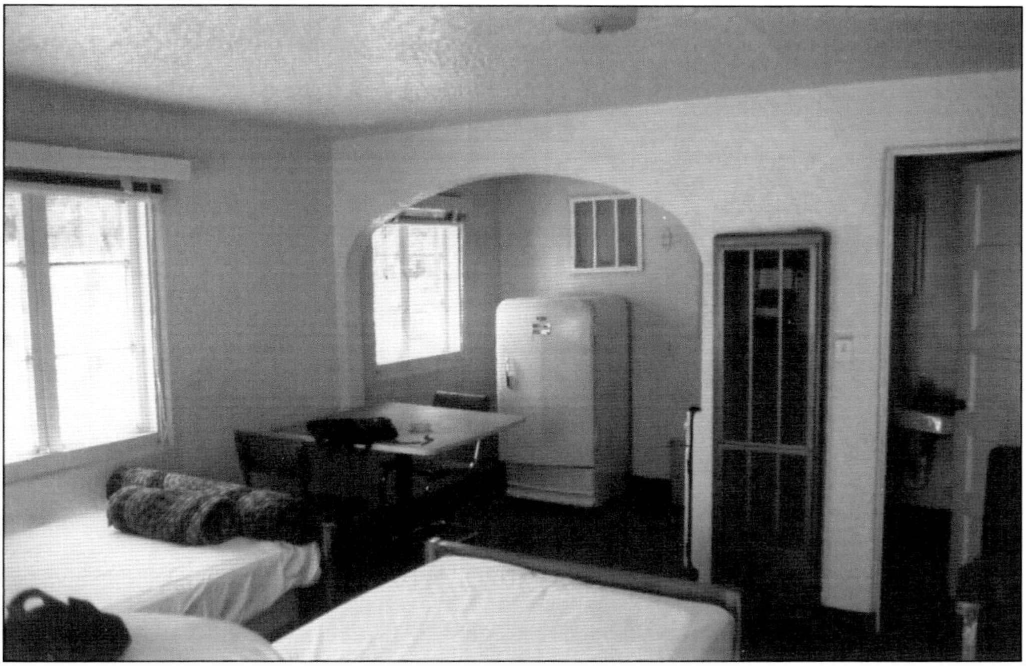

Rooms were small, clean, and simple but quite serviceable. With all its other amenities and services, the intent of the Buckhorn was to have guests spend as little time in their rooms as possible.

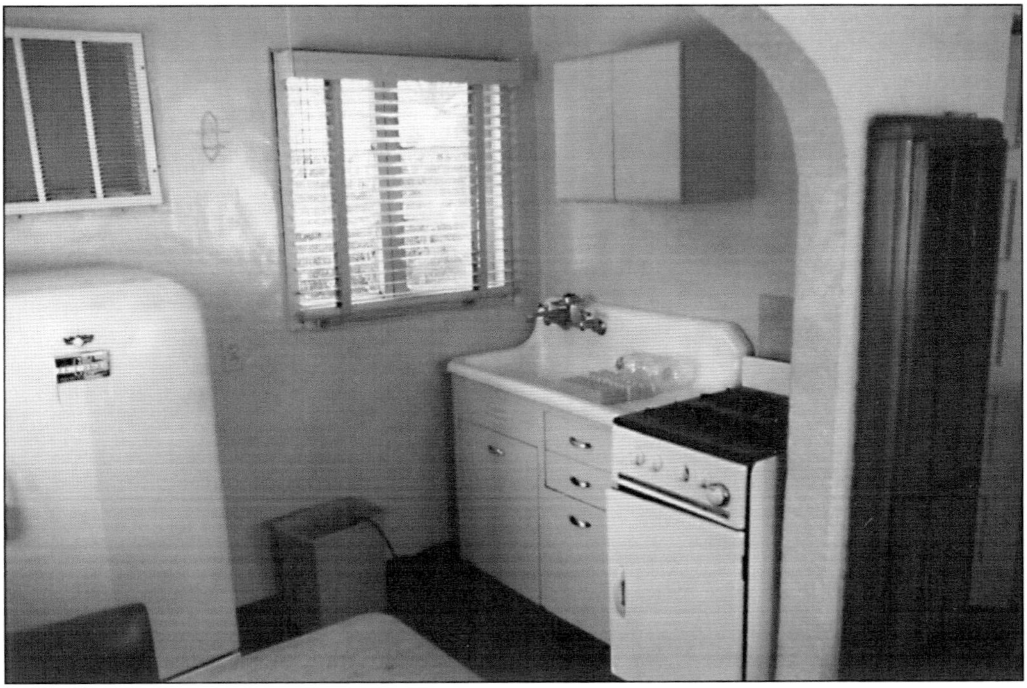

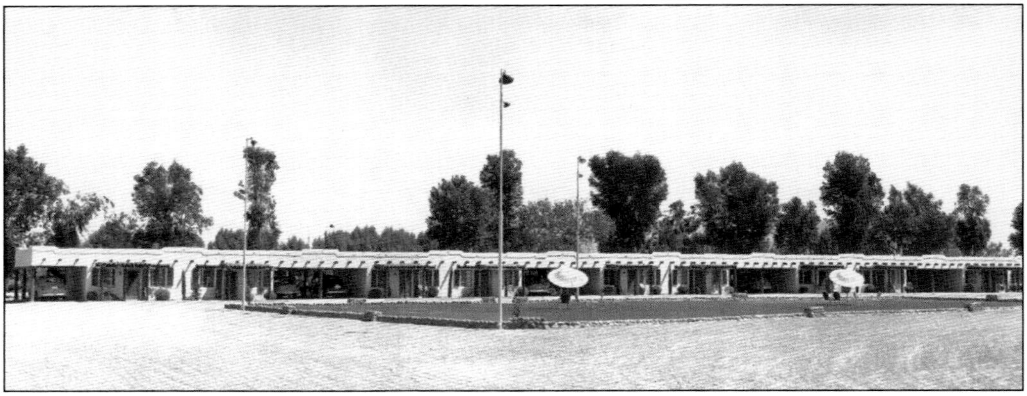

After World War II, Americans began favoring motels over old-style auto courts. The Buckhorn was at the forefront of the new era. Constructed in 1949, the motel units were an attached grouping of approximately 400-square-foot rooms with a carport separation. All but two units had one sleeping room; the others, two. Flat roofs accessed by stairs outside a back door provided private sun decks with grand desert and mountain views. Each unit had a full bath with vanity. Kitchens were fitted with metal cabinetry, a small stove, and a refrigerator. Vinyl tile covered concrete floors. Guests were encouraged, however, to use the bathhouse and dine in the restaurant. Ted Sliger continued outlining roof parapets with colorful neon lighting.

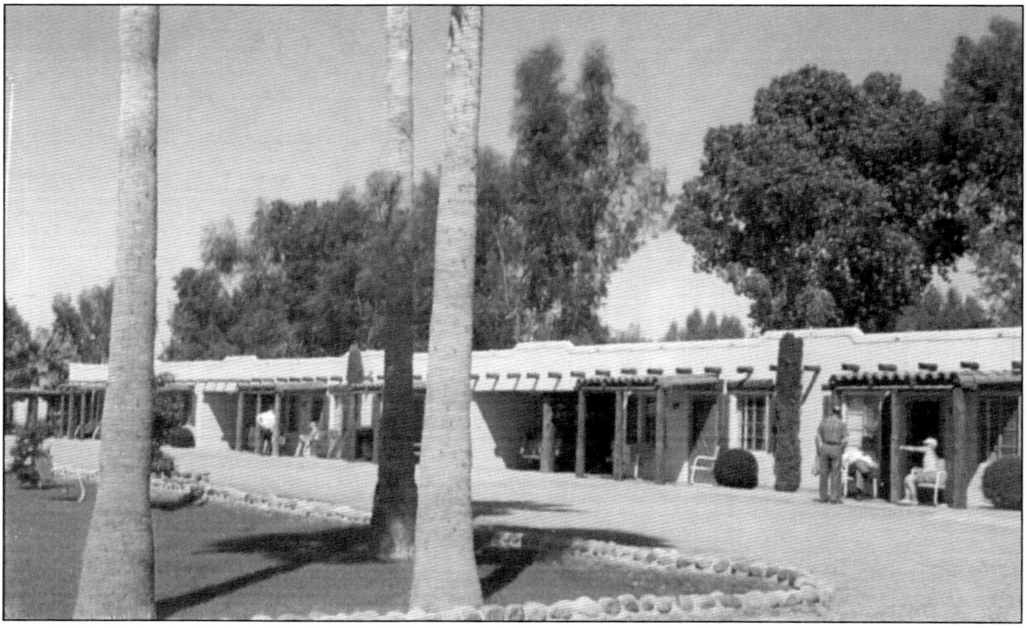

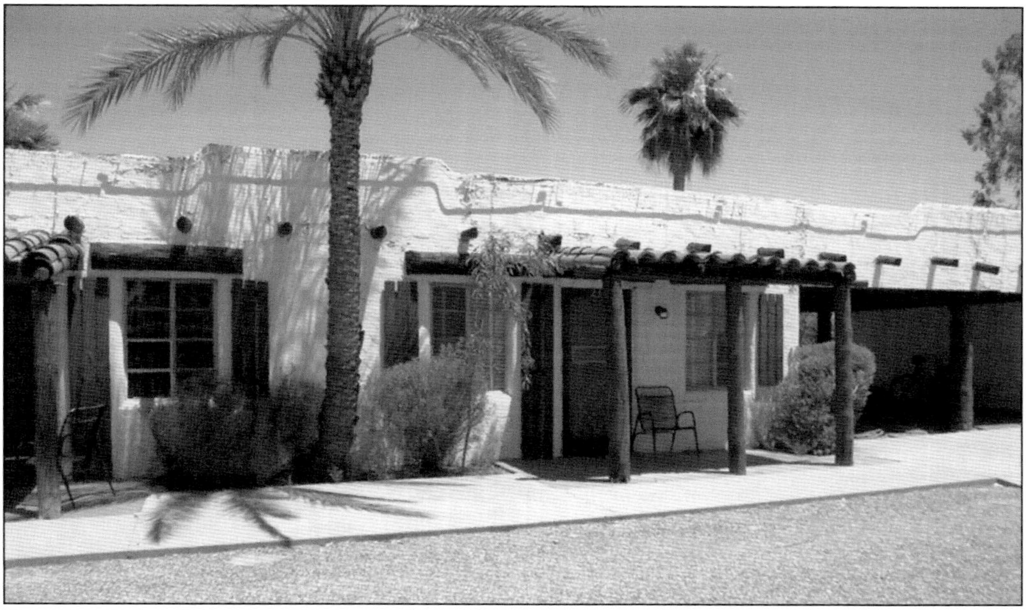

Ornamented with decorative vigas and wooden posts supporting entrance canopies, motel rooms were an inviting retreat from Buckhorn activities.

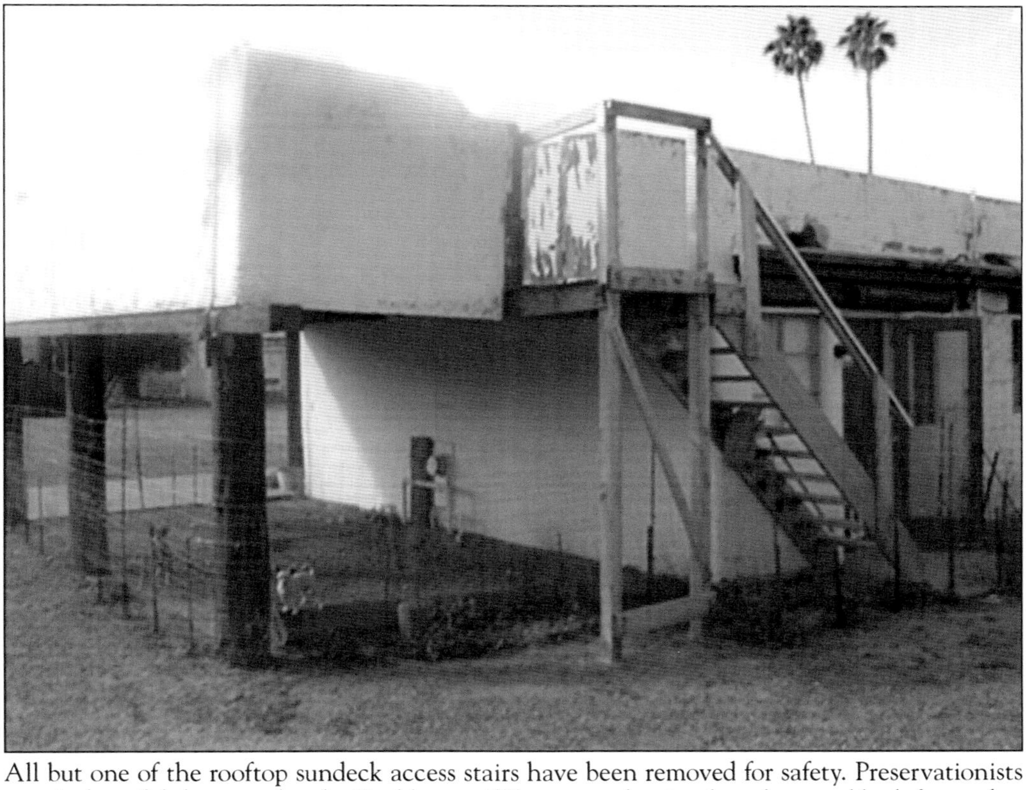

All but one of the rooftop sundeck access stairs have been removed for safety. Preservationists remain hopeful that one day the Buckhorn will be restored to its glory days, and look forward to pampered guests once again soaking up the sun's rays.

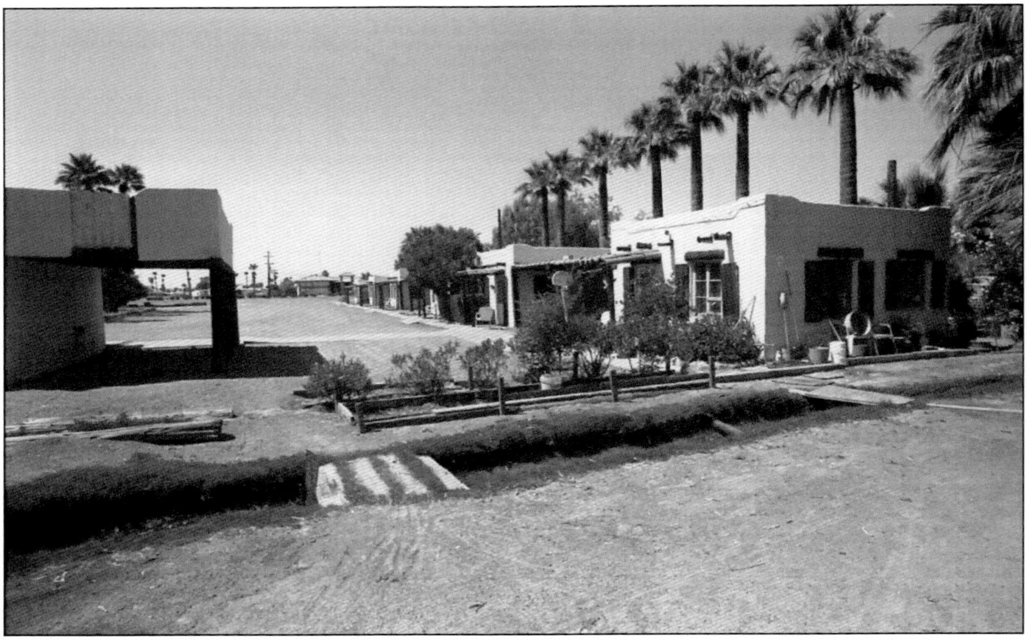

An irrigation ditch that once helped keep the Buckhorn green is now dry. Fountains that once bubbled with fresh, cooling water now stand as silent sentinels, reminders of a time when the Buckhorn was a true oasis. Stairs that led to roof-top sundecks have mostly disappeared. Years of neglect are taking their toll, leaving the Buckhorn's future very much in question.

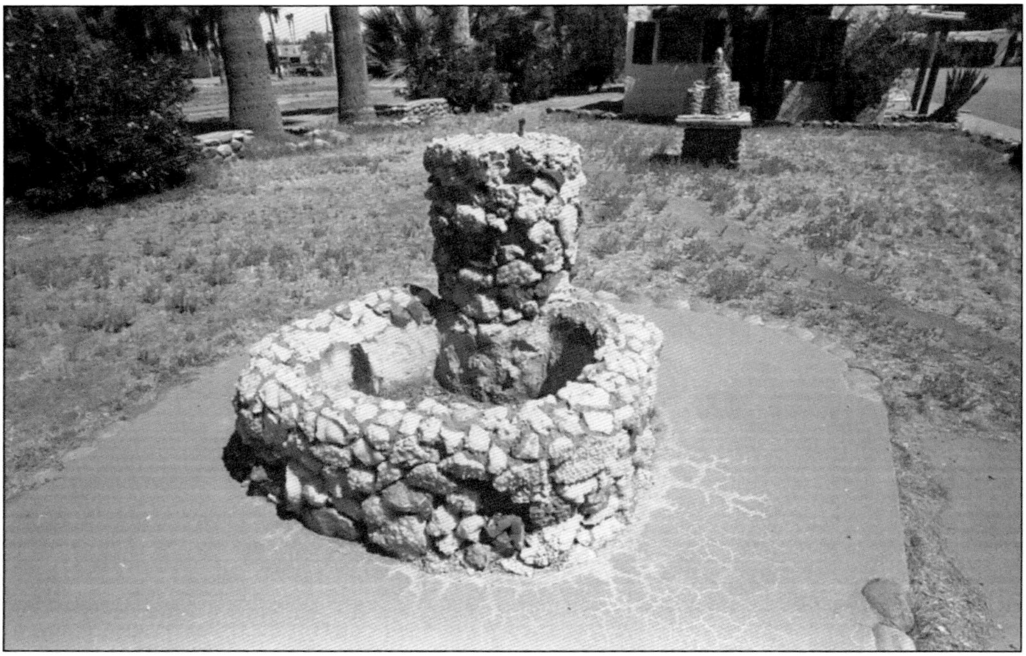

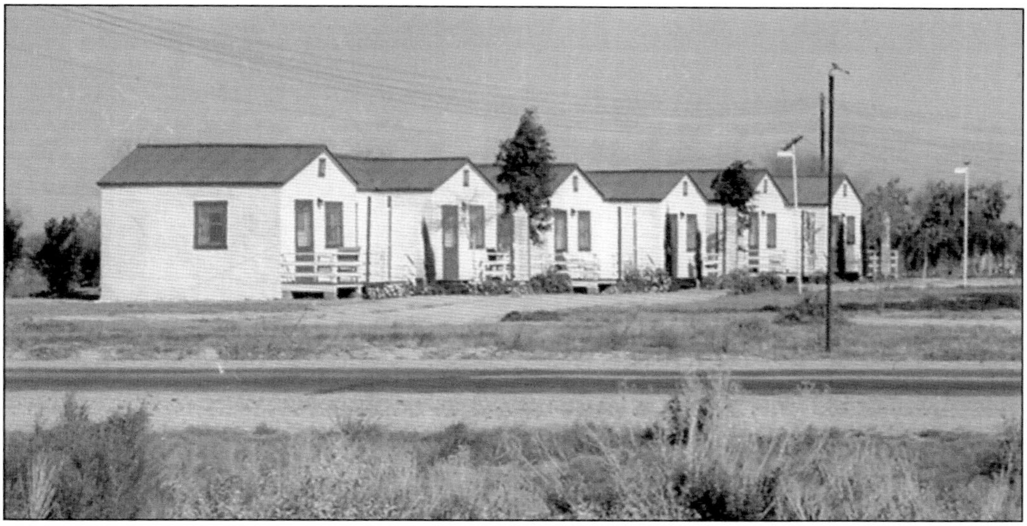

Comparative images reveal how more than seven decades of deterioration have taken their toll on the El Maro guest cottages acquired by the Buckhorn when it bought out the competing resort. The once bright, white cottages now resemble ghosts of the past. (Above, courtesy MHM.)

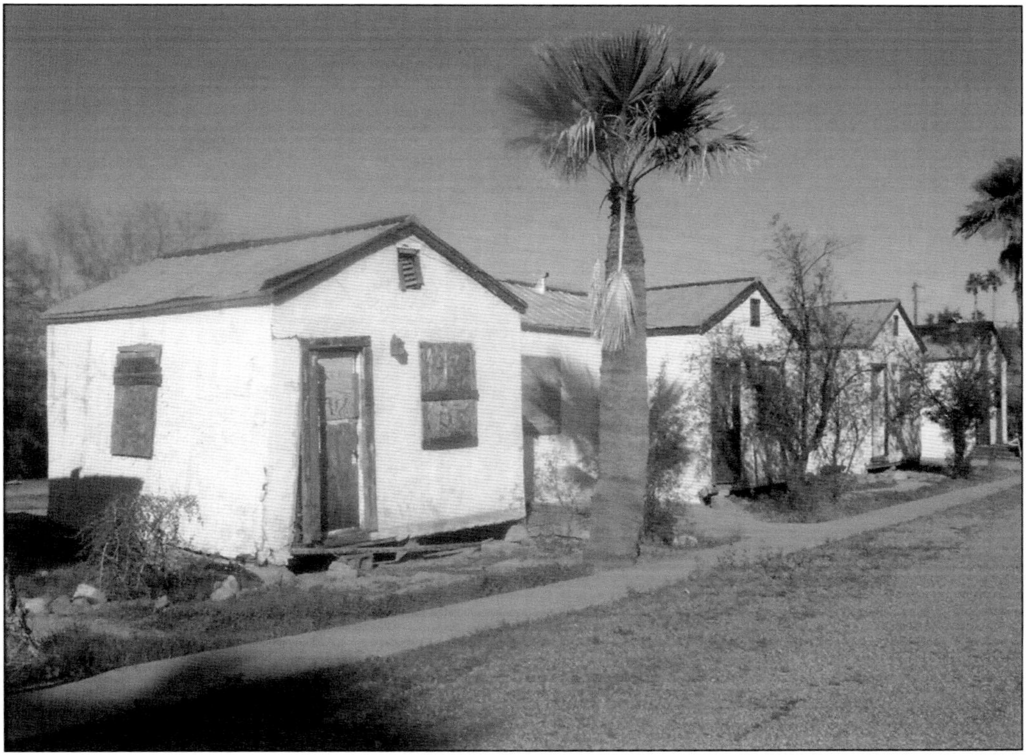

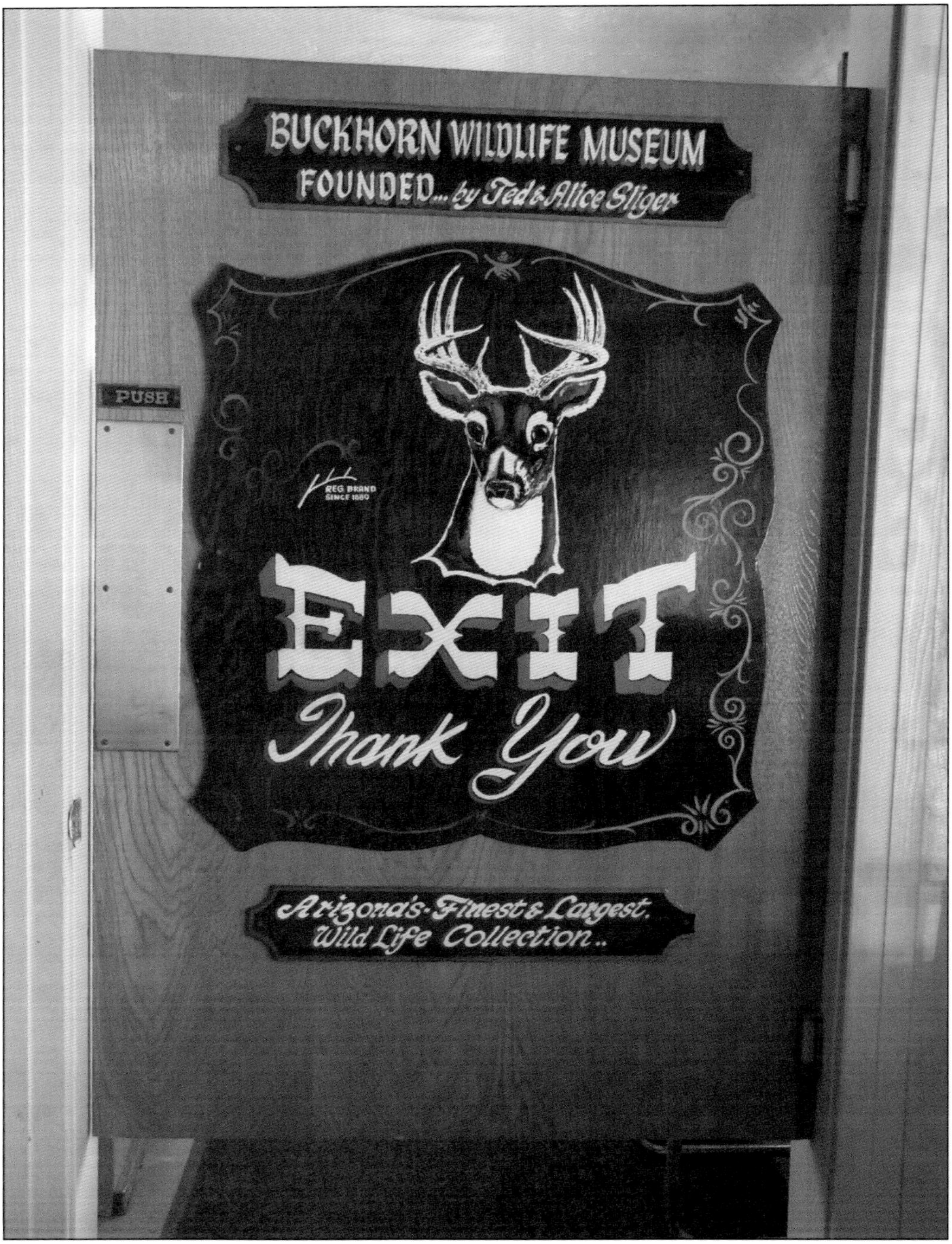

Is the Wildlife Museum's exit door a metaphor for the Buckhorn's future? Closed for nearly two decades, the Buckhorn quietly awaits what lies ahead. With minimal attention, the once glorious oasis continues to decline, its future hanging in the balance. At the time of this publication, concern for the Buckhorn has never been greater. Without immediate attention, all the remarkable accomplishments achieved by a visionary couple that built one of America's great treasures may soon be lost forever.

About the Organization

The Mesa Preservation Foundation (MPF), a 501(c)(3) non-profit organization, was founded in 2010 shortly before the death of Alice Sliger six weeks prior to her 104th birthday. For years, Alice strongly expressed her desire to see the Buckhorn preserved as a legacy to the remarkable accomplishments she and her husband, Ted, achieved in seven decades of operation. The MPF promised Alice to do what it could. Since then, it has been instrumental in raising awareness of and developing support for the Buckhorn. It has worked with many in the community to protect and preserve this irreplaceable historic property. Additionally, the MPF was instrumental in saving the iconic diving lady, a 70-foot neon sign, after a catastrophic fall in a 2010 storm. Today, the MPF is recognized as a regional leader in the preservation of historic neon. The MPF also continues its commitment to preserving historic homes, public and commercial buildings, and other structures in order to retain and strengthen community history and pride through appreciation of heritage, retaining a sense of place, and grounding economic development around irreplaceable local elements. All proceeds from the sale of this book go to the Mesa Preservation Foundation's preservation efforts. To support and follow the activities of the MPF, visit mesapreservation.org or on Facebook.